FAMILY BUSINESS

ON THE COUCH

FAMILY BUSINESS
ON THE COUCH

A Psychological Perspective

Manfred F. R. Kets de Vries
and
Randel S. Carlock
with
Elizabeth Florent-Treacy

John Wiley & Sons, Ltd

Other Wiley Editorial Offices

John Wiley & Sons Inc., 111 River Street, Hoboken, NJ 07030, USA

Jossey-Bass, 989 Market Street, San Francisco, CA 94103-1741, USA

Wiley-VCH Verlag GmbH, Boschstr. 12, D-69469 Weinheim, Germany

John Wiley & Sons Australia Ltd, 42 McDougall Street, Milton, Queensland 4064,
Australia

John Wiley & Sons (Asia) Pte Ltd, 2 Clementi Loop #02-01, Jin Xing Distripark,
Singapore 129809

John Wiley & Sons Canada Ltd, 6045 Freemont Blvd, Mississauga, ONT, L5R 4J3,
Canada

Wiley also publishes its books in a variety of electronic formats. Some content that
appears in print may not be available in electronic books.

Anniversary Logo Design: Richard J. Pacifico

Library of Congress Cataloging-in-Publication Data

Kets de Vries, Manfred F. R.
Family business on the couch: a psychological perspective / Manfred F. R. Kets de Vries
and Randel S. Carlock with Elizabeth Florent-Treacy.
       p.   cm.
   Includes bibliographical references and index.
   ISBN 978-0-470-51671-3 (cloth)
1. Family-owned business enterprises—Psychological aspects.   2. Family-owned business
enterprises—Case studies.   I. Carlock, Randel S., 1948-   II. Florent-Treacy, Elizabeth,
1960-   III. Title.
   HD62.25.K485 2007
   338.6'42—dc22   2007026418

British Library Cataloguing in Publication Data
A catalogue record for this book is available from the British Library

ISBN 978-0-470-51671-3 (HB)

Typeset in 11.5/13.5pt Bembo by SNP Best-set Typesetter Ltd., Hong Kong

This book is printed on acid-free paper responsibly manufactured from sustainable
forestry in which at least two trees are planted for each one used for paper production.

This book is dedicated to business families around the world: over the years we probably learned more from them than they did from us.

CONTENTS

ACKNOWLEDGMENTS

As this book is an interdisciplinary effort, we would like to recognize the support of two teams.

- Our colleagues in the INSEAD Global Leadership Centre (of which Professor Kets de Vries is the Director) are Agata Halczewska-Figuet (Executive Director), Sheila Loxham, Silke Bequet, Fabienne Chemin, and Nadine Theallier.
- Our colleagues in the Wendel International Centre for Family Enterprise (of which Professor Carlock is the director) are Christine Blondel (Executive Director) and centre coordinators Veronique Sanciaume and Nathalie Bogacz.

The two teams have shared original theories, and critical insights, and provided unflagging moral support; we thank them all warmly for their contributions to this book.

We are also extremely grateful to the Berghmans and Lhoist, Hoffmann and Wendel families and to the INSEAD Research and Development committee, who early on recognized the importance of our work and provided the financial support that made our research and writing possible.

We are very fortunate to have the support of Sally Simmons, of Cambridge Editorial Partnership Ltd, who worked on an early draft of the manuscript, and contributed some of the case vignettes, and we also thank her colleague Carol Schaessens for her research and editorial support. We are also happy to be working with

Francesca Warren and her very professional team at John Wiley & Sons Ltd.

Most of all, we would like to thank the families who told us their stories, taking us into their homes and businesses. When the limelight of academia shines in the dark corners of a family business, only the stout-hearted are courageous enough to speak about the issues that concern them on personal and professional levels. The families we work with often say they hope to pass on their hard-earned wisdom to other business families and the people who work for them. By sharing through this book what we have learned, we hope to repay our debt to 'our' business families.

PREFACE

As the twenty-first-century global economic model rapidly replaces the old industrial model, government policy makers, economists, and academics now recognize that entrepreneurial and family enterprises—the oldest form of commercial organizations—are a prime source of wealth creation and employment in both developed and emerging economies. Families control 95% of the businesses in Asia, the Middle East, Italy, and Spain. In mature industrial economies such as France and Germany, over 80% of the companies are family controlled. In the United States, with its strong public stock markets, families control 60–70% of the country's commercial organizations. (These figures are based on the definition of a family business as being any business organization where decisions and leadership are influenced by a family or families.)

The rise in interest in family businesses has also been a result of many social and economic forces: generational transitions; downsizing in the large corporate world; a heavily mediatized anti-globalization movement; a search for a more balanced life-style through self-employment; and the dramatic growth of Asian and other developing markets. Family businesses also represent an important untapped market for private banking, mergers and acquisitions, and recapitalizations, as well as sources of funding (for example, the investment of assets from family holding companies) for private equity and hedge funds.

As the traditional psychological contract between individual and organization has been broken, corporate loyalty has become a relic of the past. The 'organization man', the one-time mainstay of the large corporation, is rapidly becoming extinct. As a reaction to the lack of security offered by large organizations, many individuals—among them potential employees and other stakeholders—are attracted by the corporate values espoused in family-controlled firms.

In this context, a growing number of younger members of business-owning families, concerned about their own careers, are taking a second look at the job options in their father's (or mother's) company. One obvious career path for someone from a business family is to join a firm he or she already has a stake in—thereby making a kind of emotional investment that is quite different than they would make in joining a public corporation.

The career options in family firms can be interesting, for both family and non-family professionals. One-third of the companies included in the US Fortune 500 list are family controlled [1], as are some of the world's most successful firms, including Michelin, Peugeot, LVMH, Monoprix, Wendel and Carrefour in France; Tetrapak and IKEA in Sweden; Roche in Switzerland; BMW and Henkel in Germany; Barilla and Benetton in Italy; C&A, SHV, and Heineken in the Netherlands; Associated British Foods and Sainsbury in the United Kingdom; Power Corporation and Bombardier in Canada; Cargill, Koch Industries, GAP, Mars, Bechtel, and Wal-Mart in the United States; and Hutchinson Whampoa, Suntory, the Swire Group Toyota, and Hyundai in Asia. Even in large organizations such as these, the idea of family may be firmly anchored in the minds of key stakeholders, with a significant impact on prevailing leadership style and corporate culture.

Those working with family businesses in a financial or legal capacity—management consultants, bankers, accountants, lawyers, investment counselors, and other professionals—often realize that family businesses have certain unique qualities, problems, and challenges. In fact, most business issues facing family-controlled firms are similar to those faced by equivalent publicly or widely owned firms, but the challenge for the adviser working in this context lies in finding explanations for often seemingly irrational behaviour and decisions of the family about these issues. What makes many family business issues seem intractable is not the business aspects, but the emotional issues that compound them. In a family enterprise, issues like hiring, dividend payment, or succession—difficult though they may be—are really just ordinary business tasks, requiring planning and decision making. But this planning and decision-making process can be made extraordinarily complex by the dynamics of the controlling family. Personal differences in the values, motivations, and needs of different family members lead to conflict in the family's business. The ability of family leaders to adapt to the changing needs and requirements of individual family members is therefore critical, particularly when dealing with succession or other transitions.

Interview any business family and they will explain that their family's issues are particular to their family's situation. They will give examples: the senior generation will not share power with their adult children; there are family members in management positions for which they are not qualified; the owners lack influence in the business; it is impossible to have a professional relationship with Dad/Mom/Uncle Bill/the cousins; and so on. Or they'll mention the vexing issue of differences in intergenerational goals: 'They don't trust us, understand our thinking, or recognize how the world is changing.' 'They don't seem to value our experience; they want to change everything too quickly.'

So, what factors enable certain family businesses to succeed while others fail? And why are family businesses so different from other businesses? We believe in large part it is because, in a family enterprise, there is a coming together of two different systems— the business and the family. For this reason we believe it is necessary to use both economic and psychological approaches to understanding the workings of family businesses. Established means of measuring and understanding business performance can only explain so much in the family business. The rest of the story can only be uncovered by exploring the conscious or unconscious motivations that drive individuals in the business family. However, since these individuals' motivations are being acted out within a family context, it is also necessary to understand more than just the personal psychology of each family member: the way the family works as a system, and how this affects the individual psychology of each of its members, must also be looked at.

A PSYCHOLOGICAL PERSPECTIVE ON FAMILY BUSINESS

Along with using established means of measuring and understanding business performance, there is a powerful rationale for using a psychological perspective, taken from both a psychodynamic and family systemic orientation, to explore and understand business families. The motivations and drives that shape individual behaviour tell part of the story. The way a family interacts around the dinner table tells another. When insight into individual behaviour is combined with a family systemic view, we arrive at a rich understanding of what makes business families such powerful creative and destructive forces. It has been said—and we agree—that a study of the family should be included in organizational research because families 'influence behaviour at the individual, group and organizational levels of analysis' [2].

Love and Work

Sigmund Freud, the founder of psychoanalysis, argued that *lieben und arbeiten* (love and work), are 'the cornerstones of our humanness'. By this he meant that love (a feeling of affinity and connectedness) and work (a sense that one's efforts are useful) are the main sources of self-esteem and pleasure in life, and only when both are balanced do we achieve satisfaction [3].

Many family businesses experience a conflict between love (family) and work (the business) because the business is not adequately separated from the family. It has often become an extension of the family system, assuming its rules and behaviour patterns. If a family's pattern of functioning encourages clear boundaries and effective decision-making practices, it will foster sound business processes. Equally, if the family–business boundaries are blurred and family functioning is ineffective or conflicted, management processes will be adversely affected—often for no easily discernible reasons. On an individual level, the strong identification of family members with the business itself, and the intensity of emotions among the participants because of what the business represents to each one of them, may be additional sources of interpersonal conflict.

Sustaining a business over time is not an easy task even for large publicly traded companies. A simple check of the US Fortune 500 list demonstrates the point: only 77 companies have stayed on the list in their original form since 1955. More than

80% have gone bankrupt, or have been sold or acquired over the past 50 years [4]. Family business statistics offer a similar picture, with only 3 out of 10 family businesses surviving into the second generation, and only 1 out of 10 handed down to a third. The average life span of family firms (after a successful start-up) is 24 years, which coincides with the average time the founder is associated with the company [5].

What explains these rather discouraging statistics? Family enterprises face serious challenges on two fronts. There are the business issues all companies face and then there are the complex emotional and relationship issues mentioned earlier. Although they are usually experienced on the business side, many executives and family business owners need help, often in the form of outside intervention, to break ongoing stalemates in the business caused by interpersonal conflict. All too often they fail to recognize that these problems stem from the family side, or, if they do understand this, may not know where to turn for appropriate help. However, if the family can, nonetheless, survive the difficult transition to the fourth generation of family ownership, the chances are far higher that the family will continue to remain involved with the business in some form.

THE PSYCHODYNAMIC PARADIGM

The family business is pulled in several directions. Individual family members involved with it will strive to create opportunities for themselves, as well as financial gain and rewarding relationships. Their desires and motivations will affect the company. Then there are structural conflicts between the operating principles of a family and their business. However, the two systems are interdependent: the family's values and behavior affect the company's policies and decisions; and the company influences family members' careers, relationships, and finances. The mingling of family and business systems in a family enterprise explains why drawing on both psychodynamic and family systems concepts has proved to be extremely helpful in addressing family business issues that fall outside the boundaries of traditional management theory.

The psychodynamic perspective focuses on how present individual thinking and behaviour are shaped by experience and past events. The individual works towards answering some basic questions: *How do I see myself? How do I see the world around me? Is it a safe or a threatening place? How can I build on my past experience to create a better future? How can I avoid repeating past mistakes?* Because we are products of our experiences and our origins, the psychoanalyst or psychotherapist seeks to discover how these early influences affect the way we interact with others as adults. Clinical insights can help to provide a rational explanation for seemingly irrational behaviour. These insights become the building blocks for new beginnings.

The family systemic approach (which partially evolved from psychoanalytic insights, and in particular object relations theory) looks at how the family interacts *now*, and emphasizes the process of changing behaviour to create more effective relationships. The family systemic model recognizes the importance of past experiences, but focuses its intervention more on the requirements of the present situation, paying great attention to all the significant players. This is particularly useful in situations in which people must interact on emotional and cognitive levels in both family and business systems.

The advantage of these two psychological perspectives in a family business context is that they consider both the behavioral problems and the more enduring belief systems that underpin behavior at individual, interpersonal and family levels. Using these two perspectives will provide insights into the cognitive, emotional, interpersonal, and social spheres. Using these two perspectives as conceptual tools, academics, consultants, coaches, and therapists are able to address the unique human and organizational challenges experienced by family businesses. To illustrate with a business metaphor: companies use income statements to show the firm's financial trends and patterns over time, and balance sheets to show assets controlled on a certain date. The family systemic model is like a balance sheet: *This is where we are today, and here is the way we will deal with what we have.* The psychodynamic model is more like an income statement: *Here's the overview of the last 10 years; it shows where we're coming from and helps us to be more effective in predicting future trends.*

The challenge for business families, and their stakeholders, is to recognize the issues that family businesses face, understand how to develop strategies to address them, and more importantly, to create narratives, or family stories, that explain the emotional dimension of the issues to the family. It cannot be repeated too often: the most intractable family business issues are not the business problems the organization faces, but the emotional issues that compound them. Applying psychodynamic and systemic concepts will help to explain behavior and will enable the family to prepare for life cycle transitions and other issues that may arise. Examples of the psychological issues that many family businesses face include: deciphering roles and responsibilities within the family and business systems; exploring the motivations of individual protagonists and their family; and developing organizational structures and processes that support decision-making processes in the larger family business system.

Unfortunately, when analyzing organizations (including family businesses), too many people take a 'rational actor' approach, concentrating on structures and systems instead of paying attention to the human dynamics. Even when people are taken into consideration, however, most theories of individual motivation, decision making, and group behavior tend to be oversimplified. Many of these theories appear to be one-dimensional and static. Usually, differences in personality are ignored [6], and very little attention is given to the unique aspects of an individual's character: specific motives, needs, defences, fantasies, symptoms, fears, and anxieties. Completely absent from the literature of family business is any consideration of the family system's influence on individual behavior, a critical element in family firms [7].

In this book we will show that there are limitations to logical decision making. Non-rational forces can strongly influence leadership, interpersonal relations, group functioning, organizational strategy and structure, and corporate culture [8]. Our challenge is to apply both psychodynamic and family systemic perspectives to bring the human and family dimension back into our thinking about organizations.

Because the psychological forces that make up individual personality are fundamental to understanding the psychodynamics of the family firm, we will explore psychodynamic constructs such as the role of unconscious motivation, the effect of intrapsychic reality, defense mechanisms, and the impact of childhood experiences on adult behavior. We'll also look briefly at human development, and explore how life cycle transitions can affect a business family. In addition, we will apply family systemic constructs such as interpersonal relationships, family functioning, and structures and hierarchies. These concepts will support a deeper understanding of how to improve functioning and strengthen relationships in the family. They are applied to real family businesses, through case studies.

Ideas from the psychodynamic and family systemic approaches are integrated with an existing body of literature on leadership, executive behavior, decision making, group dynamics, organizational stress, power and politics, organizational design, organizational culture, strategy, and organizational development and consultation, to offer new perspectives on family business functioning. The application of concepts derived from these psychological paradigms to more traditional management theory discloses patterns that can be woven into a unified *gestalt*, helping us to explain the psychodynamics of life in family businesses.

OUR INTENDED AUDIENCE

We hope that a book offering a broader perspective on family business by addressing the human dynamics of such firms will be useful to a number of audiences.

Our most important readers will be business families themselves and their stakeholders, some of whose experiences and issues we will be sharing and exploring in this book. We hope that family executives, owners and directors, and non-family directors and executives will all find this book deepens their understanding of the unique challenges associated with a family enterprise.

Another aim is to provide business students taking a family business, strategy or organizational behavior course with a new resource to understand better the challenges and opportunities created for consultants working with family businesses. The book should also be of interest in executive seminars, and we hope, management consultants, executive coaches and other professional advisers will find it useful in their organizational diagnoses and interventions.

For the venture capitalist, investment banker, lawyer, accountant, estate planner, or tax adviser, this book should provide help in judging the stability and potential of business leaders, owners, and their companies. The case studies should also be useful in evaluating the kind of interpersonal issues that are usually not discussed in publicly owned businesses.

For the academic and research community, we hope this book will provide an in-depth understanding of human motivation and family dynamics in a business setting. It should also help in developing more realistic models of organizational functioning and enhance understanding of the influence of family concerns on individual careers.

A ROADMAP

Immersing yourself in the non-rational world of family dynamics can be a baptism by fire. The learning-by-doing experience is there, but without sound theory the understanding of the various interdependencies may come too late. The case method can prevent some costly mistakes. Rich case descriptions allow students to assume the role of the protagonists, trying to find options that improve performance and make sense of complex situations. Empathy, applied new thinking, and reflection are ideal vehicles for personal learning.

As indicated before, we offer two complementary frameworks (psychodynamic and family systemic) to help to make sense of family-run organizations. Although this book includes many conceptual models, it is first and foremost a practical book about the real world issues faced by business families. It includes many case stories, most of which we have developed from our consulting and research and use regularly in the classroom. Although the cases provide factual narrative, they are susceptible to human error and bias. For many, we offer some of our reflections on what we think is happening—but those reflections only represent our perspective. Readers should examine each case carefully and

draw their own conclusions, identifying the problems or dilemmas faced, and the options for improved business performance
and family relationships. They should ask what they might have
done in the given situation and what new insight into individual
or family behavior the case offers.

THE STRUCTURE OF THE BOOK

Part I: Questions and Observations

Introduction   We begin with a story about Steinberg, Inc., a once-
successful Canadian family company that was sold and later went
bankrupt, primarily due to conflict in the third generation. This
case study presents the kind of family business psychodynamic
processes that we question and explore in subsequent chapters.

Chapter 1   A Psychological Perspective on Business Families
proposes that understanding individual and family behavior is a
useful framework for families, advisers, students and academics. It
explains in greater depth the psychodynamic and family systems
approaches, and life cycle stages in human development.

Chapter 2   The Challenges of Love and Work is based on
our research and interviews with many stakeholders in family
enterprises. It looks at the business and human challenges that are
particularly applicable to family firms.

Chapter 3   Family Business Practices: Assessing Strengths and
Weaknesses looks at the strengths and weaknesses of family businesses from a psychological perspective. We explore some of the
advantages in working for a family firm and the particular challenges that family firms face.

Part II: Reflection and Learning

Chapter 4   The Life Cycle as an Organizing Construct is a way
of understanding the different stages in human development. The
life cycle highlights the biological aspects of psychosexual development while recognizing the impact of society, history, and culture
on personality. These life stages need to be taken into consideration when dealing with the protagonists in family firms.

Chapter 5 Narcissism, Envy, and Myths in Family Firms starts with a discussion of psychodynamic perspectives on individual development. The origin and dynamics of a reactive form of narcissism, which is quite common among people in family businesses, are explored. We also examine separation-individuation—the process of becoming a person and differentiating oneself from one's family—sibling rivalry, and Oedipal problems. The chapter ends with a discussion of envy and how it colors generational and intergenerational dynamics.

Chapter 6 The Entrepreneur: Alone at the Top. All family firms begin with an entrepreneurial act. In this chapter, we examine some of the themes that preoccupy entrepreneurs and how they affect their behavior, and address the difficulties in working with entrepreneurs.

Chapter 7 Leadership Transition: Replacing a Parent as CEO examines the psychological pressures that leaders of organizations face, and provides insight into why some leaders fail when they reach the top.

Chapter 8 A Systemic View of the Business Family places the overall family system under the microscope. We highlight how what happens in a family business is strongly influenced by the family system's structure and matrix of relationships.

Chapter 9 Diagnosing Family Entanglements introduces two conceptual instruments that will help the reader to decipher the entanglements that occur in families and family business. In this chapter we discuss the genogram—a tool that gives a quick snapshot of family relationships. Another conceptual tool that will be dealt with in this chapter is the Circumplex model—a framework that provides information about degrees of family cohesion and flexibility.

Part III: Integration and Action

Chapter 10 Addressing Transitions and Change explores how change affects individuals, families, and their enterprises. This chapter includes a review of tools and techniques for assessing and understanding change in individuals, families and organizations.

Chapter 11 The Vicissitudes of Family Business is an in-depth study of the Steinberg family, first introduced at the beginning of the book, with full commentary and analysis, and describes the way an imaginary intervention might evolve.

Chapter 12 Putting Family Business Intervention into Practice closes the book with an application of psychological thinking in a real-world situation, with examples and advice on using the techniques we present in the earlier chapters. We share our insights the ways in which coaches, consultants or counselors may help family businesses to manage interpersonal and group relationships for sustaining business performance and family harmony.

ENDNOTES

1. The term 'family controlled' is difficult to define. In many companies, the family may have a minority stake, but for historic or other reasons, they may also retain a great deal of influence in the company and in the community. We define family-controlled firms as organizations where family members retain significant decision-making power concerning strategic direction and the making of key appointments. See Carlock, R.S., Kets de Vries, M.F.R. and Florent-Treacy, E. (2007) 'Family Business' entry in the *International Encyclopedia of Organization Studies*, Thousand Oaks, CA: Sage.
2. Dyer, W.G. Jr. (2003). 'The family: the missing variable in organizational research,' *Entrepreneurship Theory & Practice*, **27** (4): 402.
3. Freud, S. (1955). *Civilization and Its Discontents. The Standard Edition of the Complete Psychological Works of Sigmund Freud Vol.21* (trans. and ed., James Strachey). London: Hogarth Press and the Institute of Psychoanalysis.
4. Carlock, R.S. and Ward, J.L. (2001). *Strategic Planning for the Family Business: Parallel Planning to Unify the Family and Business*. London: Palgrave Macmillan.
5. Beckhard, R. and Dyer, W. (1983a). 'Managing change in the family firm: Issues and strategies,' *Sloan Management Review*, **24**: 59–65; Beckhard, R. and Dyer, W. (1983b). 'Managing continuity in the family-owned business,' *Organizational Dynamics*, **12**: 5–12.
6. Kets de Vries, M.F.R. and Perzow, S. (1991). *Handbook of Character Studies: Psychoanalytic Explorations*. New York: International Universities Press; and Kets de Vries, M.F.R. (2006). *The Leader on the Couch*. London: John Wiley & Sons Ltd.
7. Dyer, W.G. Jr. (2003). 'The family: the missing variable in organizational research,' *Entrepreneurship Theory & Practice*, **27** (4).
8. Kets de Vries, M.F.R. (1984). *The Neurotic Organization*. San Francisco: Jossey-Bass.

PART I

QUESTIONS AND OBSERVATIONS

INTRODUCTION

We start this book by providing a case study of a real-life family in order to give a flavor of the kind of issues commonly occurring in family businesses. We chose this case because it demonstrates how over 50 years of entrepreneurial achievement, through two generations, can be destroyed by subsequent generations if the family fails to address the psychological issues they face.

A Family Story: The Rise and Fall of Steinberg Inc.

Act One

The Steinberg case is the story of a family who, through hard work and innovation, created one of North America's greatest retail companies [1]. In 1911 Ida Steinberg and her husband immigrated to Canada to escape the poverty and anti-Semitism in their native Hungary. The husband, never much of a provider, soon abandoned Ida and their children. Ida, an energetic and resourceful young woman, opened a small grocery store in Montreal's Jewish ghetto. The store was profitable and her son, Sam, left school at age 14 to become his mother's junior partner in the business. Over the next 20 years, Sam became a pioneer in grocery retailing, developing the concept of the full service supermarket. In 1978, at the time of Sam's death, sales exceeded $4 billion (Canadian) and the

Steinbergs had become one of North America's leading business families.

. . .

Act Two (to be discussed below)

. . .

Act Three

The final 18 months of Steinberg Inc. as an independent company were marked by a battle for control of the firm. On August 22, 1989, over 70 years after Ida Steinberg opened her first grocery store on St Lawrence Boulevard in Montreal, family conflicts that spilled over into the boardroom and business forced them to sell the business.

The new owner of Steinberg Inc. went bankrupt only three years after the takeover, having financially overextended himself, and the stores were sold off to various supermarket chains. Thousands of employees lost their jobs. And the ultimate cost? There is no longer any store with the name of Steinberg.

In presenting this family drama, we have deliberately omitted Act Two. Why? Because by doing this, we can draw your attention to the fact that it is events in Act Two that completely reverse the destiny of this company. In Act Two, the second and third generations enter the scene, and the real drama begins. Act Two also describes how family relations broke down; how non-family professional executives lost confidence in the family owners; how Sam's four daughters took their personal battles into the business arena; how the family was forced to sell; and how many key stakeholders lost money in the transaction. It tells us what happened and gives clues about why. Act Two holds important clues to understanding the family's destiny, and we will now look at it more closely.

A Family Story: The Rise and Fall of Steinberg Inc., Act Two

Act Two

The seeds of the conflicts that would destroy the Steinberg family's business were sown quite early on, in decisions that Sam Steinberg made regarding business and family governance, and ownership and management succession. Business governance at Steinberg was dominated by Sam and his friends, who followed Sam's lead on all major strategy and management decisions, including management succession—Sam appointed his son-in-law as CEO on the basis of his family membership rather than a decision based on talent. This sent a clear message to the organization that professional competence was not an important leadership selection criterion.

Sam organized his estate so that ownership of his company would be handed over to his children when he died. Ironically, part of the motivation behind his estate planning was to keep his family together after he was gone. In 1952, Sam had divided most of his assets into equal trusts for each of his four daughters and their children. The daughters all became trustees of each others' trusts. This system worked well while Sam was alive. His voting control and strong personality restrained emotional undercurrents among his four daughters. After his death, the voting shares were kept together and were voted as a block by his widow, Helen. For a few more years, the process worked smoothly. Sam's oldest daughter Mitzi took an executive role in the company, and his third daughter Marilyn took over effective control of the family trusts. There were irritations, however, because the daughters had different views on how they wanted to invest and manage their portions of the money accruing to the trusts and how they wanted to spend the proceeds.

The problems began in earnest in 1985, after a non-family CEO ousted Mitzi from Steinberg Inc. Sidelined from the business, she began to assert herself through her ownership role and the management of the family trusts. More critically, having lost the power struggle with the CEO, she seemed to have lost interest in the company and wanted to sell Steinberg Inc. Alarmed, Sam's two surviving daughters, Marilyn and Evelyn (Rita had died in 1970), joined forces to prevent Mitzi selling the company.

Attempts by other family members to mediate the resulting disputes failed, and both sides became increasingly hostile. Then, in 1987, Marilyn and Evelyn, who had cemented their voting control of the family trusts, managed to push through a motion breaking the agreement that gave Helen the voting rights for 40% of shares held by the trusts, along with the 12% left to her directly by Sam. Helen was served legal notice of the intention to break the voting arrangement in July of that year, 35 years after Sam had created the trusts. This break in the control block represented a material change for the company and had to be reported publicly. The family feud became public knowledge and front page news, and the stock market picked up the scent of a family business in trouble and a possible forced sale.

Shortly afterwards, a family business meeting degenerated into a screaming brawl, and all civil communication between the warring parties ceased. The last vestiges of privacy were stripped on December 30, 1987, when Mitzi shocked everyone by filing a lawsuit to have her sisters and their husbands removed from the management of the family trusts. In the statement of claim, peppered with catty personal comments, Mitzi accused her sisters of 'gross negligence and reprehensible neglect' in managing the trusts. A well-known Montreal cartoonist satirized the unseemly spectacle by portraying the Steinberg sisters as sodden mud wrestlers.

In many family businesses it is what happens in Act Two of the family drama (the point at which later generations get involved) that determines the continuity and success of the business, or conversely, sows the seeds of conflict and ultimate break up. Clues to what went wrong in this family drama, and its bitter ending, can be found in Sam Steinberg himself. Part of what we would seek to analyze in looking at a family like this are the following questions:

- What early experiences shaped Sam's mother?
- How did she raise Sam and his siblings?
- How did Sam's life experiences influence his leadership style?
- How did his personality steer the creation and growth of his empire? How did it influence its downfall?
- Could the mistakes Sam made have been avoided, or was Steinberg Inc. programmed to self-destruct from the time he took control (and if so, why)?
- How did Sam's parenting style and gender attitudes affect his daughters?
- What could have been done to prevent the downfall of the company?

At various points throughout this book, we will be looking at the kinds of issues raised by this family drama. We will also look at other family case studies, before returning in Chapter 11 to a more thorough analysis of the Steinbergs. We hope by this means to show how business families going through change and transition can avoid the pitfalls that endanger both family and company. Our goal is to help readers who own, work in or deal with a family business to avoid an ending like that of the Steinbergs.

ENDNOTE

1. The Steinberg family story in this Introduction and in Chapter 11 is taken from a case study written by Manfred Kets de Vries (1996). *Family Business: Human Dilemmas in the Family Firm*. London: Thompson. Other sources for the Steinberg case: Gibbon, A. and Hadekel, P. (1990). *Steinberg: The Break Up of a Family Empire*. Toronto: Macmillan; National Film Board of Canada documentary *The Corporation: After Sam*; Mintzberg, H. and Waters, J.A. (1982). 'Tracking strategy in an entrepreneurial firm,' *Academy of Management Journal*, **25** (3), 465–499; and Steinberg Inc.'s annual reports and corporate communication materials. Arnold Steinberg, a former executive vice president at Steinberg Inc., and a nephew of Sam, was also a valuable resource.

CHAPTER 1

A PSYCHOLOGICAL PERSPECTIVE ON BUSINESS FAMILIES

In most societies the family is a fundamental institution for transmitting values to succeeding generations, and for ensuring their physical and emotional development. Families are usually driven by a deep concern for both the well-being of individual family members and for the family legacy. However, in a business family, normal family goals may come into conflict with the business's economic goals because an important theme within the family system is to meet the human and psychological needs of its members rather than to arrive at the best economic return.

It is a truism that human beings are subjected to many elusive, out of awareness processes that affect how they make decisions. We all know that executives (including people working in family businesses) do not always act rationally, logically, or sensibly [1]. However, we have discovered that many leaders of family businesses seem to be especially prone to irrational behavior (as will be illustrated in the various case studies that appear in this book) [2]. Clinical investigation has shown that many problems in family businesses stem from the fact that their leaders (as well as other family members employed in key positions in the business) are often unknowingly acting out their deepest conflicts, desires and fantasies in the larger arena of the family business. The task for anyone studying family businesses is therefore to look at deep structures: the inner motives, fantasies, desires and defensive reactions of the principal actors. What drives them? What makes them act the way they do? How can we make sense of their behavior?

In a family business (particularly one in crisis) there will be a need at some point for its members to reflect on how their family is organized and to tease out the structures and rules that drive their interpersonal relationships. They will have to discover which of their interaction patterns are functional and which are dysfunctional. Carl Jung often asked his troubled patients, 'Is this behavior working for you?' If the answer is 'No,' it may well be time for the family to consider other approaches to relating to each other.

A very effective conceptual way of understanding individual behavior and motivation is psychoanalytic psychology, particularly objects relations theory [3]. However, when studying family businesses we have found that this orientation to understanding complex human processes needs to be enhanced by theory from the more recent fields of systems analysis and family therapy—known as family systems theory [4]. We have discovered that combining psychodynamic thinking with family systems ideas into a psychodynamic-systems approach can be invaluable as a key to unlocking many of the knotty problems faced by business families.

PSYCHODYNAMIC AND FAMILY SYSTEMIC PERSPECTIVES

One of the challenges we faced in writing this book was overcoming some of the institutional or academic barriers to working across the boundaries between psychodynamic and family systemic therapy. In 1998, Christopher Dare, in a paper on the practice of psychodynamic and family systemic therapy, commented:

> The two disciplines of family therapy and psychoanalysis remain organizationally and conceptually disassociated from each other despite the two subjects having considerable overlap, plying adjacent trades and using theoretical ideas which show considerable parallels [5].

At the time, Dare encouraged a stronger link between the two disciplines. But in fact, a rapprochement of these two ways of looking at human behavior is increasingly becoming a reality. In practice, we have found it extremely useful to establish a link to the inner psychological theater of the individual and explore how the scenes of this inner theater are enacted in the larger family system.

To have a greater impact in family business interventions, this book is designed around the application of psychodynamic and family systemic frameworks for studying human behavior [6]. Applying these two perspectives creates a more complete and balanced view of individual behavior and interpersonal relationships. It is an ideal way to bring a degree of rationality to what can, at times, be extremely perplexing behavior.

Because of this orientation, we use theories, concepts, methodologies, techniques, and vocabularies that are more often used in psychology than in discussions of management issues. In particular, we draw on concepts and theories taken from psychodynamic psychology (particularly object relations theory, self-psychology, and ego psychology), dynamic psychiatry, developmental theory, cognition, and the study of narrative.

In this search for rapprochement between various disciplines we like to emphasize that object relations theory, an offshoot of psychoanalytic theory that emphasizes interpersonal relations, primarily in the family and especially between mother and child, will be especially helpful to bridge the gap between classical psychoanalytic psychology and family systems theory. Object relations theorists are interested in inner images of the self and other, and how they manifest themselves in interpersonal situations. Consequently, there is a degree of overlap between this derivative of classical psychoanalysis and family systems theory. As Christopher Dare said, 'Psychoanalysis and family therapy can come together now, [. . .] by agreeing that both are preoccupied with the therapeutically useful, ethically apt re-creation and telling of stories' [7].

KEY IDEAS FROM THE PSYCHODYNAMIC APPROACH

The psychoanalyst Sigmund Freud postulated that the human mind functions through the interaction of opposing forces. A person has wishes and fantasies that evoke anxiety, leading to defensive reactions that range from relatively normal to dysfunctional. The conflict between these forces is mainly unconscious, and yet can have a huge impact on people's emotional life, self-image and relationships with other people and larger organizations [8].

Children are born with certain innate desires that cause them to seek pleasure and avoid pain. These desires become transformed into mental images that govern their feelings and behavior. As their parents attempt to socialize and fit them for society, children inevitably experience frustration of such desires as they learn what is allowed and what is forbidden. Gradually their childish impulses are modified and transformed more in line with societal norms. During this process many of the original desires and anxieties associated with them are seemingly forgotten. However, these unacceptable wishes and desires are not really forgotten but continue to linger below the surface, retaining the potential to affect adult behavior significantly in later life.

Freud later went on to formulate a general theory of mental development, part of which involved defining ideas such as the unconscious, defenses (the desire of the conscious mind to cope with wishes and fantasies emerging from the unconscious), and character patterns. He also described the developmental stages of childhood in his 'psychosexual stages of development' (which we look at in more detail in Chapter 4) and the idea of transference.

THE ROLE OF TRANSFERENCE AND COUNTERTRANSFERENCE

Everyday conversation consists of one person attempting to transmit feelings to another. We talk about 'putting something across,' or giving someone 'a piece of our mind.' For example, when we are in distress, we may try to convey to another person our distress in such a way that he or she can literally *feel* it. The normal communication process consists of fairly rapidly oscillating cycles of projection and introjection: as one person communicates with words and demeanor (projection), the other receives and interprets the communication (introjection); then the listener, having understood the speaker's message, reprojects it to the original speaker, perhaps accompanied by an interpretation [9].

Similarly, at some stage in any research or process involving the investigating of human behavior, the subject of that investigation is likely to evoke certain responses in the researcher—responses that in a therapeutic encounter between a client and therapist are usually referred to as 'transference' and 'countertransference.' This cycle of projection and introjection—a ubiquitous phenomenon—is what transference and countertransference processes are all about.

Transference is normally used to describe the way in which a client perceives or experiences in their therapist characteristics or behavior that belong either to an important figure from the client's own past (a parent, for example), or that are a denied part of their own personality (for example, the client perceives the therapist as being angry or sad when in fact these are the client's subconscious feelings 'projected' on to the therapist).

The term 'countertransference' is normally used to mean the feelings that a client evokes in a therapist—again, possibly relating to an important figure or figures from the therapist's past. It describes feelings that therapists become aware of that do not seem to belong to themselves but which they experience as a result of being with the client. For example, at the end of a therapy session the therapist may feel inexplicably frightened, sad, confused, or worried. This may be due to the subtle transference of these feelings to the therapist by the client.

In short, transference refers to the feelings of the client about the therapist, countertransference refers to its mirror image: the feelings that a patient arouses in a therapist [10]. In this book we will use these terms to apply to the feelings that the subject (the business family) arouses not only in the researcher, therapist, coach, or consultant, but also in the individual members of a family organization toward one another.

For example, a typical example of a transference reaction can be found in the case of two colleagues at work, say a young woman and her much older boss, who can barely stand to be in the same room with one another. Both are competent, responsible individuals but when together they seem to regress into dysfunctional behavior. Even though their acrimonious personal relationship has been addressed directly, agreements reached and boundaries set, the effectiveness of both women is compromised. The younger woman harbors a permanent grudge against her boss that she herself cannot rationally explain. Moreover, the older woman takes the bait, and the younger woman brings out the worst in her.

One approach to solving this problem would be to evaluate the possibility of a transference reaction on the part of the younger woman. Perhaps, as a child, she had a difficult, unresolved relationship with her mother or another older, female relative—many of whose mannerisms her boss shares. Forced to deal with her 'mother' at work, the young woman's unconscious emotions may spill over into her relationship with her unwitting superior.

Thus careful evaluation of transference and countertransference reactions provides us with *another source of information* that can be used concurrently with more conventional data. Although countertransference reactions can be confusing, we need to be aware of them and understand why they are happening, as they can be great assets to us in our 'detective' work.

Transference and countertransference are critical concepts in interpersonal understanding because they are ubiquitous elements of the human condition. They are processes whereby (as we indicated) there is a confusion of person, place, and time, due to the reliving of earlier relationships, usually in an attempt to resolve earlier development problems that were not successfully dealt with by someone earlier in life. They can be viewed as a kind of repetition, resulting in persistent, stereotypical behavior patterns that have their roots in privileged relationships with early caretakers. These two concepts are organizing activities, indicating the continuing influence of a person's early life experiences throughout the life cycle. The challenge is for us to understand that this pattern—useful as it may have been when we were young—may no longer be appropriate at a later stage of life.

Psychological Defenses

An individual's personality is largely determined by the particular way that person balances his or her intrapsychic view of the world with the impact of external reality. In dealing with the stress and strain of daily life we use 'psychological defenses' to help us to cope with emerging anxiety [11]. These defensive reactions are mostly unconscious (although we can learn to become aware of what we are doing), and have the effect of preventing us having to face aspects of ourselves that we find threatening, preventing us from being overwhelmed by feelings that are too disturbing. These often work well because through them we are able to find a mental equilibrium—albeit somewhat limited in some areas [12]. Of course, these defenses contribute to behavior that is not always easily understandable. A classic example is the 'kicking the dog' phenomenon—returning from work at the end of a frustrating day and shouting at the children or the dog. This pattern can be viewed as a displacement defense: we displace our anger from the person to whom we cannot safely express it (a likely candidate being the boss) onto a safer target, one that is less likely to retaliate.

A number of 'mechanisms of defense' are now part of everyday language—for example, projection and denial. Other terms often mean different things to different theorists and overlap: ideas such as 'rationalization,' 'intellectualization,' 'displacement,' 'reaction-formation,' 'introjection,' and 'splitting'. We take a closer look at splitting later in the book.

The Idea of Texts

One particular clinical research concept in psychodynamic therapy that is especially useful in understanding the family business is the notion of texts (in family systemic therapy they are known as 'scripts' or 'narrative') [13]. Texts are the grouping of interrelated information and all types of data containing messages and themes that can be systematized. When decoding family-business texts, significance is extracted from interrelated factual, cognitive, and affective units constructed from the researcher's experiences with people in the business.

Texts can include obvious things (like managerial statements, writing, and observable behavior) and implicit things (like symbolic behavior, organizational myths and stories, specific strategic decisions, particular interpersonal styles, and the type of organizational structure that characterizes the company). When analyzed, these give clues to what life in a family or an organization is all about. Understanding these texts adds a further dimension to our analysis of organizational phenomena. If we are alert to underlying themes, to meanings behind the metaphors used by family members and other stakeholders, to the reasons for the selection of certain words, and to the implications of certain activities, our knowledge of family and organizational life becomes much richer [14].

A number of rules are helpful when decoding these texts. First, there is the 'rule of thematic unity.' When we try to analyze an organizational story, we have to shape the different observations into an interconnected, cohesive unit, a *gestalt* or whole. We need to identify themes.

Second, we are engaged in pattern matching, looking for structural parallels, for a fit between present-day events and earlier incidents in the history of an individual or organization; we are watching for revealing repetition [15]. These patterns demonstrate how individuals may misinterpret the present in terms of the past and relive the past through present actions. Transparently anachronistic repetitions probably indicate some form of transference reaction and when these happen, it is time to sit up and pay attention.

Third, interpretations need to be guided by the 'rule of psychological urgency,' which assumes that an individual's most pressing needs, intentions, or ways of acting can be identified somewhere in the family text. We need to tease out the operational code—what drives the individual—of a person's life [16]. The challenge is to identify pervasive relationship patterns, what have also been called 'core conflictual relationship themes' [17]. To understand what is going on, it is essential to identify these constantly repeated patterns. There are always consistencies in an individual's relationships.

Finally, there is the 'rule of multiple function' [18]. Depending on the psychological urgency of the matter at hand, part of the text can have more than one meaning and can be looked at from many different points of view. Sometimes organizational resistances and defensive processes stand out. At other times, the key dynamics may be related to the way people manage aggression or affectionate bonds. Processes evolving around shame, guilt, envy, jealousy, and rivalry can also be important. To complicate matters even further, these issues can occur concurrently at the individual, interpersonal, group, intergroup, and organizational levels. It is therefore necessary to seek out meanings at multiple levels and to tease out the individual and organizational roots and consequences of a family business's actions and decisions.

THE FAMILY SYSTEMIC PERSPECTIVE

Family systemic thinking is derived from many different streams of social science research on how individuals interact and relate to each other in groups. For example, in sociology, Kurt Lewin's work on group dynamics led to the awareness that group work can be an effective tool for changing ideas and behavior. The development of his field theory demonstrated how groups experience conflict, and how they communicate [19]. His conceptual ideas have informed psychologists working with families on interpersonal and relationships issues.

In a similar vein, Wilfred Bion, a psychiatrist and psychoanalyst also working on group dynamics, identified three tactics that groups use to avoid dealing with the real task at hand: entering into fight/flight mode, pairing, or resorting to dependency reactions [20]. Although a group of people is supposed to engage in real work, it became clear from Bion's observations that groups could be extremely creative in resorting to other, more regressive activities that complicated progress on the task at hand. Executive coaches, consultants, and other advisers need to pay attention to group phenomena—and the role they play in their clients' fantasy life—when dealing with family businesses.

Family systems theory makes it very clear that the therapist is not a detached observer of what happens in the family. He or she becomes very much part of its dynamics. Understanding the role of the therapist in the system is fundamental to understanding the systemic approach to families. Early family therapists assumed that the therapist could change the system while remaining detached and unaffected by what happened in the family [21]. But as research in the field progressed, it became obvious that there is a process of mutual influence that develops between the therapist and the family [22]. The development of this second-order cybernetic thinking supports the realization that there is no objective reality, and that the therapist, interacting with the family, constructs his or her own understanding of the family that is observed [23]. As we have suggested before, therapists, consultants, and coaches should be prepared to engage in a process of self-reflection and analysis in order to turn these interactions to their advantage; they should constantly think about what is happening to them while engaged in an intervention with a family.

Although, clearly, family systems thinking has a different focus from the psychodynamic approach, there is now an increasing convergence between family systems theory and psychodynamic ideas, in particular those of the object-relations theorists [24]. (See Table 1.1 for a comparison between the family systemic and the classical psychodynamic approach.)

Table 1.1 gives a sense of the nuances in client orientation: past versus future, individual versus the group, a more participative role versus a more detached role, and being directive versus being reflective. But because of the convergence between systemic family therapy and relational psychoanalysis we have to bear in mind that all that we are talking about are nuances. The mingling of family and business systems within a family enterprise explains why drawing on both the psychodynamic and the family systems approach has proved to be extremely helpful in addressing family business issues that fall outside the boundaries of traditional management theory.

Table 1.1 A comparison of family systemic and classical psychodynamic perspectives

Family systemic	Psychodynamic
• Focuses on family relationships	• Focuses on the individual
• Explores present to future	• Explores past to present to build for the future
• Focuses on behavioral changes in behavior	• Develops new insights as a prerequisite for change
• Addresses problems in the system	• Focuses on the problems of the individual, taking a relational perspective
• Therapist collaborates in the system	• Therapist has more of a detached attitude
• Works with actual family	• Explores symbolic family through the individual family members
• More directive approach	• More reflective approach

The psychodynamic perspective focuses on how individual thinking and behavior are shaped by experience and past events. Because we are all products of our experiences and our origins, the psychotherapist seeks to discover how these early influences affect the way clients interact with others as adults. Clinical insights can help to provide a rational explanation for seemingly irrational behavior. These insights become the building blocks for new beginnings.

In contrast, the family systems approach looks at how the family interacts *now*, and emphasizes the process of changing behavior to create more effective relationships. The family systems model recognizes the importance of past experiences, but focuses its intervention more on the requirements of the present. This is particularly useful in situations where people must interact on emotional and cognitive levels, as is the case in both family and business systems.

The advantage of using these two psychological perspectives in a family-business context is that they consider both the behavioral problems and the more enduring belief systems that under-pin behavior at individual, interpersonal, and family levels. Using these two perspectives provides insights into the cognitive, emotional, interpersonal, and social spheres.

THE THERAPEUTIC ALLIANCE

A crucial factor in the success of a therapeutic or consulting intervention is the establishing of a good therapeutic alliance—the collaborative relationship a therapist is able to form with a client. It concerns the shared ability of the patient and the thera-pist to understand and to relate to each other on a deep level, being prepared to work on the task at hand [25]. It is this rela-tionship that enables the client and therapist to explore together issues that are anxiety-provoking for the client and therefore usually avoided.

The working alliance is established by the therapist's ability to build relationships (allowing clients space to talk, empathy, demonstrating positive regard) and by the personal qualities of the therapist. This alliance is also established by the therapist's ability to maintain what is called the 'therapeutic frame,' a set of rules of working together, usually delineated in the initial meeting. The frame deals with practical matters, such as times of meeting, length of therapy sessions, the fee, confidentiality, regularity of meeting, and the setting of boundaries between the two parties.

Building the Alliance with a Family

When working with a family rather than an individual the thera-pist needs particular training in how to establish an alliance that provides a level playing field that will allow all participating generations to work as a family of adults. A family meeting facilitated by an external adviser needs to meet the needs of the senior generation (for example, by showing that their ideas are respected) and the younger generation (for example, by allowing them to express their frustration, or other emotions, in a con-structive way). As part of creating the therapeutic alliance, the adviser needs to provide the family with a 'safe space'—a reas-suring environment that needs to be suitable in both physical terms (e.g. quiet, and where clients will not be overheard if strong emotions are expressed) and emotional terms (one in which clients feel they trust the therapist with their inmost anxieties). Only when this is available will family members' anxiety be suf-ficiently reduced for them to feel able to experiment with new ways of doing things.

A family meeting, or series of meetings, with a professionally trained facilitator can provide the family with opportunities to think about and test new ways of working together. For example, a family considering appointing the youngest son as managing director, or a daughter as the first woman board member, may have to overcome both the power of family scripts and the larger society's biases and traditions of business leadership.

A SUMMING-UP

This chapter has provided some basic understanding of the prin-ciples and theories we will refer to throughout the book. We will demonstrate how using a psychodynamic-systems approach can help the family to prepare for life-cycle transitions and other psychological issues that family businesses face, including:

- deciphering roles and responsibilities within the family and business systems;
- exploring the motivations of individual protagonists and their family; and
- developing organizational structures and processes that support decision making in the larger family-business system.

A critical value of family systemic therapy is the acceptance of the role of the therapist, consultant, or coach as a part of the system [26]. For the purposes of this book, we suggest that you, the reader, are also a researcher [27], especially if you are from, work for, or have experience with, a business family. Instead of ignoring factors like personal emotions, you should recognize and welcome them, viewing your own reactions as important sources of data. By engaging in a process of self-reflection and self-analysis, you can turn these feelings to your advantage. Try to sharpen your skills in self-observation. You should constantly think about how you react as you work through the ideas in this book: Do you agree with what you are reading? Disagree? Why? And what kind of associations bubble up when you are reading?

ENDNOTES

1. Zaleznik, A. and Kets de Vries, M.F.R. (1975). *Power and the Corporate Mind.* Boston: Houghton-Mifflin.
2. Levinson, H. (1972). *Organizational Diagnosis.* Cambridge, MA: Harvard University Press; Levinson, H. (1981). *Executive.* Cambridge, MA: Harvard University Press; Levinson, H. (2002). *Organizational Assessment: A Step-by-Step Guide to Effective Consulting.* Washington, DC: American Psychological Association; Zaleznik, A. (1966). *Human Dilemmas of Leadership.* New York: HarperCollins; Zaleznik, A. (1989). *The Managerial Mystique.* New York: HarperCollins; Hirschhorn, L. (1988). *The Workplace Within: Psychodynamics of Organizational Life.* Cambridge, MA: MIT Press; Kets de Vries, M.F.R. (1989). *Prisoners of Leadership.* New York: Wiley; Kets de Vries, M.F.R. (2006). *The Leadership Mystique* (2nd edn). London: Prentice Hall/Financial Times; Kets de Vries, M.F.R. (2006). *The Leader on the Couch.* London: John Wiley & Sons Ltd; Gabriel, Y. (1999). *Organizations in Depth.* London: Sage.
3. Freud, S. (1933). New Introductory Lectures. *The Standard Edition of the Complete Psychological Works of Sigmund Freud Vol 21* (trans. and ed., J. Strachey). London: The Hogarth Press and the Institute of Psychoanalysis. **22**; Sandler, J. and Rosenblatt, B. (1962). 'The concept of the representational world,' *Psychoanalytic Study of the Child,* **17**: 128–145; White, R. (1966). *Lives in Progress.* New York: Holt, Rinehart & Winston; Greenberg, J.R. and Mitchell, S.A. (1983). *Object Relations in Psychoanalytic Theory.* Cambridge, MA: Harvard University Press; Lichtenberg, J.D. and Schonbar, R.A. (1992). Motivation in psychology and psychoanalysis. *Interface of Psychoanalysis and Psychology* (eds Barron, J.W., Eagle, M.N. and Wolitzky, D.L.). Washington: American Psychological Association, pp. 11–36; Lemma-Wright, A. (1995). *Invitation to Psychodynamic Psychology.* London: Whurr Publishers.
4. Minuchin, S. (1974). *Families and Family Therapy.* Cambridge, MA: Harvard University Press; Bowen, M. (1994). *Family Therapy in Clinical Practice.* New York: Jason Aronson; Lusterman, D.D., McDaniel, S.H. *et al.* (1995). *Integrat-*

ing Family Therapy: Handbook of Family Psychology and Systems Therapy. Washington, D.C.: American Psychological Association; Sexton, T.L., Weeks, G.R. *et al.,* (eds) (2003). *Handbook of Family Therapy.* New York: Brunner-Routledge; Harway, M. (ed.) (2005). *Handbook of Couples Therapy.* Hoboken, NJ: John Wiley & Sons Ltd.

5. Dare, C. (1998). 'Psychoanalysis and family systems revisited: the old, old story?' *Journal of Family Therapy,* **20**: 165–176.

6. Dyer, W.G. Jr (2003). 'The family: the missing variable in organizational research.' *Entrepreneurship Theory & Practice,* **27** (4), 402; Kets de Vries, M.F.R. and Miller, D. (1984a). 'Narcissism and leadership: An object relations perspective,' *Human Relations,* **38** (6), 583–601; Kets de Vries, M.F.R. and Miller, D. (1984b). *The Neurotic Organization: Diagnosing and Changing Counterproductive Styles of Management.* San Francisco: Jossey-Bass; Kets de Vries and Associates (1991). *Organizations on the Couch.* San Francisco: Jossey-Bass.

7. Dare, C. (1998)—as note (5)—p. 174.

8. Freud, S. (1920). *A General Introduction to Psychoanalysis,* Boni & Liveright; Freud, S. (1933)—as note (3).

9. Kets de Vries, M.F.R. (2007). Are you feeling mad, sad, bad, or glad? INSEAD Working Paper, Fontainebleau, France.

10. Epstein, L. and Feiner, A.H. (eds) (1979). *Countertransference.* New York: Jason Aronson.

11. Freud, S. (1933); Freud, A. (1966). *The Ego and the Mechanisms of Defense.* Madison, Conn.: International Universities Press; Vaillant, G.E. (1992). *Ego Mechanisms of Defense.* Washington, D.C.: American Psychiatric Press.

12. Jacobs, M. (1999). *Psychodynamic Counselling in Action* (2nd edn). London: Sage Publications Ltd.

13. Loewenberg, P. (1982). *Decoding the Past: The Psychohistorical Approach.* New York: Alfred A. Knopf; Kets de Vries, M. and Miller, D. (1987). 'Interpreting organizational texts,' *Journal of Management Studies,* **24** (3): 233–347; Rennie, D.L. (1994). 'Storytelling in psychotherapy: the client's subjective experience,' *Psychotherapy,* **31**: 234–243.

14. Kets de Vries, M.F.R. and Associates (1991). *Organizations on the Couch: Clinical Perspectives on Organizational Behavior and Change.* San Francisco: Jossey-Bass.

15. Geertz, C. (1983). *Local Knowledge.* New York: Basic Books; Spence, D.P. (1982). *Narrative Truth and Historical Truth.* New York: Norton

16. Leites, N. (1953). *A Study of Bolshevism.* New York: Free Press; George, A.L. (1969). 'The operational code: A neglected approach to the study of political leaders and decision making,' *International Studies Quarterly,* **13**: 190–222.

17. Luborsky, L. (1984). *Principles of Psychoanalytic Psychotherapy.* New York: Basic Books; Luborsky, L., Crits-Christoph, P., Minz, J. and Auerbach, A. (1988). *Who Will Benefit from Psychotherapy?* New York: Basic Books.

18. Waelder, R. (1936). 'The principle of multiple function,' *Psychoanalytic Quarterly,* **5**: 45–62.

19. Lewin, K. (1951). *Field Theory in Social Science.* New York: McGraw-Hill.

20. Bion, W.R. (1948). 'Experiences in groups,' *Human Relations,* **1**: 314–329.

21. Bateson, G. (1972). *Steps to an Ecology of Mind: Mind and Nature*. New York: Ballantine Books.
22. Von Forester, H. (1981). *Observing Systems*. Seaside, CA: Intersystems.
23. Anderson, T. (ed.) (1990). *The Reflecting Team*. New York: W.W. Norton.
24. Kohut, H. (1971). *The Analysis of the Self*. Madison, Connecticut: International Universities Press; Greenberg, J.R. and Mitchell, S.A. (1983). *Object Relations in Psychoanalytic Theory*. Cambridge, MA: Harvard University Press; Fonagy, P., Cooper, A.M. and Wallerstein, R. (1999). *Psychoanalysis on the Move: The Work of Joseph Sandler*. London/New York: Routledge.
25. Greenson, R.R. (1965). 'The working alliance and the transference neurosis,' *Psychoanalytic Quarterly*, **34**: 155–181; Sandler, J., Dare, C. *et al.* (1973). *The Patient and the Analyst: The Basis of the Psychoanalytic Process*. New York: International Universities Press; Castonguay, L.G., Constantino, M.J. *et al.* (2006). "The working alliance: Where are we and where should we go?" *Psychotherapy: Theory, Research, Practice, Training*, **43**(3): 271–279.
26. Howe, R. and von Foerster, H. (1974). 'Cybernetics at Illinois,' *Forum*, 6.
27. Glaser, B. and Strauss, A. (1967). *The Discovery of Grounded Theory*. Chicago: Alpine; Devereux, G. (1967). *From Anxiety to Method in the Behavioral Sciences*. New York: Humanities Press; Turner, R. (1974). *Ethnomethodology*. Harmondsworth, UK: Penguin; Edelson, M. (1984). *Hypothesis and Evidence in Psychoanalysis*. Chicago: Chicago University Press; Schein, E. (1987). *The Clinical Perspective in Field Work*. Newbury Park, CA: Sage.

CHAPTER 2

THE CHALLENGES OF
LOVE AND WORK

All businesses—family controlled or otherwise—find it difficult to remain profitable over the very long term. Many factors contribute to a company's demise or its inability to continue independently: businesses mature; markets and technologies change (eliminating the need for various products and services); or competitors quickly copy successful strategies. But, as already suggested, in family businesses, more often than not, it is the family itself that is the main threat to long-term continuity. Unresolved personal conflicts, lack of trust, difficult interpersonal relationships, sibling rivalry, generational issues, the family's demands on the business—any or all of these issues can affect a family firm's success.

Although conflict is a natural element of the human condition, unfortunately, in some families, intense psychological conflict becomes a regular pattern. When a family allows unresolved or recurring conflicts to diminish communication and trust, it becomes difficult for family members to share ideas, discuss issues or make decisions effectively.

In this chapter we look at the structural phenomena of family business relationships and the special challenges these pose for leadership and ownership. We also examine the issues of human motivation, patterns of interaction between family members, and the potential competitive advantages of family-owned firms over publicly traded corporations.

CONFLICTING GOALS IN THE FAMILY BUSINESS

We saw earlier in the Preface (p. xvi) how Freud identified love and work as being the keys to human satisfaction [1]. Psychoanalyst Erik Erikson later interpreted '*lieben und arbeiten*' as meaning 'a general work-productiveness which would not preoccupy the individual to the extent that he loses his right or capacity to be a loving being' [2]. Erikson argued that in order for an individual to find satisfaction in life, he or she must experience love and work in a balanced, and not mutually exclusive, way. Often, family members expect (albeit unconsciously) to get both these forms of satisfaction from the family business, despite the fact that this is primarily concerned with work. (In some senses, however, this is a legitimate hope because a family business is a unique form of business organization since it involves the overlap of a system structured on rational economic principles with a system organized and driven by emotions.) It is important to recognize that strategic thinking and business practices in a family business will often be affected by the 'love' needs of the family.

Consider the case of a father and son working together in a family business that the father founded and owns. When the father considers management and succession, he probably thinks first of his son. Indeed, he may have been fantasizing about the two of them running the business together from the day the boy was born, and is looking forward to his son succeeding him as CEO. He loved showing his little boy round the factory; later, he made sure his son got a lot of experience working in different areas of the company.

Now let's consider the son's perspective. While he was growing up, his father took his son to the factory whenever the boy was free. While his friends played sports with their fathers, he had to stack boxes or sweep the floor. At university, he worked part time at the business on special projects while his friends were at the beach. He feels that every moment he spends with his father is diluted by some aspect of the business, which appears— to the younger man—to come first. Consequently the son sees the business as being his father's first love. It would not be surprising to learn that the son has very ambivalent feelings about the business. Although he realizes that it does provide a way for him to interact with his father, at the same time he may feel he has always had to compete with the business for his father's love and attention.

This story need not necessarily hint at future tragedy but it does illustrate the kinds of ambiguities in relationships and perceptions that can be both great strengths and potential liabilities for family businesses. When the input or ability of individual family members is taken for granted, the business's strength and future can become compromised. On the other hand, the family's emotional involvement with each other can be the glue that holds the business together through many critical events, including generational transition. The following case illustrates one way in which these ambiguities can be confronted.

A Family Story: The Prodigal Son

An entrepreneur (we'll call him Jack Williams) created a very successful family business in the 1980s, an eponymous supermarket that was very well known in the region in which it was located. Jack Williams won many national marketing awards: for the produce department's inviting presentation of fresh fruit, for the store's innovative dairy ideas, and for customer loyalty. Customers would send Jack holiday postcards, which he displayed on a 'wall of fame' at the front of the store. Along with the postcards were photographs of customers in exotic locations, proudly displaying a Jack Williams shopping bag.

Jack Williams had two sons. His older son, Tom, graduated from university with a degree in accounting, and went to work for a public accounting firm. After three years, he earned his certified public accountant certificate, and began a master's degree program in management. Working part time, he earned an MBA in two years. When he had finished his studies, he asked his father if he could work in the family business. Jack was thrilled that Tom expressed an interest in working with him. It coincided nicely with his plan to open a second store.

So Jack invited Tom to join the business, expecting Tom to become the managing director of the new outlet.

Jack's younger son, Kevin, didn't share his father's and brother's business orientation. He enrolled at the University of Colorado at Boulder, and skied until the end of the winter, at which point he was kicked out. He then transferred to the University of California at San Diego to work on his surfing. At the end of the year, having successfully completed a semester of surfing, he was asked not to return.

Frustrated, with no career opportunity on the horizon, and with no real goals, Kevin returned home and asked his father for a job. As a good father, Jack hired Kevin to unload trucks for the produce department. The produce department was the most demanding area of the business, because fruit and vegetables are fragile and perishable. Kevin agreed to give it a try.

A few weeks later, the produce manager asked to see Jack. He reported that Kevin was not doing particularly well. He 'was not meeting expectations' and he didn't seem to be very committed to his work. Jack told the produce manager to treat Kevin like any other employee. He should be given a warning notice, and Jack should be kept informed of the situation.

The next month, the produce manager asked to speak to Jack again. Kevin's performance had not improved; in fact it was worse. Jack assured him that Kevin would not be at work the next day. On his way home that afternoon, Jack walked through the produce department and found his son. 'Kevin,' he said, 'why don't you stop by the house tonight after work? I need to talk to you.'

Kevin showed up at his parents' house a few hours later. Jack invited him to sit down, then told him in no uncertain terms that his performance was unsatisfactory, and he was fired. Kevin was taken aback, and didn't know what to say.

Then Jack got up and took two large towels off a nearby shelf. He threw one to his son, saying, 'Son, I heard you just lost your job. Let's go out to the hot tub and talk about your life and career. I really want to hear your ideas, and I want to know what I can do to help.'

Jack Williams had a successful business *and* strong family relationships because he treated the family like a family and the business like a business. He could have made a mess of things by placing the needs of the family before the requirements of the business and allowing his son to keep his job, despite his lack of commitment and poor performance. This story would then have had a very different ending because if Jack had allowed his son to keep his job, Kevin's career and life would have continued on a low-performance trajectory. Within the business, non-family employees and executives would have seen the family compromised by Kevin's low performance, and eventually his older brother would have had to deal with the fact that Kevin was failing to contribute to the business's success. The 'hot tub solution' is an important signifier—Jack was prepared to help his son to find an activity more to his liking (although it might be worth considering what had contributed to his son's lack of a work ethic in the first place).

Because family businesses are often multigenerational, the senior generation's unwillingness to make tough decisions about the next generation may come back to haunt a firm long after the senior generation has retired. The greatest challenge for committed and high-performing siblings is having to work with a brother or sister who has no emotional investment in the business and is only there to collect dividends or a paycheck. The parent who allows a child to 'get by' is setting the scene for chronic conflict when their children become significant owners, and begin to struggle with each other over performance and rewards.

THE THREE-CIRCLES MODEL

So, we know that conflicts between family and business systems are to be expected because these two systems operate according to different values, and are oriented toward conflicting goals, all within a context of overlapping individual and organizational relationships. However, another issue is that families as systems tend to focus inwardly, and generally resist change (are homeostatic), while business systems, if they are to succeed, must take the opposite approach—focusing on the external environment, and looking for ways to exploit change.

We will now look at further conflicts of interest in family businesses by examining the three-circle model, which looks at the three subsystems that comprise the family business system: family, business, and ownership [3]. By showing the different interests of the different elements in the family business we can get a better idea of why businesses that overemphasize the business system at the cost of the family system often end up in a mess.

The Family Circle

Family members put a high priority on *emotional capital*—the family's shared experiences working across generations. Family members are also concerned with *social capital* (their reputation within the community) and *financial capital* (dividends and wealth creation). The family's values, relationships, and communication style are all elements contained in the family circle. Everyone in

Figure 2.1 The three-circle model of family business

the family (in all generations) obviously belongs to the family circle, but some family members will never own shares in the family business, or work in it.

The Business Circle

Executives in a business are concerned about strategy and *social capital*—the reputation of their firm in the marketplace. The business circle typically includes non-family members who are employed by the family business. Family members may also be employees. An employee has a stake in the social capital (reputation), and the financial capital (business performance as it affects career opportunities, bonuses and fair performance measures). The business system is similar to that in all for-profit organizations, i.e. it is driven by the firm's mission and strategy as implemented by the management team. The business circle includes structure (reporting relationships), systems (information or human resources), and processes (quality, communications).

The Ownership Circle

Owners are interested in *financial capital*—performance in terms of wealth creation (business performance and dividends). The ownership system is driven by the shareholder-value proposition that articulates the owners' expectations for profitability, risk, growth, and type of industry. The owners' goals are often codified in governance processes (board of directors, legal structure) and ownership distribution. The ownership circle may include family members, investors, and/or employee-owners.

The Need for a Multi-Faceted Approach

It is important to note that traditional management literature focuses on the role of the executive, whereas in the family-business world, ownership is an equal, or even more important, element. Executives have the opportunity to influence a firm through their direct involvement in the decision-making process. Their role is important but temporary. Owners, on the other hand, have a lifetime relationship with the firm; they name the board members who hire and fire the firm's leadership, and they also decide on the nature of future ownership according to whom, and by what process, they transfer their stock. (Historically, and across cultures, women in family firms are often owners but not executives. But as owners, they may have tremendous influence, a fact that is often underreported and underestimated.) In the long term, ownership is the mechanism for exerting family influence on a firm.

Family, ownership, and business roles clearly involve different, and sometimes conflicting, values, goals, and actions and in a family business people may have multiple roles and priorities A few people—for example, the founder or a senior family member—may hold all three roles: family member, owner, and employee. These particular individuals are thus obviously intensely connected to the family business, and it is the conflict of interests presented by their having several different roles that can lead to problems.

HOW CONFLICT CAN DEVELOP

In a company that is still at an early stage of development, decision making is typically dominated by the founder-entrepreneur who leads and owns the business and is also head of the family. This individual combines the key roles in the three family, business, and ownership subsystems, though at this stage we talk about a 'one-circle family business.'

Maintaining a unified family group becomes more difficult as the family grows, and as multiple generations assume leadership and ownership positions. In succeeding generations different individuals start to play different roles. As the roles diverge, and the number of family members increases, differences in the family's interests can create new opportunities for siblings or cousins in an ownership group.

In a three-generation family there are likely to be family members who are owners but not employees (for example, the grandparents), or family members who work in the firm but are not owners (young adults or in-laws). As the roles diverge and the family increases in size, the differences in the family's interest can create powerful clashes between siblings or cousins who are required to work together.

There can be many reasons for conflict. A diverse group of family shareholders with little or no direct connection to the business may not have the expertise or values needed to support a shared vision. As the number of descendants increases, more time may be spent on political activities rather than on thinking about how to move the business forward. In entrepreneurial firms, the first (founding) generation will have no experience of generational transition, so may fail to plan ahead to ensure that the family's relationships and values will continue to support the business. In poorly planned generational transitions, family politics can become a major diversion as emotion overpowers rational decision making.

Businesses with any public ownership are required to hold shareholder and board meetings, and resentful family members could use such meetings as a forum for expressing previously suppressed conflict from the family system. We, in our role as family-business advisers, have been present at board meetings that have quite literally turn into brawls, with punches—and on one occasion, a chair—being thrown. Occasionally, family conflicts end in litigation, and very bitter and very public fights over assets—fights that ultimately destroy the company and the family. More commonly, unhappy family members react by blocking the decision-making process—thus making their point but simultaneously endangering the business.

The 'family-first' principle makes sense for entrepreneurs, who start their business, and work hard at it, usually in order to support their families. But, ironically, an emotionally distant entrepreneur committed to such an approach may create a situation in their business where the children end up wanting to destroy the business because they believe their father and mother loved the business more than they loved the children. Less common, but equally destructive, are multi generation family businesses driven by the family-first principle. Family members in such organizations expect to be given work in the firm, however incompetent they may be; they might also insist on prioritizing steady dividend income over strategic investments, thereby placing unreasonable financial restraints on management. These companies are often weakened by a lack of financial and managerial resources—and talent.

Key Areas of Conflict

To summarize the three-circle model, it's clear that the overlap of the family, business, and ownership circles can create conflict in five critical areas (as represented in Figure 2.2). Parallel planning action [4] in these particular areas, to align business and family goals, can help to ensure that business success doesn't precipitate a family disaster (or vice versa). The five areas are:

1. **Capital**: How are the firm's financial resources allocated among different business and family demands?

2. **Control**: Who has decision-making power in the family and firm? Is the board of directors the real decision maker, or do the father and mother make decisions at the kitchen table?

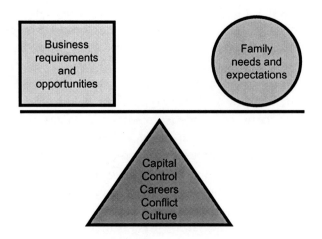

Figure 2.2 Balancing family and business needs in five critical areas [5]

3. **Careers**: How are individuals selected for senior leadership and governance positions in the firm or family? Is family membership an overriding factor, a consideration or a disqualification? Can in-laws be included?

4. **Conflict**: Can the family stop conflicted human relationships spilling over into the business system? If two family members have a disagreement about compensation, can they attend a family social event without fighting?

5. **Culture**: What values are primordial to the family and business systems, and how are these values transmitted? Does business performance influence the power of individual family members?

The media is full of dramatic examples of conflict involving one or more of these five critical areas in prominent family businesses, and in the Reliance Group, India's largest publicly traded company (the family are the largest shareholders), we see hints of where problems could arise in all five areas at once.

A Family Story: The Reliance Group

When the news broke that the feud between the warring Ambani brothers had been settled, the Indian business community breathed a sigh of relief and stocks rocketed to new heights. Mukesh and Anil Ambani, heirs to the $22.5 billion Reliance Group, had been at loggerheads since the death of their father, Dhirubai, in 2002.

Dhirubai Ambani, one of India's most flamboyant businessmen, rose from humble beginnings to establish India's largest industrial empire. He became not only one of his country's greatest entrepreneurs but also one of the world's richest men. Born in Gujarat in 1932, Ambani left his village for the Arabian Peninsula in 1949 where he first worked as a petrol station attendant. He soon demonstrated considerable business acumen by representing people whose insurance claims had been rejected, taking a cut from any settlement he managed to negotiate.

By the age of 25 he had made enough money to return to India and set up the Reliance Commercial Corporation, a trading company exporting spices to Yemen. Before long, Ambani had established a textiles mill, and continued as a textile manufacturer until the early 1980s, when he seized the opportunities presented by the fast-growing Indian economy to set up world-scale facilities for the manufacture of polyester and textile intermediates, and plastics and polymer intermediates. The company continued to expand: in just three decades it had developed into the Reliance Group, with interests in petrochemicals, energy, and telecommunications.

Reliance Infocomm was the result of Dhirubai Ambani's vision to change the way Indians live, by creating a digital revolution across the country. His mission, stated in 1999, was to 'make the tools of information communication available to people at an affordable cost. They will overcome the handicaps of illiteracy and lack of mobility.' Working at impressive speed, from late 1999 onward Reliance Infocomm laid 60 000 kilometers of fiber-optic cables, spanning the entire country. The network was commissioned on December 28, 2002, the 70th anniversary of Ambani's birth—although Ambani had died six months earlier.

Ambani's two sons, Mukesh and Anil, joined Reliance in the early 1980s. Voted India's most admired Chief Executive in 2004, for the sixth year in succession, Anil has been Chairman of Reliance Capital and Reliance Infocomm and Chairman and Managing Director of Reliance Energy Limited. Previously, he was the Vice Chairman and Managing Director of Reliance Industries Limited. His brother Mukesh was ranked 42nd among the *World's Most Respected Business Leaders* in 2004 and voted 13th in The Most Powerful People in Business by *Fortune* in the same year. Mukesh has been Chairman and Managing Director of Reliance Industries Limited.

In 1986, the brothers took over the day-to-day running of the business, when their father suffered a stroke. Then in July 2002 Dhirubai Ambani died, leaving no will. Many people predicted that it would only be a question of time before his two sons would start to fight. Their ownership issues, simmering quietly behind the scenes, and managed by the media-cautious Reliance organization, finally spilled over into the public domain.

One reason for the dispute was the Reliance board's attempt to redefine the role of managing directors. Item 17, as it came to be known, gave Mukesh the power to reduce Anil's role in the company. Other reasons have also been cited, ranging from Anil's dalliance in politics, and the fact that the brothers' two wives do not appear to get along, to the more fundamentally divergent views of the two brothers on certain key business and personal issues.

Anil and Mukesh's battle carried on for seven months, during which time their mother, Kokilaben, attempted to broker a deal. With the help of family friends, and advice from astrologers, Kokilaben produced a solution that divided Dhirubai Ambani's empire as fairly as possible between the two brothers. Mukesh and Anil were awarded 30% each, and 10% was split between Kokilaben's two daughters Neena and Dipti, with Kokilaben herself retaining 30%.

The deal effectively divided the original empire into two distinct parts, but less than a year after the original deal was made, the brothers were once again locked in a struggle over the control of a gas reserve, and were beginning to compete in the same industries. The *Hindu Times*, stated: 'The world of business appears much too small to accommodate the two brothers and their ambitions' [6].

As the Reliance case study demonstrates, even two brothers can face challenges in balancing the demands of the business and their own personal expectations. A central issue in this case is control: Who makes decisions about the business and its strategy? Strategy formulation will also have implications for how the brothers allocate capital. The brothers are also experiencing a significant conflict about their careers and the roles that the two of them will take in the family business. Conflict becomes an issue because their father did not articulate clear guidelines or family agreements on how shareholder disputes should be settled.

Probably underlying the brothers' problems may have been the absence of a safe 'holding environment' provided by the parents, resulting in feelings of not having received a fair share of attention from one or both of them. It may have accentuated rivalrous feelings between the brothers that remained submerged as long as the father was alive. With his death, the 'containment' provided by the father was no longer there and the submerged conflicts came to the surface. Throughout the case, we can see the difficulties that business families face when their personal psychology and relationships impact on the business and the larger family group.

So far, we have presented case stories that highlight some of the disadvantages of family-owned or family-controlled firms, with the undoubted successes of the Steinberg and Ambani families clearly undermined by the family dramas. It would, however, be extremely shortsighted to underestimate the myriad advantages of the family firm. In the next chapter, we therefore consider the unique strengths of the typical family firm, as well as look at how these can sometimes act as weaknesses.

ENDNOTES

1. Freud, S. (1955). *Civilization and Its Discontents. The Standard Edition of the Complete Psychological Works of Sigmund Freud Vol.21* (trans. and ed., James Strachey). London: Hogarth Press and the Institute of Psychoanalysis.
2. Erikson, E.H. (1950). *Childhood and Society* (p. 264). New York: W.W. Norton & Company.
3. Tagiuri, R. and Davis, J.A. (1982) 'Bivalent attributes of the family firm.' Working Paper, Harvard Business School, Cambridge, MA. Reprinted 1996, *Family Business Review,* **IX** (2): 199–208.
4. For a full description of parallel planning, see Carlock, R.S. and Ward, J.L. (2001). *Strategic Planning for the Family Business: Parallel Planning to Unify the Family and Business.* London: Palgrave Macmillan.
5. See Carlock, R.S. and Ward, J.L. (2001).
6. Case vignette written by Sally Simmons, based on: Srinivasan, R. (2006). 'The argument continues,' *Business Line (The Hindu),* February 12.

CHAPTER 3

FAMILY BUSINESS PRACTICES: ASSESSING STRENGTHS AND WEAKNESSES

Despite the vital role that family businesses play in the world economy, little is really known about how family ownership or management affect the behavior and performance of firms. One recent study published in the *Journal of Finance* stirred up general interest in the topic: using the financial performance for the Standard and Poor's 500 as a base of comparison, Ronald Anderson and David Reeb concluded that family firms outperformed non-family firms in the US [1]. These findings, according to the authors, contradict anecdotal accounts that family businesses perform poorly. Other students of family firms have questioned these findings, however. Thus the jury is still out as academics continue to research and defend both viewpoints [2].

While the studies on financial performance continue, historical data concerning the longevity of all firms, although limited, do appear to show several psychological dimensions where family businesses may develop practices that create competitive advantage, provided they can overcome inherent structural and interpersonal issues (not all best practices are appropriate in every cultural or family context). Once we acknowledge that the two systems in family firms—the family and the business—are not necessarily compatible, we can work to exploit the strengths of each and establish structures and processes to neutralize the weaknesses created by the interface.

Although it is not difficult to draw up a list of ways in which family-controlled organizations have particular advantages or disadvantages when compared to publicly-owned companies, it is not always evident *why* they have these advantages or weaknesses, let alone how to exploit them or, conversely, limit the damage [3]. It is certain, however, that families who own or control businesses can be more thoughtful and effective if they understand the core human issues that create family and business challenges.

The above discussion suggests that family firms have unique competitive advantages over non-family firms. This so-called 'family effect' would mean that there are family or business practices that result from family ownership and management, and positively affect performance [4]. Performance can have many dimensions but in terms of the financial discussions above, it relates to the ability to efficiently use assets and effectively position the firm in profitable market opportunities. We will argue that family dynamics at both the individual and the family levels influence family values and behavior in five dimensions that contribute to improved performance.

The easiest way to understand the psychology of a family business is to imagine the individual family business member at the center of a number of concentric circles (see Figure 3.1). Individual psychology is influenced by unique, innate personality characteristics—but no man or woman is an island. The individual is steeped in the values and beliefs of that person's family of origin, and the family itself behaves in a way that is formed by shared history and modulated by societal rules. In a family business, these concentric spheres of influence interact not only in terms of family practices, but also intrinsically affect the business practices of the family firm. Therefore, when trying to tease out explanations for business practices, it often makes sense to work down through the concentric circles to identify the core issues motivating *individual* family members.

For example, if an individual sees the world as a threatening place (as a result of early life experiences), it may be harder for him or her to fully trust his or her brothers and sisters, let alone non-family members. If some of his siblings have the same world view, the family as a whole will be low on the trust equation. As a consequence, it is very likely that they will feel that,

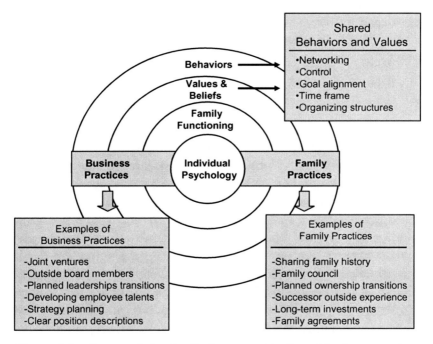

Figure 3.1   Concentric levels of influence on family and business practices

in business, you cannot trust other people. These beliefs will be expressed in behaviors such as requiring a family member to personally open and close the warehouse every day. It will also have a direct impact on the organization's culture, as employees sense that the family's managers and owners do not trust them.

Family practices and business practices are often interrelated because they are shaped by the same psychological influences. For example, advisers often recommend that next generation family members work for several years outside the family firm to gain knowledge and experience. Many older generation family members will argue that outside experience is not really necessary, since the family firm offers unique opportunities for younger adults. Here it is important for both advisers and families to realize that the *core issue* is not the merit of outside work experience, but rather a young adult's basic need to become autonomous and develop confidence in his or her own abilities. Similarly, when the business goes through a leadership succession period or forms a board of directors (business practices), these events will be shaped by the *family's* values and behavior—with a reciprocal, and cyclical, influence on the individuals in that family.

- Why do family businesses sometimes outperform the markets?
- Why do family businesses sometimes fail after years of success?
- Why do the strengths that create competitive advantage in one area sometimes become a disadvantage in another?

To put these questions in context, consider some typical examples. We know of one successful Asian real-estate developer who enjoys competing against large international groups. While they are drafting a capital project request to circulate to senior management, he is calling his network to secure the necessary funding for a cash offer. He shakes hands on a deal in the morning, raises the money during the day, and wires the funds that evening. His competitors are starting their management review of the project when he goes home to dinner, deal done. However, this flexibility drives his brothers and management team crazy. They recently learned of a €250 million project, which they co-own, after reading about it in the morning newspaper. Long-term strategic perspectives provide another example of what can be both a strength and a disadvantage in a family business. Such a perspective allows a family business to invest in projects that competitors cannot accept because their company is publicly traded and has a short investment cycle. However, if the family's long-term perspective also means that senior executives hang on to their jobs for decades, blocking careers and new thinking, then a shorter time frame in some areas would be more helpful to that business.

THE INTERFACE OF BUSINESS AND FAMILY PRACTICES

Drawing on the deeper understanding of the psychology of families we outlined above, we propose a framework to help to find practical answers. We have identified five dimensions that are relevant to all businesses, but in addition have special relevance within family-controlled businesses. The five dimensions are:

- *Networking* Deep information sharing and strong relationships developed within the family and business systems.
- *Goal alignment* Balancing individual and collective goals.
- *Control* Identified family power in the company, board and ownership group.
- *Time frame* Long-term commitment to family investment and business strategy.
- *Organizing structures* Using both flexible and rigid controls to support a clear family business philosophy.

Using these dimensions (which will be described in detail below) as an organizing construct, we can direct our attention to the areas in which family values and beliefs (as formed by the concentric layers within the family) have a primal influence on business practices.

Networking

All organizations depend on systems of external and internal networks: formal and informal, as well as long-term and punctual. In a public organization, networks are constantly being created and dismantled as a part of strategic moves that seek, for example, to optimize market movement or reduce costs through outsourcing. Individuals seek to create parallel internal networks to advance their own or the organization's goals. External networks are maintained in direct relationship to their importance to the organization, with the best networks providing clear communication and just-in-time delivery. Networks that no longer perform according to agreed standards are likely to be cut off or redistributed.

A successful family business will obviously have similar networks; like any business, they develop networks as a part of their value chain, and these networks regulate their interaction with the outside world. However, in some family businesses, certain external networking relationships may be determined by family-influenced, rather than strictly strategic, criteria. The Asian real-estate developer we mentioned above has kept in touch with individuals who made deals with his grandfather, and still speaks their dialect. When he wants to make a deal, these networks often provide a shortcut. In this type of situation, the nature of external networks and business relationships are influenced by ethnicity, language, and family experience.

As we see in the case of the Asian developer, a multigenerational family business has the advantage of shared history, experiences, and success within the family, which provide a *de facto* framework for selecting and maintaining networks. In addition, there is often a sense of mutuality between employees, key customers, suppliers, and others—a strong social network that enables the family business to identify opportunities and develop ongoing relationships—thereby creating economic value for both the business and its shareholders. There are precedents for determining which external relationships are beneficial, and which are not. A family that has a clear sense of purpose will be more open to outside perspectives, and actively develop networks in unlikely areas. In family firms with a well-defined and responsible ownership group, external partners are attracted by the family's mutuality of shareholder commitment and the value of interacting with identifiable owners.

On the other hand, a family in which the business purpose is not clearly defined, or in which the family's immediate needs are given top priority, may have a 'family first' philosophy that complicates the development of networks. Although it may be evident to the family concerned that the family's practices benefit the family as a whole, to outsiders, this philosophy appears to foster secrecy in decision making, and closes the options for exploring outside perspectives or novel ideas. A company that values dominance of family over business logic, or overtly accepts nepotism, is not likely to be sought out by external partners.

Consider the concentric circle model again. In family firms, individuals are the critical success factor in maintaining effective internal networks. If the family members communicate well and treat each other as autonomous adults, these family practices will encourage a culture of trust and openness in their business. In fact, trust has been identified as a primary factor in providing family firms with a competitive advantage [5]. The family's ability to communicate can also be an important factor in developing the talent and capabilities of the next generation, because 'strong ties to senior family members . . . will likely lead to greater context, access to information, resources, and career sponsorship, which are positively related to career success' [6]. There is also value added when the internal networks insure that information is distributed from the business to the family (especially shareholders), and from the family to the business. This form of knowledge sharing strengthens the alignment between family and business practices, and creates relationships built on openness and trust.

Goal Alignment

For family members, one of the obvious advantages of working for the family firm is the perception (illusory though it may be) of controlling their own destiny. Running an organization in which you have a personal stake creates a special feeling of independence, and the narcissistic pleasures inherent in this should not be underestimated. Having your name on a building gives a sense of stewardship and responsibility, and it also brings competitive advantage. As one member of a family media conglomerate said, 'My name has certainly helped me to get access to top executives of companies—people who under other circumstances would have kept their doors shut.'

Even more significantly, the quality or image of the company and its products can affect the identity of the family. Association with defective or inferior products is then perceived as a reflection on the self. When a family has been producing wine for many generations (like Torres in Spain) or trading grain (like Cargill in the United States) family members want to be proud of their products. Their involvement with the company product adds to the company's competitive advantage.

A family's internal understanding about its values and goals often determines the kind of behavior that will be acceptable or unacceptable in their organization. Fair process in decision making and planning helps families to develop a higher level of trust and unity in both their business and family practices [7]. The family's values also direct their approach to stewardship of assets, and affect their attachment to the family legacy, which in turn helps to establish a sense of identification and commitment of the firm's non-family employees.

In this case, employees often feel like part of the family and are actually treated that way, creating a much more caring organization than would typically exist in large publicly held companies. Flexible structure allows employees to have easy access to senior management and, in many cases, to the ownership group. The result is a real sense of connection and mutuality of goals.

A legendary example of the overflow of shared family values into the family firm is the furniture manufacturer Herman Miller Inc. This company has repeatedly been listed as one of the best-managed companies in America. D.J. De Pree founded the company in 1923 and was succeeded first by his son, Hugh, and then by Hugh's son Max.

A Family Story: Herman Miller, Inc.

At Herman Miller, Inc. there is a group of people strongly committed to the beliefs and ideas of the senior family members, particularly those of Max De Pree. Employees share the family's outlook toward customer service, quality, and productivity—a covenant that works both ways. Family members back up their strong belief in the potential of people with a corporate code of conduct that determines the psychological contract between workers and management. Included in the ground rules for working at Herman Miller, Inc. are the right to be needed, the right to be involved, the right to understand, the right to affect one's own destiny, the right to be accountable, and the right to appeal decisions perceived as arbitrary or unfair.

This focus on rights goes beyond mere talk: it affects everyone's wallet. The company has a long-standing reward system that entitles workers to a share of financial gains resulting from their suggestions for improving design, customer service, quality, and productivity.

The atmosphere and leadership style established in this family company remained intact even after the company went public. A stock-option plan grants stock to all regular employ-

ees who have worked in the firm for at least a year, and there
are silver parachutes for *all* employees in the case of an
unfriendly takeover (not just golden parachutes for top management). Herman Miller Inc. continues to function less
bureaucratically than a company that had been publicly held
since its inception. The family culture makes the firm much
less impersonal. Because employees feel like part of the family,
even the lowliest production worker has no difficulty knock-
ing on Max De Pree's door [8].

The importance of unity in goals and purpose in the family
and organization can be even better illustrated by looking at situations in which these factors are weak or absent. Blocked communication, bad relationships, and poor planning within the
family can erode the family's alignment on values and strategy.
Sometimes the family firm just has to live with the colorful, and
forceful, personality of the chairman, who, having stepped down
from operational responsibilities, suddenly has plenty of time on
his hands to negotiate maverick acquisition schemes. Senior family
leaders may no longer be effective because the firm has moved
into a different phase of the business life cycle. Conflicts within
branches of the family may be spilling over into the business,
creating deadlock. As younger generation family members become
adults and owners with their own set of values, coalitions may
begin working together to block a carefully planned family initiative. Competition and envy among next-generation family
members, as they pursue leadership roles in the firm, may lead to
accusations of nepotism. A powerful family leader may run amok
because there are no independent advisers with enough control to
stop him. Children might have inherited valuable assets without
having any idea of how to manage or divide them fairly.

Any of these problems can erupt with high drama in a family
business and, indeed, are a perennial source of inspiration and
discussion in popular entertainment, for example in Greek tragedies; many of Shakespeare's plays; Arthur Miller's *Death of a
Salesman*; television shows (*Dallas*); the media (CNN, *The Financial Times*, *Wall Street Journal*); and in court (Parmalat).

Control

The saying goes that the hand that rocks the cradle rules the world. This holds true, in various ways, in the family business. In no other area are family and business practices as intertwined as in the dimension of control. Family businesses often face a difficult decision on whether responsibility and control should be held by management, the board, the ownership group or some combination of all these groups. And when families control blocks of shares in several companies, conflicts of interest may arise, as illustrated in the following case study.

A Family Story: Ferdinand Piech and Volkswagen

In the first six months of 2006, Volkswagen (VW) was rocked by sex and corruption scandals, attacks on the company's corporate governance, and poor performance figures. While CEO Bernd Pischetsrieder tried to deal with the fall-out from these scandals, and kick-start a stringent restructuring program in the face of powerful union opposition, he had to deal with an attack on another front. His predecessor and chairman of the VW supervisory board, Ferdinand Piech, far from giving him his support, was conducting a systematic campaign to unseat him.

Ferdinand Piech became CEO of VW in 1993 and transformed the company's fortunes, reintroducing the Beetle and launching improved versions of the brand's most popular models. But his ambition led the company into near disaster. Piech wanted to move VW upmarket and compete at the luxury end of the business. He made hubristic bids for Rolls-Royce and Bentley but lost out to BMW, then headed by Pischetsrieder. Huge investment in unpopular luxury models also failed to pay off. Going upmarket went against the whole ethic and image of Volkswagen—'the people's car'—and the products were not up to the mark. It also pitched VW against Audi and Porsche, companies with which VW already had lucrative ties, creating a conflict of interests.

Pischetsrieder's attempt to bring VW down to earth, downmarket, and downsized, was welcomed by industry commentators, but this refocusing effort was a slow process and immediately brought him into conflict with Piech, as it was the complete reversal of Piech's strategy. Piech retained enormous power at VW, independently of his role on the supervisory board. His family controls 100% of Porsche, of which he personally owns about 13%. Porsche, is the largest shareholder in VW. Porsche also has interests in VW's distributing companies. In the months leading up to the Annual General Meeting in May 2006, Piech made no attempt to hide his canvassing for support to oust Pischetsrieder and replace him with his own man.

At the Annual General Meeting, numerous small investors accused Piech of ignoring the conflict of interests his positions at VW and Porsche created, of systematically undermining the CEO, refusing to talk to investors, and failing to address people's concerns about VW's corporate governance. They also asked for an inquiry into reports of deals made between Porsche and Lower Saxony, the state where VW has its headquarters, who together owned 40% of the company.

Piech declined to respond to their charges and the shareholders, incensed by his arrogance and damaging interference in the running of the company, demanded his resignation. But Piech refused to go. However, his campaign against Pischetsrieder failed and Pischetsrieder's contract was extended until 2012. The following day, newspapers carried pictures of both men shaking hands—but despite his tarnished public image the AGM had assured Piech's position for at least another 12 months, and Pischetsrieder was already attracting negative comments, unable to shake off rumors that he had secured his job by scaling down his restructuring program to appease union representatives on the board.

The uneasy situation in the company continued for a further six months. Then, in November 2006, Piech mounted a surprise boardroom coup and ousted Pischetsrieder. Five of the six members of the VW governing presidium spoke against Pischetsrieder, including union representatives aggrieved at his restructuring plans. The powerful VW presidium consists of a representative from Lower Saxony (Pischetsrieder's only supporter at the November meeting), Piech, Porsche AG CEO Wendelin Wiedeking, and three members of the workers' council. Martin Winterkorn, previously CEO of Audi, was brought in, hand-picked by Piech, to take Pischetsrieder's place.

Industry commentators interpreted the move as an important development in Ferdinand Piech's yet-to-be-revealed endgame. 'Few doubt the billionaire engineer will stop before he wields full control,' *BusinessWeek* reported. In March 2007 Porsche announced it was increasing its stake in VW to 31%. Meanwhile, the company's future strategy has already begun to resemble the direction the company took under Piech's leadership when he was CEO.

The Volkswagen case demonstrates both the advantages and disadvantages created by a controlling family shareholder group. One of the advantages of family firms is the existence of identified shareholder(s) who can articulate the ownership group's expectations and/or has the power to force management to act. Too often in widely traded firms there are agency conflicts, where the goals of management are in conflict with the goals of the shareholders, resulting in value expropriation by the management group to the disadvantage of the ownership group [9]. The disadvantage with dominant family shareholders, especially in publicly-traded companies, is that a powerful individual may not represent the other shareholders, either in his family or in the public markets, and propose strategies that are based more on his personal motives than on creating shareholder value.

Another issue related to control in family firms is the identification of the next generation of senior management. Sometimes within a family, the oldest son is not the most capable successor— but he *is* the oldest son. Another serious issue involves nepotism, where family members win executive positions based on family membership rather than potential or performance. Individual rivalries and competition in the family can lead to power plays in the family firm that ultimately destroy the company [10]. All too often, a leadership transition doesn't occur until after a funeral. In firms in which certain family owners have unlimited or ill-defined access to power, non-performing family executives may be tolerated or even moved about the company like chess pieces. Obviously, there is little attraction for outside talent in a company like this.

A Family Story: The Incompetent Son

Pierre LaMotte, founder of a thriving chain of clothing stores, had suffered a severe coronary incident that he barely survived. His worried wife insisted that their only son, Lucas, should be given a senior position in the company, so that he could take on some of his father's responsibilities and reduce the stress for Pierre of running the company on his own. Lucas, who was living at home and had failed to find a job, was happy to take on his father's responsibilities.

Unfortunately, Lucas had an unjustifiably high opinion of himself, despite the fact that he had no senior-level management experience, and had dropped out of business school after failing his exams. It was not long before his arrogance and incompetence soured the atmosphere in the company. His worst traits were his tendency to blame others and his refusal to accept responsibility for his own mistakes. If a deal fell through, it was because someone had failed to follow up the clients. If new product ideas did not take off quickly, developers were demoted. Some of the most promising and competent employees left the company.

It became clear that Pierre was blind to his son's shortcomings. Eventually, Lucas acquired a firm with outdated product lines and obsolete machinery without informing his father or anyone else in the company. At this point, the concerned CFO managed to alert Pierre to the looming crisis. Pierre reasserted his control, and reassumed his old responsibilities—and the additional stress of having to deal with his son who almost brought the company to the verge of disaster. The prognosis for his own health, and that of the company, was not good.

For better or worse, family businesses often (although not always) have greater certainty than publicly held companies about what kind of leadership will prevail in the firm. It is often clear, quite early on, who is next in line. In many companies this is an advantage: when leadership development and succession are properly handled, there tends to be less political in-fighting and more stability than in a publicly-traded organization.

In fact, leadership development within a family business often begins (as it should) when the future leaders are young children. Breakfasts, dinners, outings, family gatherings, after-school work, and summer jobs are devoted to talking about, or working in, the business. It is an intrinsic part of the education process.

One executive recalled how, as a child, he would take long walks with his father, during which they would visit stores to look at competitors' products. Afterwards, his father would ask him which products he liked most, and this would lead to lengthy discussions about each product's quality. The expertise the son gained during those informal outings proved invaluable later in life when he took his father's place at the head of the company.

This in-depth business knowledge can help to give family members a head start over executives entering the business at a later stage. Early training like this helps to explain the sometimes puzzling appointments of very young family members to senior positions. When these younger executives are supported and mentored by older family and non-family executives, power responsibility is shared by a greater number of people with diverse ideas, but shared goals. The older executives and other family owners often have a strong commitment to merit, and impose a rigorous level of accountability—thereby creating a system of checks and balances that work to maintain a power equilibrium in the firm and in the family.

Time Frame

The CEO of a leading family-controlled Hong Kong bank described to us the competitive advantage that Asian family businesses have over western publicly-traded companies doing business in Asia. He commented wryly that Asian family businesses recognize 5- to 10-year cycles of economic growth and decline and yet, despite this well-known fact, western firms often sell their plants or freighters at a hefty discount during business downturns simply to reduce their exposure to the contracting Asian market. The banker explained that this has always been a great wealth-creation opportunity for Asians, who simply buy the assets during distress periods and hold them until the economic cycle improves, when they are then well positioned to exploit new opportunities for growth and expanded market share.

Because families think in generations, family firms generally take a longer-term, and arguably more objective, view of their planning and decision making than do their publicly-traded counterparts. This strategic openness creates opportunities for change. Appropriate timescales support value creation; the board of directors is not preoccupied with meeting quarterly earnings projections or avoiding new investments because of their effect on the next year's earnings—they are looking further ahead.

Moreover, in comparison to publicly-quoted companies, these family firms are less vulnerable to the scrutiny of the stock market and their shareholders, contributing to a longer-term orientation to the business. In addition, they are not subjected to regulations like the US Sarbanes–Oxley act, a set of rules that has created additional corporate board responsibilities, subjecting executives in case of non-compliance to criminal penalties, or having government bodies such as the US Securities and Exchange Commission implement rulings on requirements to comply.

This more long-term perspective is also shaped by the fact that family firms often look at wealth creation not as a goal but as a *consequence* of investing in their business and the people who manage it. This long-term perspective involving the next two or three generations allows current shareholders multiple options when looking at capital investments for expansion. In addition, a recent McKinsey study indicated that family companies in their study sample were 'performance oriented but risk averse, which might make them less successful in boom times but keeps them alive, with healthy profitability, over the very long term' [11].

Furthermore, a tendency toward a long-term strategy supports the development of relationships with suppliers, market channels, and creates economies of scale. Because of their loyalty to their employees, family businesses are also more careful in downsizing their organizations during difficult economic periods. As a result, family organizations tend to sustain their core organizational abilities, including the intellectual property and experience of their employees. When markets recover, family organizations are thus often better prepared to exploit the upside potential.

The danger inherent in a long-term time frame is that a perceived lack of urgency may lead to entrenched paternalistic or autocratic leadership, particularly if there are few non-family executives or truly independent directors at the top of the organization. For many reasons—for example, a historical event that traumatized an older generation—a family may have a shared value of risk avoidance. Resistance to change within the family is likely to encourage a lack of innovation in the business. In a strongly patriarchal family of which the grandfather will remain the undisputed head until he dies, the older generation may be strongly opposed to *business* transitions that bring in the younger generations, thereby leading to a concentration of authority and blocked careers for promising family and non-family executives.

What starts off as well-meaning behavior on the part of controlling owners may end up as a stifling or even perverted imposition of their desires and demands on the firm, and on their children. The family may be able to keep control of the company for a time, but the next generation will struggle not only to assume responsibility as owners or employees of the company, but also to develop their own identity.

Although less common now in Europe and North America, the paternalistic model is still the organizational structure of choice for family businesses in many regions, for example, in parts of Asia, Africa, the Middle East, and South America. (It should be pointed out that paternalistic organizations may offer a kind of social safety net, and despite the restrictions, this type of organization is often supported by the stakeholders, including many employees and family members.)

Organizing Structures

There is a certain informality associated with family organizations that can allow flexibility, even in large-scale or global family businesses. This is partly because responsibility sharing between family and non-family executives, board members, and even family owners, is often based on mutual trust and support, rather than a predetermined organizational structure or policies. A family business might be run by two brothers who work as co-CEOs; in a larger family, the senior leadership role might be rotated among qualified family members on a three-year basis. In some families, the business is run by non-family executives, with family members serving as executive directors responsible for different business units.

These organizational relationships or structures are unheard of in publicly-traded companies, where there is greater organizational rigidity. Flexibility works best with the kind of personal relationships and trust that come with a member of a family. Many successful family businesses see such trust as a core organizational value, and design flexible organization structures to exploit it. Conversely, publicly-traded firms with short management tenures, especially at the top, often build structures that assume *distrust*, and design defensive controls to protect against self-serving behavior and conflicts of interest.

Informal organizational structures, and the sharing of roles and responsibilities, also improve the timing of decision making in family firms. While public or widely traded companies must depend on a series of checks and balances, a clear decision-making process, and a hierarchy of reporting relationships, family firms with a strong alignment between the owners and the managers can move quickly to make strategic acquisitions or invest in new market opportunities. One family owner-director attending an INSEAD family business executive program closed the acquisition of a major competitor during a family training session. After he left the classroom several times for telephone calls, one of us followed him out to inquire if there was a problem. His reply was: 'No problem, only a quick deal to close.' It turned out that his telephone calls were to transfer millions of dollars from his and his father's bank accounts to complete an acquisition. This international family business was acquiring the number two US player in their industry from a classroom—hardly the typical Wall Street approach.

A flexible organization structure also helps to exploit new opportunities where there is uncertainty about opportunity size, or the risks involved. For example, one leading European beer manufacturer began to trade in Russia simply by moving equipment from a discontinued European plant to a small plant there, setting up the operation and testing it. Instead of doing market research, attempting to determine sales sensitivity and undertaking complex information seeking, they tested the market using a low-cost probe—creating a brewery and selling beer. The results were outstanding and they soon became leaders in the emerging Russian market.

The potential weakness inherent in an overly-flexible structure is that authority and responsibility may not be clearly defined and jobs may overlap, with executives holding a number of different positions. Such an organization can be confusing to outsiders: reporting relationships are haphazard; structures and processes are often undeveloped or ignored; job descriptions, planning, and budgets may simply not exist.

A comparison between the official organization chart in a family business and what really happens on a daily basis might well reveal that decisions are made at the dinner table rather than at the quarterly board meeting. Research on privately-held family firms showed that firms that employed more structure (such as strategic planning, formal compensation systems and outside directors) outperformed their less-formalized counterparts [12].

Consider the case of three brothers who each own one-third of a business and who all work in the business together. Although one brother is designated managing director, his two brothers frequently give different and sometimes countermanding instructions to the firm's employees. For these two brothers, the firm's management hierarchy is easily bypassed. They see their ownership as giving them equal or even greater authority than the firm's official leader. Such a Byzantine management structure complicates succession and transitions, muddies financial compensation decisions, and demotivates employees.

Another potential problem with family businesses is that sound business practices can be affected by issues of family loyalty. Family businesses often promote from within, among family and non-family executives. Part of this selection process is practical.

The lack of formal organization in family-business structure means that only those who understand these informal relationships, and can exert their influence in them, can function effectively. Family members often play a dominant role in these organizations, where the lack of clear responsibility and accountability can become a source of serious weakness. The situation becomes uncontrollable when it is unclear where individuals' loyalties lie.

The Evolving Family Enterprise Philosophy

Inherent in the discussion of these five dimensions are the family's values and beliefs about their relationship with the family business. This family business philosophy, or, to put it another way, how the family balances their desires and the requirements of the business, shapes the family and business practices. Some families put a stronger emphasis on one or the other. Strong family values are obviously important for aligning goals and behavior in family firms, but these values must reflect the nature and scope of the family business. Therefore the organizing structure of 'family first' or 'business first' may work well, or fail, as a function of the changing demography of the family, and the environment in which the company operates [13]. As both the family and business grow, a family enterprise philosophy that mediates between a family-first or business-first approach offers a more balanced framework for decision making and planning.

Some families make it very clear that their business exists to benefit the family. Millions of families own and manage a small business with a family-first philosophy, meaning they put their highest priority on providing jobs and income for family members. This philosophy reflects the earliest and most common form of business (think of small shops and farms, for example).

Problems arise when the business grows and the number of stakeholders increases but the philosophy continues to be 'family first'. Business and strategy decisions are made on the basis of what is best for the family, or simply on what they want, rather than the requirements of a large or growing enterprise. Unqualified family members may assume key jobs with control over company assets; salaries may be unrelated to performance; and dividends may be seen as a right rather than a reward. Any of these practices can drive a company into bankruptcy.

As the following story shows, family-first companies can also sometimes be turned into a kind of summer camp for a spoiled next-generation of family members. But how did they get so spoiled? Who created the problem in the first place? We will look at that later.

A Family Story: The Spoiled Kid Syndrome

Soon after inheriting a company with a market-leading brand, the CEO and controlling shareholder, who was the son of the company's founder, led it into bankruptcy during a recession in the early 1990s. His family was unable to see the catastrophe coming, although with hindsight all the signs were there. The young CEO drew a large salary, drove company-owned sports cars, flew the company jet, and lived in a company-owned mansion. He spent most of his time at a company-owned fishing camp or on the golf course, participating courtesy of company-sponsored memberships.

For a while, the company, a highly profitable private-label manufacturing business, ran itself. Not surprisingly, the occasional hours the CEO spent at the office did more harm than good as he invested in pet projects that took resources away from the family's 'boring' (his word) main business. However, his lack of vision meant that investments were not made appropriately, and the company began to lose money. But the CEO refused to accept reality, in spite of warnings by other shareholders, and in due course the company went bankrupt and was purchased by a competitor.

A likely explanation for the family's indulgence of the younger generation in this case study was the parents' desire to compensate for their guilt at not being available (emotionally or otherwise) when their children were growing up. The parents may have given their children first teddy bears, and then Porsches, never helping them to internalize the values of work and taking responsibility. Predictably, with this kind of upbringing, such parents end up with spoiled kids who do not really have the capacity to run the business. And if the parents would simply accept that fact, all would be well. There are always other ways their children could spend their time.

The problem comes when the parents do not want to see, or accept, the consequences of their actions. This is when faulty logic comes into play: the parents feel that the new generation should be kept busy. However, since these children have not acquired many useful skills, the only place they can be kept busy is in the family company, but when a number of family-member employees add little or no value, the company risks turning into a welfare institution.

Companies cannot afford to have unproductive people around for long. Apart from the financial strain, unproductive hangers-on can lead to serious problems of morale: hard-working employees who pull their weight also have to carry the hangers-on, and they become increasingly resentful and may leave. Furthermore, as owners, these hangers-on can have an unhealthy influence on strategic decision making, self-assuredly backing policies that reinforce their position, and often having to deal with issues they know little or nothing about.

This situation is particularly, and damagingly, ironic if (as is often the case in family firms) family members demand a high level of commitment from non-family members. These demands are acceptable if management gives non-family members due credit for work well done; they are unacceptable, however, if the existing incentive system is heavily biased toward non-contributing family members. It is essential for leaders to 'walk the talk' in any situation, and a family business is no exception. If they do not do so, they lose their credibility. It also becomes difficult to attract capable managers, endangering the company's future. The people who are willing to stick around in these circumstances may not be the people the company actually needs.

On the other hand, the 'business first' philosophy can be damaging because it is likely to impact adversely on the personal lives of those who run the business, and affect their performance at work. In a typical example the principal protagonist is a hard-working entrepreneur completely involved in the business. He (it is usually a man) works long days and after a quick dinner with his family, works late into the night answering e-mails. He is a real visionary in the business, and is greatly appreciated for his leadership skills. Unfortunately, his intense focus on the growing business leaves him very little time, and even less energy, to devote to his family. Although he is aware of this, he cannot see how he can change the situation: the demands of the business are too overwhelming. He rationalizes his behavior by saying that he is working in the best interests of the family. The children are in good private schools; the family spends a week together at their vacation home every summer; they have a full-time house-keeper. He looks forward to the day when he has enough money, and can spend more time relaxing with the family.

He fails to realize, however, that he may be cannibalizing the future of both the business and the family. There may be no 'later on,' because he is growing out of touch with his wife and children. He is not passing *positive* personal and business core values on to his children, or educating them to become responsible stewards of the family business, or even well-balanced, happy adults. Often, the wake-up call for an individual in this situation comes in the form of a heart attack, an out-of-control teenager, or a spouse who wants a divorce.

ASSESSING THE HEALTH OF A FAMILY BUSINESS

As we have shown, the most challenging and dangerous situations arise when family and business systems become enmeshed. If the boundaries between these two systems are not clear enough, needs of individual family members—emotional closeness, stability, and time away from the business—may become mere footnotes on the business agenda. This can weaken the cohesiveness that should hold the family and company together through subsequent generations.

Internecine family disputes that spill over into the business can be devastating. If a family has not developed its own patterns of communication and procedures to address conflict, family disagreements will be played out in the business arena. The business is forced to address the issues, rather than the family. Two brothers who do not get on may choose never to speak to each other again as a means of 'resolving' their conflict. But two brothers fighting for control in a family business are likely to end up in court if they cannot find a way to resolve their conflict. All too often family members choose to sacrifice the business rather than find a solution to conflicts that arise among themselves. The stories of the Gucci and Steinberg families, which appear later in this book, illustrate dramatically how a family in dissolution can destroy its own business.

In this chapter we have broadly outlined some of the characteristics of family firms that can either hinder or help their operations. However, there are many other factors and circumstances specific to individual family firms that could be viewed as both strengths and weaknesses. When attempting to judge the attributes of a company, it is helpful to ask the following questions [14]:

- Does the overall family enterprise appear healthy (family and business subsystems)?
- Is there a strong sense of family commitment to the business and to working together?
- Is the business performing well, relative to its goals and peer group in its industry?
- Does the business have a reputation for quality products, a motivated workforce, strong customer relations, and innovation?
- Are the family and business efforts supporting a shared vision?
- Does the family add value to the business?
- Are there clear boundaries between the family and business systems to ensure effective decision making?
- Does the business create social, emotional, and economic value for the family?
- Are the family's and business's strategies aligned to ensure that the needs of both systems are sustainable in the long term?

If the answer to most of these questions is yes, then it is most likely that *whatever* the family is doing, and *however* they are doing it, is apparently working for them, and will work for their company.

ENDNOTES

1. Anderson, R.C. and Reeb, D. (2003). 'Founding family ownership and firm performance: Evidence from the S&P 500,' *Journal of Finance*, **58** (3): 1301–1328.
2. Villalonga, B. and Amit, R. (2006). 'How do family ownership, control and management affect firm value?' *Journal of Financial Economics*, **80** (2).
3. Dyer, G.W. Jr (2006). 'Examining the "family effect" on firm performance: a comparative study,' *Family Business Review*, **19** (4, December).
4. Dyer, G.W. Jr (2006).
5. Davis, P. (1983). 'Realizing the potential of the family business,' *Organizational Dynamics*, Summer.
6. Dyer, G.W. Jr (2003). 'The family: The missing variable in organizational research,' *Entrepreneurship Theory and Practice*, Summer, p. 407.
7. Van der Heyden, L., Blondel, C. and Carlock, R.S. (2005). 'Fair process: Striving for justice in family business,' *Family Business Review*, **8** (1; March).
8. De Pree, M. (2004) *Leadership is an Art*. New York: Doubleday; Labich, K. (1989). 'Hot company, warm culture.' *Fortune*, Feb. **27**: 44–47.
9. Jensen, M. and Meckling, O. (1976). 'Theory of the firm: Managerial behaviour, agency costs and ownership structure,' *Journal of Financial Economics*, **3** (2).
10. Dyer, G.W. Jr (1986). *Cultural Change in Family Firms*. San Francisco: Jossey-Bass.
11. Elstrodt, H.-P. (2002). 'Keeping the family in business.' *The McKinsey Quarterly*, **4**: 100.
12. Gomez-Mejia, L.R., Nunuz-Nickel, M. and Gutierrez, I. (2001). 'The role of family ties in agency contracts,' *Academy of Management Journal*, **44** (1): 81–95. cited in Dyer, G.W. Jr. (2003).
13. Carlock, R.S. and Ward, J.L. (2001). *Strategic Planning for the Family Business: Parallel Planning to Unify the Family and Business*. London: Palgrave Macmillan.
14. Carlock, R.S. and Ward, J.L. (2001).

PART II
....

REFLECTION AND LEARNING

CHAPTER 4

THE LIFE CYCLE AS AN ORGANIZING CONSTRUCT

As we progress between childhood and old age, our outlook, goals, and roles in life change. Several psychodynamic theorists have proposed models representing the different life stages that individuals go through as they progress to maturity and eventual death, and identified how the successful (or otherwise) negotiation of problems in early life affect an adult's later functioning. This thinking was later built on in the family systems body of theory to produce the idea of life cycles—the stages all humans go through.

The idea of life cycles can be applied to both families and business structures. We believe that they are a particularly important issue in family businesses because the life cycles of the business, the family, and individual family members will all interact. Transitions might occur at the same time in someone's personal life as in his or her work life—for example, where an entrepreneur is facing retirement and the business is simultaneously faced with a change in its leadership [1]. The coincidence of various life cycle transitions can lead to particular stresses in family businesses.

In this chapter we start by looking at life cycle interaction in family businesses, before going on to review some of the most important psychodynamic models for life stages. The chapter ends with a case study illustrating the effect of life cycles in one particular family business.

THE MULTIPLE LIFE CYCLES OF THE FAMILY BUSINESS

In Figure 4.1 we have mapped the life cycles of individuals, organizations, industries, and families to show how they often move through transitions in parallel—something that can create excessive strain when two life cycles move out of sync.

Looking first at the various axes in the figure, we can see how each one shows a variety of transition points.

- Starting with the ownership axis, we see how ownership typically moves from sole ownership, to family partnership, to sibling partnership, to cousin collaboration, toward a family syndicate structure.
- On the individual axis, we see the progression from young adult, to settling down, mid-life transition, with late adulthood as the final stage.
- The family axis begins with having children, continues through the stage when children become independent, to grandparenting and retirement.
- In the industry and organizational axes we see how organizations and industries grow, mature, and decline—and also how organizations can renew themselves.

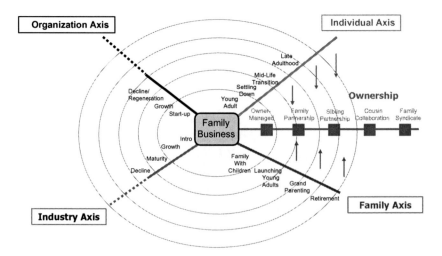

Figure 4.1 Life cycle forces impacting on strategy, structure, management and ownership in family businesses [2]

Obviously, not every individual or business will move through every single one of the stages illustrated. Equally, some businesses might actually go through multiple cycles of stagnation, regeneration, and growth.

We show all these axes on a single diagram because this illustrates the real complexity that arises when there is parallel progression in different life cycles. Beginning at the centre of the diagram with the founding of a family business, we typically see an entrepreneur—often a young adult—who has identified a new or unexploited business opportunity. In the start-up phase, the entrepreneur may be the sole or controlling owner. As the business develops, the entrepreneur's family may also begin to grow. From then on, family and business demands on the entrepreneur's energy and financial resources will increase. As the business matures, adult children may join the company. Decisions about leadership succession should be made during these years but often are not. Ownership becomes more complex as children and cousins inherit their parents' shares and responsibilities, at a time in the business life cycle when the need for regeneration may become acute.

Transitions in family businesses differ from those in publicly-traded firms. For example, if a CEO dies while at the head of a publicly-traded firm, the board will meet and either promote another employee, or conduct an external search. The details of the deceased CEO's plans for the distribution of his personal estate are of little consequence for the future of the firm.

However, imagine a family business in which the founder-CEO, and controlling shareholder, has led the firm for 30 years but has never outlined a plan for leadership or ownership succession. The death of a powerful family member can then create a financial and leadership vacuum at a time when his family face a devastating emotional loss. Family members will be grieving over the loss of an important figure in their lives (irrespective of the quality of their relationship with him) at the same time as they try to develop strategies to fill the deceased's central role in the company. If the family and board have not planned for life cycle events such as succession, regeneration, changes in industry, and evolving ownership responsibilities, then conflicting demands for their emotional resources combined with confusion in leadership roles can have serious repercussions for both the business and the family.

At this point, it is worth making a short detour to explore two fundamental theories of human development that shed some light on why transitions can be so difficult for people to face.

KEY MODELS OF HUMAN PSYCHOLOGICAL DEVELOPMENT

Understanding the life cycle concept helps to make sense of the way individuals and families develop. In business-owning families, individual life cycle development takes place within a matrix of business and family needs, as members struggle to define and negotiate their roles and relationships over a lifetime. The life cycle concept is very important, and it is worth taking a little detour to explore some fundamental theories of human development. The two most influential models from psychodynamic theory are those developed by Sigmund Freud [3], the founder of psychoanalysis, and the psychoanalyst Erik Erikson, whose major work, *Childhood and Society*, was published in 1950 [4].

Freud's Six Phases of Psychosexual Development

It was Freud who first suggested that personality development corresponded to different periods of chronological age. His model of human development focused on development from infancy to childhood, over six phases (see Table 4.1).

Freud believed that the human psyche could be explored using empirical methods. He posited a life cycle explanation that encompassed physical development and psychological processes, arguing that every human being has to pass through the consecutive psychosexual phases outlined in Table 4.1. An individual whose early development was hindered or arrested in one of these phases might show related dysfunctional behavior later in life.

Table 4.1 Freud's six-phase model of human development

Phase	Age	Characteristics	Developmental indications
Oral	Birth to 18 months	Needs and pleasures centered around the mouth	Capacity to give to and receive from others; early development of sense of trust and self-reliance
Anal	1–3 years	Coincides with development of sphincter control	Autonomy; struggle for control; self-determining behavior; capacity for cooperation
Urethral	Transitional	Transition between anal and phallic stages	Growing gender identity and identification
Phallic	3–5 years	Focus on genitals	Development of sexual identity; curiosity without embarrassment; initiative; resolution of Oedipal Conflict
Latency	5–11 years	Inactivity of sexual drive	Consolidation of previous psychosexual development; basis for adult satisfaction in work and love
Genital	11 to young adulthood (beginning of puberty)	Maturation of sexual characteristics; increase in libidinal drives produces regression and reopens unresolved conflicts from earlier stages	Sexual and psychological foundation of mature individual

Erikson's Eight Ages of Man

Building on Freud's thinking, Erik Erikson developed an expanded life cycle model of individual development that offered several new insights by taking a psychosocial perspective (see Table 4.2). First, his lifelong model considered human development from birth to death, not just childhood to young adulthood. Second, he used an epigenetic principle, that is, progress in each

Table 4.2   Erikson's eight ages of man

Stage		Psychosocial crisis	Behaviors	Psychosocial learning
1	Infant (0–1)	Trust versus mistrust	Mostly experiencing safety and reliability	Trust
2	Toddler (2–3)	Autonomy versus shame and doubt	Acting on their own within limits	Determination
3	Pre-school (3–6)	Initiative versus guilt	Play and interact with others	Purpose
4	School-age child (6–11)	Industry versus inferiority	Work with others, complete tasks	Competence
5	Adolescence (12–18)	Ego identity versus role confusion	Becoming and sharing oneself	Fidelity (fitting in your community)
6	Young adulthood (18–20s)	Intimacy versus isolation	Developing close relationships	Love (acceptance)
7	Adult (20s–50s)	Generativity versus stagnation	Balancing needs of others and self	Giving/caring
8	Late adulthood (60+)	Ego integrity versus despair	Recognizing life's value	Wisdom

successive stage is determined by success, or lack of success, in dealing with the challenges from the previous stage. Third, he considered the interaction across generations, which he called mutuality. Previous thinkers had noted that parents and other caregivers influence their children, but Erikson observed that children also influence the growth and development of the adults who care for them [5]. The concept of mutuality is important for business families, where the different generations may interact at work or in the boardroom, as well as in the family setting.

Erikson's description of the early stages of human development closely parallels Freud's psychosexual phases, and emphasizes the importance of the parent–child relationship. Erikson saw later stages as being oriented toward the external world outside the family. He theorized that each stage presents developmental challenges or crises, presented as polarities that the individual needs to address successfully in order to move to the next stage. Development in each stage is affected by the social context in which the person operates. He also suggested that a person can overcome developmental problems faced earlier in life [6].

In stage 1, infants normally trust that their needs (food, warmth, contact) will be met (the 'oral stage' in Freud's developmental scheme). At the heart of this sense of trust is the mother–child interaction, which the infant later extrapolates to the larger environment where he or she operates. Loving parents and a generally responsive environment will teach the infant that he or she lives in a world that can be trusted—a world in which help, care, and love are available; a world that nurtures hope and a belief in the attainability of desires. It is up to the parents to ensure that their child develops this way of looking at the world. Where there is a failure in parental care, strong feelings of distrust are generally the consequence.

In stage 2, the child learns to explore and develop a sense of independence from caregivers. As the child gains sphincter control (Freud's anal stage), he or she has a choice to 'keep' or 'let go,' with implications about where the body ends and where the outside world begins. If parents are supportive and not overprotective, children gain autonomy, and feel that they can control themselves and their world. If parents are constrictive, a child will feel ashamed and/or doubt its ability to be independent. Battles may ensue about who will be in control, and these battles may continue later in life. Again, balance is the critical parenting activity: children should push (but not be pushed) and be allowed to fail, but not see themselves as a failure. They need to internalize a perception of being able to control events in their lives.

In stage 3, children move more and more into a play world, often of their own creation. They can initiate their own learning, motivated by curiosity, and have social interactions with peers and adults. If they are allowed sufficient physical and intellectual freedom, their sense of initiative will be reinforced. Play is an important factor in practicing the new freedom that increased motility brings. Although much of children's play is solitary, their ability to play is enhanced by the willingness of the other family members to engage the developing child—to enter his or her fantasy world [7]. Such encouragement contributes to the child possessing an adventurous attitude toward life. During this period, children attempt to undertake many adult-like activities and learn how conscience governs initiative. When that exploration takes them over the limits set by their parents, they develop a sense of guilt. Children who are held back have a more prudent, conservative way of dealing with the environment at large, while children allowed to engage in role experimentation develop a sense of purpose. The way in which children are cared for at this stage also helps to determine whether guilt is a dominant emotion as the child experiences an awakening of sexual interest.

In stage 4, the child comes into direct contact with external social influences (school and community) and begins to use reason, language, tools, and machines for building, creating, and accomplishing. The play world of stage 3 is replaced by the real world of rules. Teachers' concern and peer support, along with the parents' unconditional encouragement, are vital if the child is to feel that his or her accomplishments are worthwhile. A harsh environment can lead to a sense of inferiority.

In stage 5, adolescence begins. This is always a phase of struggle because of the dramatic physical, emotional, and social changes facing the adolescent (Erikson wrote reassuringly that this phase is 'traversable'). The child, still strongly connected to the parents, develops a personal identity influenced by how well the individual fared in previous stages. Teenagers will measure themselves against their own role models and will cling together in an attempt to experience a group identity because they are struggling to develop their own individual identity. Children who have experienced a great deal of turmoil early in life may have trouble coping with the rapid changes that are part of adolescence. Young people can be supported in this stage if they engage in honest, adolescent-led communication and in academic, religious, sports, community, or family rites of passage.

Stage 6 sees the arrival of young adulthood (the 20s and 30s). The challenge for young people in this stage is to create significant interpersonal relationships in many settings: work colleagues, adult friends, and romantic partners. A person with a well-established sense of self will be able to enter into intimate relationships without feeling threatened by the loss of his or her own identity. However, internal conflict will arise during this stage if a sense of identity has not been firmly established. The ideal outcome of this stage, according to Erikson, is the ability to love, as well as to address and accept differences and antagonisms—the capability of forming a commitment to a relationship, whether it is a marriage, or a relationship between friends or co-workers.

The seventh stage is the longest, covering the middle adult years from the late 20s to late 50s. This is also the most difficult stage to define because of the ebb and flow of life events and activities. Establishing a career and child-rearing are two markers for this period as the individual's focus moves from 'the future' and 'me' to 'the now' and others. The crisis in this period is the classic struggle of personal life balance—how we can best use our energy and talents. Erikson coined the term 'generativity' to describe a mature adult's impulse to teach, mentor, and guide younger generations (not limited to one's own offspring), and/or to work to improve social conditions. Erikson termed the counterbalancing position 'stagnation,' meaning being preoccupied with one's own needs and desires. The ideal, once again, is a balance between the two: people who try to save the world, or who impose their views too forcefully on younger people, are often as ineffective as those who make no effort to give back at all.

This period of the human life cycle is filled with many events that force us to renegotiate our personal goals and interpersonal relationships. Marriage and birth, divorce, illness, and death all affect how we see ourselves and the world around us. As we progress through this long stage, we begin to measure our lives in terms of time left to live instead of time since birth. People may experience a midlife crisis as the reality of their lives conflicts with the dreams and aspirations that have motivated their actions. There is a struggle between generativity and self-absorption. It is a period in time that marks a greater search for meaning. The classic question, 'What am I doing this for?' reflects a focus on oneself, while 'Who am I doing this for?' reflects a concern for others. Success at this stage is about balance and recognizing that getting older without having experienced or accomplished your dreams does not reduce your capacity for caring about others.

Stage 8 covers the end of working life into retirement (starting at 60 plus). The crisis here is how to attain what Erikson called 'personal ego integrity' with a minimal amount of despair in the face of dramatic changes. Many things work against balance in late adulthood: connection with our communities weakens; our careers wind down, and physical illness increasingly becomes a reality rather than a hypochondriacal fear. The death of friends and family members brings the knowledge of our own mortality ever closer. Despair can result from this if an individual feels there has been little purpose to life, or that his or her life has been a failure. This can deepen when the realization that death lies inescapably ahead is accompanied by a fear of dying. However, if this can be faced and dealt with, ego integrity will result: recognizing and accepting the wisdom of a life well lived, with satisfaction. Erikson believed that this wisdom is our final gift to younger generations, who need role models.

Having considered some ideas about stages in an individual's human development we will now look at stages in the family, by returning to the idea of the life cycle.

THE FAMILY LIFE CYCLE

An understanding of human life cycles allows us to understand better life cycles in other systems and organizations. As Erik Erikson put it, 'Each successive stage and crisis has a special relation to one of the basic elements of society, and this for the simple reason that the human life cycle and man's institutions have evolved together' [8].

A family is a unique social system because it has gone through its own particular cultural, geographic, and historical experiences, although it will have been influenced by factors that all families experience, such as birth, marriage, and partnership. The family system creates a strong emotional connection between family members that can never be completely broken—and which is often, in fact, made stronger by death or disconnection in the family [9].

Economic and social changes in the twentieth century have forced continual redefinition of the concept of family, which can no longer be exclusively represented by the traditional nuclear model (two parents of the opposite sex, in a long-term marital relationship financially supported by one partner, and living with their own (shared) children). It must now embrace same-sex couples, step-families, different financial and psychological structures, and flexible membership.

All families experience transitional events such as marriage, childbearing, the empty nest, retirement, and death [10]. As they attempt to address the challenges associated with each new stage, they need to be able to renegotiate their family hierarchies and relationships to reflect the changing conditions and new roles in the family. When a family is unable to navigate such changes, the result is often conflict or other inappropriate behaviors that cause the family to remain stuck. For example, parents who exert strong parental leadership when their children are small may need to learn to take a less directive approach as their children become teenagers and to hand over to them a reasonable degree of decision making. If parents remain unreasonably authoritative, their children are likely to develop either a continued dependency on them, or go to the opposite extreme, resorting to rebelliousness with dysfunctional consequences.

CARTER AND MCGOLDRICK'S FAMILY-BASED LIFE CYCLE MODEL

In 1989, family therapists Elizabeth Carter and Monica McGoldrick [11] developed a six-stage model of the family life cycle. Although, because of the wide variety of modern family structures that now exist, this model cannot always be usefully applied, the concept is helpful because it examines the development of individuals within the context of the family system.

One of the challenges that all family members face is the development of emotional autonomy and separation from the family of origin—often described in psychodynamic terms as the 'process of separation–individuation' [12]. In a family-systems model this is termed 'differentiation'—the stage when individuals in a family system move from being a family of children and parents to being a family of adults.

The first phase identified in this family life cycle model describes the years from the birth of the children through to their adolescence. In this phase, children are affected by experiences in the family of origin, the interaction of their parents, and their own interactions with siblings and extended family. School and the larger community are also strong influences on the development of individual family members.

The second phase of the family life cycle model is leaving home. Young people leave for university or careers, thereby differentiating themselves from their family of origin. The outcome of this stage should be the creation of new, adult-to-adult relationships with their parents. The concept of differentiation is important because if young people are not able to differentiate from their parents (for example, as we mentioned earlier, because their parents have been over-authoritarian) they will have difficulty developing intimate adult relationships with their peers.

In most (but not all) cultures, leaving home signals the desire for starting a life away from the family of origin. If we apply this framework to business families, the potential for conflict immediately becomes apparent. What happens when a young person begins to work in the family firm? If there are foggy boundaries between the family and its business, a young person's struggle to become an autonomous adult can be complicated. This is because the children are left with no outside arena in which to test their abilities and differentiate themselves from the family of origin.

The third life cycle stage includes the premarital (or pre-partnership) years. Young people are looking for partners, testing different relationships, experimenting with intimacy, and make decisions about marriage or other life commitments.

In the fourth stage, they solidify their relationship with another individual and negotiate the shared experience of living as a couple. During this period the young couple also renegotiates and realigns their relationship with their families of origin, siblings, and peer group, to include their new spouse or partner. Again, this can be complex: there is now a combination of three families. Each partner brings a family of origin to the mix, to which is added the new family the partners are creating together. In business families, strong ties to the family of origin of one or both partners may interfere with the development of the couple's new marital family.

Phase five begins when a couple have children. This involves a significant renegotiation of roles, because the couple's relationship changes dramatically as they make space and time for the newcomer(s) and as their roles adapt to the fact that their own parents are now assuming grandparenting roles. In this phase the needs of the spouse, children, and professional life should all, ideally, be kept in balance. The family moves into the next phase when children become adolescents. During the teenage years, the parents are challenged to develop a parenting relationship that is mutually rewarding and supportive, as their own children attempt to differentiate from them. Adolescents are particularly effective at creating conflict within the family system, and at creating conflict between their parents.

As the individuals in the couple mature, their relationship begins to shift its focus as they start to realize the limits to their career dreams, and to recognize other reduced opportunities. In addition, they may have to re-enter their family of origin to provide care and support for aging parents. In cultures where extended families live in close proximity, this is still a natural process. But in families where members do not live in the same geographical region, or even the same country, this may require significant sacrifice on the part of one or both of the partners. Having simultaneous responsibilities toward both children and elderly parents creates additional stress in the family system.

The sixth phase begins as the couple launch their children into the world, and move firmly into their own mid-life period. The couple must, again, renegotiate a new relationship based on the two of them as a couple. There are further adjustments ahead as their children find partners. The partners of their children, and eventually grandchildren, must be drawn into the family circle. Their own parents will die, leaving the couple to deal with this life passage as well. The realization of their own mortality, of being next in line, increasingly becomes a reality.

Carter and McGoldrick call this last phase 'later life'. In this phase, both partners cope with their own physical and psychological decline and have to learn how to deal with loss, as life partners and old friends die. It is a time for preparing for (or denying) death, reflecting on personal successes and failures, family experiences, and for finding final opportunities to support children and grandchildren.

The family life cycle model proposed by Carter and McGoldrick was based on the same principles as Erikson's eight-stage model but puts the emphasis on the family system. An important premise of Erikson's work is that individual psychological and developmental tasks are made easier if the preceding task has been resolved effectively. In Carter and McGoldrick's family systems model, the family's influence and relationships with individuals are added to the mix. It shows how the family system is an important factor in helping or hindering a person's achievement of life tasks and in influencing his or her consequent psychological development.

APPLYING THE LIFE CYCLE IN FAMILY BUSINESSES

To illustrate how one might use these various models in the family business context, let's consider the story of a typical business family as its members move through their various life cycle phases. While you read this case, try to identify points at which the business stages and individual life cycle phases overlap. On the surface this can appear to be a simple story, but carefully studied it can reveal certain specific events and experiences that influence the way the protagonists act. What do you see happening in the immediate future for this family and their business?

A Family Story: A Mother and CEO's Life Cycle

Margaret Brompton, her father, and her husband Steve had started a small local trucking company in the 1970s. Margaret was her father's only child; his wife had died when Margaret was 5. The founders of the trucking firm were very ambitious, and despite a meager cash flow in the early years, had been able to develop the company into a strong regional trucking and logistics support firm. Margaret's original plan was to work part time in the business so she could care for her three children. Unfortunately, when the first, her daughter, was still a baby, the business's success and her father's illness forced her to take a more active role. The fact that she and her husband gave the business a high priority later added to their children's commitment to the family firm.

Thirty-five years later, Margaret was more involved with the company than ever. After the death of her husband in 1990, Margaret had taken on his and her father's roles as chairman and chief executive officer. All three of her children also worked in the business, as she had always wished. For Margaret, the business was an important legacy, and a lingering connection to both her husband and her father, and she was proud that her children were a part of it.

However, Margaret saw the children facing major challenges. Her daughter, now president of the company, had two pre-teen children, one of whom was having serious trouble in school. Margaret's first son had married a successful entrepreneur, but the couple divorced after five years. The Bromptons' passion for their business was criticized by their son's former in-laws; according to them, the business had been one of the reasons for the divorce. To outsiders, the Brompton family appeared to be overcommitted to their business. Although Margaret worried about the happiness of her children and grandchildren, she felt that overall they were a close and loving family, fortunate to have a business that could support them.

Now in her late 70s, Margaret was thinking about retiring. Not completely—she would still stay on the board—but she wanted to have enough time to see her friends and get to know her grandchildren better. She had always assumed that her daughter, now 50, would be the next chairman and CEO, and had made that clear to her children. But recently both her sons had expressed an interest in running the company.

Her younger son, the only one in the family with an MBA, wanted to take the company in a new direction: he was very concerned about the growing competition from an air freight company that had set up a hub at their local airport. Margaret continued to put off a decision about who should succeed her. She began to consider whether the solution might be to split the company into two divisions.

'This company has been an important part of my life,' said Margaret. 'I know I need to think about retiring, but I'm not sure I'm ready to move on. I'm not sure my daughter is ready to become CEO. And what about my sons? I want to avoid conflict that could harm the company. It looks like I will have to remain in charge for a while yet.'

A case study like this raises a number of questions:

- Margaret worked closely with her father and husband all her life, and has now stepped into their shoes. What does this tell us about her relationships with them?
- Margaret had to become quite involved with the business, and this meant she was less available for her children. Do the decisions her daughter and sons made reveal evidence of a family script, which they are following? For example, was

their commitment to the business a conscious choice, or a continuation of the only life they had ever known?

- Was it actually the case, as the accusations of one son's former in-laws stated, that the family's overcommitment to the business contributed to the divorce?
- From a family systems perspective, what should Margaret do about succession?
- Do the established relationships mask other problems?

We can also consider the parallel process of the family's individual life cycles, and the business life cycle. Consider Margaret's age. As Erikson explained, our 70s is a time of life when most people have moved into, or through, a phase of generativity as a way to develop a legacy, by teaching and learning from younger generations. And yet Margaret does not seem to want to give up any control in the family business. Could it be that, working in her father's and husband's shadows most of her life, she never fully developed her own identity?

Furthermore, her company is 35 years old: so why isn't she analyzing the market situation more closely, as her younger son is encouraging her to do? Could it be that she still thinks of her son as the awkward teenager he once was?

Clearly, there are no definitive answers. The point of this exercise is to demonstrate how, when studying family businesses, we search for underlying themes, meanings, and metaphors, and explore the implications of certain activities and behavior in order to throw light on what is going on in the business.

In the next chapter we will be going on to look in more depth at the individual process and how particular character styles of family members can affect a family business, especially when a family member is the CEO.

ENDNOTES

1. Kets de Vries, M.F.R. (1995). *Organizational Paradoxes: Clinical Approaches to Management*. London: Routledge.
2. Carlock, R.S. and Ward, J.L. (2001). *Strategic Planning for the Family Business: Parallel Planning to Unify the Family and Business*. London: Palgrave Macmillan:

adapted from Sigelman, C.K. and Shaffer, D.R. (1991). *Life-Span Development*. Belmont, CA: Brooks/Cole Publishing; Levinson, D.J. (1978). *The Season of a Man's Life*, New York: Balantine Books; Eggers, J.H., Leahy, K.T. and Churchill, N.C. (1994). 'Stages of small business growth revisited: Insights into growth path and leadership/management skills in low and high growth companies,' in Bygrave, W.D., Birely, S., Churchill, N.C., Gatewood, E., Hoy, F., and Wetzel, W.E. (eds), *Frontiers of Entrepreneurship Research* (pp. 131–144). Boston: Babson College, 131–144.

3. Freud, S. (1905). *Three Essays on Sexuality*. In Strachey, J. (transl. and ed.), *The Standard Edition of the Complete Psychological Works of Sigmund Freud Vol. 7*. London: The Hogarth Press and the Institute of Psychoanalysis.

4. Erikson, E.H. (1950). *Childhood and Society*. New York: W.W. Norton.

5. Erikson (1950).

6. Erikson (1950).

7 Winnicott, D.W. (1971). *Playing and Reality*. New York: Basic Books. See also Winnicott, D.W. (1975). *Through Pediatrics to Psycho-analysis*. New York: Basic Books.

8. Erikson, E. (1950), *Childhood and Society* (p. 250). New York: Norton.

9. Walsh, F. (1993). *Conceptualization of Normal Family Processes*, New York: The Guilford Press.

10. Duvall, E. (1977). *Marriage and Family Development*. Philadelphia: Lippincott.

11. Carter, E. and McGoldrick, M. (1999). *The Expanded Family Life Cycle: Individual, Family, and Social Perspectives*. New York: Allyn & Bacon.

12. Mahler, M.S., Pine, F. and Bergman, A. (1975). *The Psychological Birth of the Human Infant*. New York: Basic Books.

CHAPTER 5

NARCISSISM, ENVY, AND MYTHS IN FAMILY FIRMS

We have already looked in earlier chapters at some of the issues with which family businesses struggle. In this chapter, we will look at the etiology of the intrapersonal, interpersonal, and group processes that people in family businesses have to face. The best place to start is with a discussion of individual development. This will enable us to explore the challenges of developing a life and relationships separate from our parents, and will help us to understand why working with parents or other relatives can be difficult. Later we will look at the larger issues of family dynamics and how parents and children become a family of adults.

PERSONALITY TYPES

As we saw in the previous chapter, Freud and Erikson argued persuasively that the human personality is shaped by very early experiences in our lives. Developmental psychologists argue that what happens in our early years not only influences the ways in which we behave and defend ourselves later in life but also leads to people developing specific 'personality types' or 'character styles' [1]. More recent writing about character styles endorses the idea that different 'psychic wounds' during childhood contribute to the character development of the adult.

Narcissism

The issue of early development brings us to the topic of narcissism. The term derives from the Greek myth of Narcissus, a youth who falls in love with his own reflection and pines to death. Freud described the very early stage that all infants go through as 'primary narcissism'—a period of childish self-absorption and attention seeking that is a necessary precursor of the child's ability to develop love for others.

In the child's development, parents (particularly the mother or primary caretaker) will be the first agents of socialization. In the beginning, to the totally dependent infant, the mother will be the universe, the object of primary attachment, of love and adoration. It is through the mother that the child will first exercise his or her senses: the tactile, the olfactory, and the visual. It is through the mother that the child will explore the answers to the most important existential questions that will shape his or her entire life—how loved he or she is, how lovable, how independent he or she can become. The mother becomes the benchmark against which everything will be measured. She will be idealized and internalized, thereby turning into a mythical creature that continues to play an important role in the person's internal theater.

To understand the psychological process by which an infant becomes an individual, it is also important to realize that our development plays on two stages: our inner theater of intrapsychic dramas, ruled by our desires, wishes, and needs, and an outer theater, where we interact with the physical world with its human relationships and demands. As indicated earlier, an individual's personality begins to be shaped in childhood, particularly during the first three years. This is when the core patterns of character are developed, and we emerge as individuals with a sense of our own body, gender identity, name, mind, and personal history. This is a period in time when we are very malleable, and the foundations are laid for the kind of person we are going to become (and the kind of behavior patterns that will stay with us for the rest of our life). Of course, this does not mean that later life experiences are of no importance, but they have a different kind of impact to those of our earliest years.

The clinical term for the changes that take place during these early years of life is narcissistic development. The term 'narcissism' has a negative connotation, evoking egotism, self-centeredness, and exaggerated self-love. However, it is important to realize that a healthy dose of narcissism is essential for human functioning and that it helps to constitute the basis of self-esteem and personal identity. Oscar Wilde's comment that 'loving oneself is the beginning of a lifelong romance' has a grain of truth in it. But narcissism is a double-edged sword. Having either too much or too little of it can throw a person off balance, and when equilibrium is lost, instability about the sense of self may develop in the core of an individual's personality.

Narcissistic development refers to an infantile stage through which we all must pass and during which the growing child derives pleasure from its own body and functions. This early stage is an extremely delicate time in a child's life, and the kind of treatment it receives during this period will color its view of the world all the way through adulthood.

Obviously, the role of parents and caretakers during narcissistic development is very important. Are they supportive and consistent, or rejecting and inconsistent? Do family circumstances expose the child to traumatic experiences? Support and care are a *sine qua non* for the foundation of a secure sense of identity and positive self-regard. In contrast, not having these caring experiences can have a devastating effect on the child and later adult.

Freud once noted: 'If a man has been his mother's undisputed darling he retains throughout life the triumphant feeling, the confidence in success, which not seldom brings actual success along with it' [2]. Whatever may be the mother's role, her influence will linger on, having an impact on the person's aspirations and achievements.

Of course there is no such thing as a perfect parent, and becoming a person is completely different from the comfortable period of intrauterine existence when the child's every need was automatically taken care of. Growing up cannot take place without a certain degree of frustration; fortunately, normal development requires frustration to occur in tolerable doses.

In an attempt to deal with their frustration at not receiving perfect care—that is, having every wish taken care of instantly—children try to retain their original impression of the perfection and bliss of their early years by creating both a grandiose, exhibitionistic image of themselves and an all-powerful, idealized image of their parents, with the latter taking on the roles of saviors and protectors. Psychoanalysts call these two narcissistic configurations the grandiose self and the idealized parent image [3]. Over time, if children receive good enough care, these two configurations are tempered by reality. Parents, siblings, and other important figures modify children's exhibitionistic displays, channeling grandiose fantasies of power and glory in proper directions and laying the foundation for realistic ambitions, stable values, well-defined career interests, and a secure sense of self-esteem and identity.

Constructive narcissistic development implies good-enough care and age-appropriate frustration. When individuals experience sufficient support from their caretakers they will end up well balanced [4]. They will go through life with the kind of inner strength that includes a capacity for introspection, empathy, and a positive outlook toward life. People who have these experiences can become excellent leaders.

But not everyone is lucky enough to establish a special caring bond within the family or to receive age-appropriate frustration. Many things can go wrong in the process of growing up. Prolonged disappointment due to parental overstimulation, understimulation, or highly inconsistent, arbitrary behavior, for example, can lead to problems of a narcissistic nature. And if violence and abuse are the norm in the family, the stage is set for an inner theater peopled with malevolent players.

Children who have been exposed to inadequate or dysfunctional parenting may later believe that they cannot depend on anyone's love or loyalty. As adults, they will act according to that conviction. These are people who, despite their claims to self-sufficiency, are troubled in the depth of their being by a sense of deprivation, anger, and emptiness. In order to cope with these feelings, and perhaps as a cover for their insecurity, some people allow their narcissistic needs to turn into obsessions, becoming fixated on issues of power, beauty, status, prestige, and superiority. They can end up with a grandiose sense of self-importance (exaggerating their achievements and talents), require excessive admiration, have an unrealistic sense of entitlement, can be interpersonally exploitative, and are unable to recognize or identify with the feelings of others. Furthermore, their attempts to maneuver others into strengthening their shaky sense of self-esteem makes them appear manipulative and arrogant [5]. In many instances, people with narcissistic disorders are preoccupied with thoughts of getting even for the injuries (real or imagined) that they experienced while growing up, and they can be extremely envious. When public figures have narcissistic disorders, all these negative and destructive ways of relating to the world are acted out on a large stage.

Reactive Narcissism

Many people in leadership positions reach the top because they can perceive and seize a historic moment: they are the right people with the right ideas at the right time. But clinical studies of leaders have also shown that a considerable percentage of these people become what they are because they are driven by negative motivations. For some, including many entrepreneurs, they are motivated by a desire to compensate for past hurts. Because of the hardships they encountered in childhood, when they were belittled or mistreated, they are driven to prove the world wrong and show everyone that they are a force to be reckoned with [6].

A Family Story: Reactive Narcissism

Many saw Johan Sanders [7] as a brilliant visionary with the street savvy to make things happen. As a descendant of the founder of the family firm, he had succeeded in building up a successful newspaper venture in Eastern Europe. To others, however, he was nothing more than an extremely abrasive individual, who constantly complained about all the 'inept people' working for him, people who 'were out to sabotage,' in his words, everything he tried to do.

Although Johan deserved credit for getting the venture off the ground, his job was eased by substantial financing from the family business and the help of a number of very capable people seconded from head office. Without them, Johan's abrasive leadership style—characterized by fear and intimidation—would have killed off any commitment and enthusiasm. With more and more people working in the venture, his leadership style became an increasing liability.

The situation came to a head when the members of his senior team complained to Johan's uncle, the CEO of the family firm, and told him that he had to choose between retaining them or his nephew. They pointed out that Johan's presence had become an obstacle to progress, referring to his intimidating manner, his inability to listen, and his conviction that he knew more about anything than anybody else. His uncle had no choice but to remove Johan from his position, to limit the damage his nephew was causing.

Johan Sanders is a good example of a reactive narcissist. Although driven and achievement-oriented, his bravura was a veneer for his insecurity and lack of self-confidence. When dealing with others whom they perceive as adversaries, people like Johan can be uncooperative, irritable, hostile, and resentful. They are prone to giving unreasonable criticism, being scornful toward people in authority, and displaying envy and resentment.

As a middle child in a family with parents who were not very empathic, Johan always felt unappreciated and misunderstood. Growing up, he had been very envious of his younger sister (his father's favorite) and his older brother (his mother's favorite) who was not only an excellent student but also a very good athlete. Johan's sense of being wronged, misunderstood, and unappreciated (which was, in fact, to some extent a realistic assessment) involved him in unending power struggles with his parents. His feelings about himself would oscillate between self-loathing and a sense of entitlement or moral superiority. Johan always felt that other people interfered with his freedom. Being controlled by others was intolerable; he wanted to do things his way.

Johan's main driving force in life was 'I'll prove the bastards wrong.' This outlook made him difficult to live with: his childhood was filled with verbal aggressiveness, interpersonal conflict and manipulative behavior, all of which continued to characterize his behavior in adulthood. He was infamous for his argumentativeness, anger, and confrontational behavior, his tendency to reject people, and his directing of his aggression toward those unlikely to retaliate. Although he was the author of much of his own misery, he would never take personal responsibility for his actions and seemed completely unaware of the effect his behavior had on others. The only people who could survive working with him were 'yes-men and women', because he allowed no opportunity for constructive give-and-take. Most of the projects he engaged in ended badly.

Although some reactive narcissists eventually overcome their feelings of bitterness, true reactive narcissists never reach this stage. They retain their grandiose sense of self-importance, habitually take advantage of others in order to achieve their own ends, fish for compliments, and continue to believe that their problems are unique. They never lose the feeling that they deserve favorable treatment and that rules are there for others, not for them. Their envy of others, and their rage when they cannot get their own way, can be formidable [8].

As a caveat, it needs to be said that while many reactive narcissists continually try to boost their defective sense of self-esteem and are governed by envy, spite, revenge, and vindictive triumph over others, it is entirely possible for a person with this kind of narcissistic disposition to channel it in a positive way. Some people can become capable of recognizing, through therapy or other interventions, that although they may have had a bad deal while growing up, they do not need to continue such a pattern. Often these people experience a great desire to break the downward cycle and become focused on 'reparation,' repairing or overcoming the hurts of childhood by helping others.

MANAGERIAL IMPLICATIONS OF DYSFUNCTIONAL NARCISSISM

Reactive narcissism is one of the most common causes of defective leadership. It is at the center of a host of character problems, such as paranoid, schizoid, passive-aggressive, antisocial, abrasive, histrionic, and compulsive behavior [9]. Parallels can also be drawn between the individual pathology of reactive narcissism and organizational pathology, or neurotic organizations [10]. Irrational characteristics exhibited by the principal decision makers in an organization can seriously affect the overall management process. The Russians have a pithy proverb for this: 'Fish start to stink at the head.' At the top of a neurotic, toxic organization (especially one in which power is highly centralized, as is usually the case in entrepreneurial and family businesses), one is likely to find a top executive whose rigid neurotic style is strongly mirrored in the inappropriate strategies, structures, and organizational culture of his or her firm. If this situation continues for too long, the leader's toxic actions may sow the seeds for the organization's decline or even self-destruction. In many entrepreneurial and family businesses, the peculiarities of the person in charge are strongly reflected in the company's corporate culture. Two destructive leadership styles—'dramatic' and 'suspicious'—frequently surface in entrepreneurial and family firms.

A dramatic organization is one run by the kind of narcissist who needs constant attention, excitement, activity, and stimulation and who has a tendency toward extremes. Leaders like this can be highly impulsive and dangerously uninhibited in their ventures, while dramatic organizations tend to attract dependent subordinates who have limited influence on policy making. Leaders who favor the dramatic style hoard power. Consequently, their organizations are overcentralized, and the organizational structure and information systems are often too primitive for the firm's many products and broad markets.

In a suspicious organization, leaders feel constantly under threat and act accordingly, with neurotic vigilance, suspicion, and distrust. The organization becomes secretive, in extreme cases even transforming into a kind of police state, with elaborate information systems set up to monitor all internal and external trends.

The impact of these two kinds of leadership on an organization can be devastating. Leaders prone to reactive narcissism do not create mature, innovative, learning organizations: quite the opposite—they force their personality on their subordinates until relationships become enmeshed and uniformity the norm. In organizations like this, it is difficult to maintain a sense of being an individual, one's own person. Those who need to do so leave the company, while those who decide to hang on often regress to infantile, dependent behavior patterns.

THE IMPORTANCE OF INDIVIDUATION

A major challenge in any child's developmental process is that of becoming a person in its own right. In the psychodynamic model this is referred to as the early life process of separation–individuation [11], whereby the child acquires a sense of separateness, the perception that he or she is a discrete entity, apart from the mother, emerging as a unique individual, with a name, a body, a mind, and a personal history. To become a whole person with a coherent sense of identity, the young child begins a process of differentiation. For this, the child first needs to attain the capacity for intrapsychic separateness, the ability to feel adequate in the absence of the other person.

As mentioned earlier, according to psychodynamic theory, we all inhabit two worlds—our intrapsychic world and the external world in which we interact with others. Early in life, it is hard to separate these two worlds, but eventually, when the child's reality testing [12] becomes more sophisticated, his or her outer and inner worlds become truly separate and distinguishable. Before this happens, however, the child also has access to an important third world: a space of fantasy and illusion, where connections can be drawn between the other two spheres. This imaginary world is a transitional place, an intermediate area of experience, a play area between reality and fantasy [13].

This world is inhabited by transitional objects, like strings, blankets, and teddy bears. These objects may be an almost inseparable part of the child, from which it cannot bear to be parted: however, they can also be viewed as the first 'not-me' possessions. These familiar objects help a child link his or her outer and inner realities. When the mother is absent, transitional objects prolong the soothing and calming experience her presence provides. Over time, the child is able to let go of transitional objects, as the capacity to internalize the soothing functions of the mother develops.

The ability to explore and investigate, and the development of an inner sense of cohesion and an external sense of reality, have their beginnings in the illusory transitional space of childhood. This transitional world is also the incubator for creative thought. This is where processes like symbolization, make-believe, illusion, daydreaming, playfulness, curiosity, imagination, and wonder all begin.

Transitional objects and transitional space play a major and very basic role in our development: they help us establish who we are. This transitional world is part of the process of resolving the developmental tasks of childhood so that we can arrive at adulthood and maturity with a unique sense of self.

THE FAMILY FIRM AS TRANSITIONAL OBJECT

One way of looking at a family business is to see it as a kind of transitional object, a stage between the comforts of family life and the realities of the harsh outside world. This space becomes a safe haven from possibly painful experiences. It becomes a place where one does not really have to grow up. However, one could argue that the business also offers a chance for family members to take on the challenge of moving from dependence and symbiotic attachment to individuation, autonomy, and interdependence. Nonetheless, one of the paradoxes of family firms is that they offer enormous opportunities for taking up responsibilities at an early age. At the same time, they can block some individuals' personal development if the older generation continues to treat the younger adults like children, thereby preventing the process of personal growth and healthy individuation. Such an outcome will be more likely, if a child's early environment was insecure. If parents failed to provide the right conditions for the separation–individuation process, the child may have a shaky sense of identity as it moves into adulthood—and the need for a transitional object will continue. A family business is not a teddy bear and hanging on to it as if it were one is bad business practice.

When the family business is used as a transitional object, dysfunctional processes can be transferred to the business and behavior patterns perpetuate themselves in a recursive cycle. In this way, family firms actually enhance the risk of arrested psychological development: the proximity and familiarity they provide add to dysfunctional behavior. In some family businesses, people become stuck, and never attain a true sense of separateness.

The story of Samuel C. Johnson, of S.C. Johnson & Son, Inc., provides us with an example of how a business, or a business object, can influence the trajectory of a person's life.

A Family Story: S.C. Johnson & Son, Inc.

S.C. Johnson & Son, Inc. [14], is best known in the United States for its eponymous product Johnson's Wax. The company was founded in the late 1880s when Samuel C. Johnson Sr transformed his hardwood parquet floor business into a company selling prepared floor wax. The company thrived and grew under the leadership of the founder, his son, and later his grandson Herbert.

Herbert Johnson was forced prematurely into leadership at the age of 28, when his father died unexpectedly. The year was 1929, and Herbert found himself at the head of a company with 500 employees and $5 million in sales. Herbert managed the business well during the difficult Depression era, but he had trouble at home. One of his daughters died at the age of

4, and his wife became an alcoholic. Herbert and his wife divorced in 1931, and shared custody of their two surviving children, Karen and Samuel C. Johnson Jr.

The earliest memory Samuel C. Johnson Jr recalled was of his parents' divorce. Herbert told his son that Samuel's mother was an alcoholic, and that there was nothing more to be done to help her. From that point on, Samuel's father came and went in his life intermittently. Samuel said in a filmed interview, 'My biggest doubt was: did my father love me as much as he loved the company? Maybe I was just an instrument to carry on the family name in the company' [15].

Samuel eventually took his father's place as CEO of the company, although his father was controlling until his death and was critical of Samuel's decisions. As an adult, Samuel, too, developed a drinking problem. Eventually he checked into a top rehabilitation center. As part of his recovery process he realized that he needed to reconnect to his memory of his father as a passionate, creative businessman. And so Samuel decided to retrace a journey his father had taken in an amphibious plane through the jungles of Brazil in 1935 to discover steady supplies of wax (a key ingredient in the company's products) from the carnauba palm tree.

The original plane, a Sikorsky S38 named *Carnauba*, had later crashed at sea, and by the time Samuel wanted to undertake his journey there were no other Sikorsky S38s in existence. Samuel, an experienced pilot, decided to build a replica using the original Sikorsky specification. More than 60 years after his father's historic flight, he made the same journey at the controls of the plane, with his own two sons as co-pilot and information officer. 'I felt,' he said, 'as if my father were flying with me.' In Brazil he found two carnauba palms that had been planted by his father 60 years earlier. 'I took this trip to spend more time with my father, after all these years. Looking up at the palms my father had planted brought back the feeling I had looking up at my dad when I was a young boy. I knew that I had fulfilled his wish for me.'

As Samuel Johnson's story shows, S.C. Johnson & Son, Inc. offered the young man huge responsibilities at an early age; at the same time, Samuel's enmeshed and conflicted working relationship with his father, and his cut-off relationship with his mother, undermined the development of his own sense of identity and became a block to his autonomy. He was trying to deal with this unfinished business many years later as he explored his relationship with his father through rebuilding his father's plane, and retracing his voyage of discovery. This story shows how family firms may contribute to arrested psychological development, and how they can turn into transitional objects. But it also demonstrates how one son attempted to free himself from developmental arrest and move on.

THE POWER OF ENVY

The high dramas of adult life often have deceptively innocent beginnings. As we have seen, early childhood experiences (both painful and pleasurable) have great significance for later family entanglements. To understand the potentially destructive consequences of these entanglements, we have to understand their emotional origin—in which envy often plays an important part.

Although it can sometimes be useful in spurring us on to greater efforts to achieve what we want but do not have, envy can often bring unpleasant feelings of helpless yearning to possess what someone else has—wealth, power, status, love, beauty, belongings. Often unacknowledged as such, envy can give rise to further deeply negative feelings of frustration, anger, self-pity, greed, rivalry, and vindictiveness.

The first component of envy is clearly the wish to equal, imitate, or surpass the envied individual. The second component seems to be a narcissistic wound—a sense of something lacking—connected with feelings of inferiority, inadequacy, and injured self-esteem. To be consumed by envy involves self-devaluation as well as longing for a desired possession. There is anger at the possessor, perhaps expressed mildly (in chagrin or discontent), moderately (in resentment or ill will), or severely (in malicious and spiteful acts of spoiling or destruction) [16]. There are elements of envy in Samuel C. Johnson Jr's story, as he struggles to become a great man like his father, while creating an unholy alliance with his mother.

Envy is one of the most primitive and fundamental emotions. It starts to evolve as soon as the infant sees the mother's breast as the source of all gratification and good experiences. The infant wants complete possession and access to this wonderful thing all the time. But soon the infant realizes that it is not possible to control of the 'object', which comes and goes. Often, just as the child is coming to terms with all this, a new baby arrives, aggravating the situation and stirring up envious feelings.

The older child begins to see that there are winners and losers in love because when the new baby receives more of its mother's attention, the older child has less. With this realization, envious feelings become intensified in the older child. The arrival of this third person—the younger child—into the original mother–child dyad transforms the older child's rather simple envy into jealousy. Jealousy is a protest against a loss of a loved one and characterizes itself by the wish to hold on. Unlike envy, jealousy never pertains to a two-person situation. It is a complex group process involving three or more people. In contrast, envy is a destructive feeling about needing to *have*; when someone else possesses something desirable, envy feeds the wish to spoil and take away whatever it is the other person has. Due to the effect of envy, rivalrous feelings build up and lead the older child to compare its own qualities with those of the new baby. The result: a sense of competitiveness and sibling rivalry that can extend far beyond childhood.

Because of the narcissistic injury (the deflation of the older child's self-image) that accompanies envy, the wish to return injury for injury may become a central theme of an individual's character, and vindictive triumph—the satisfaction that comes with restoring injured pride—the only thing worth living for.

The intensity of envy that a child feels is very much determined by the environment provided by his or her parents. The adequacy or otherwise of the parents' nurturing skills affect the child's relationships to its siblings and to other people later in life. One of the great challenges in parenting is to minimize sibling rivalry. This necessitates a considerable amount of maturity on the part of the parents: they must have a certain tolerance for conflict if they are to be able to neutralize it in and between their children. They should also be able to make their children feel that their treatment of them is fair. But parents differ greatly in their ability to contain their children's envious feelings [17]. (Given the difficulties many parents have in managing their own emotional lives, it is no wonder that they sometimes have difficulty handling their children's emotions well.) Children whose parents are poor at managing emotions may find, however, that destructive rivalries continue throughout their whole life, with potentially disastrous results if they own a business together.

Another factor that can influence how children develop and handle envy and rivalry is the emotional availability of their parents. If parents are preoccupied with themselves, children may begin to fight for the little quality time that is available. Sibling rivalry and competitiveness then become the dominant patterns in the family. Children in such households become expert judges in who has preference in the love equation. When children's early feelings of envy and jealousy are unresolved, their dysfunctional entanglements are likely to linger throughout life, becoming as troubling a handicap as a chronic disease. And these feelings will flare up in the family business setting.

In normal circumstances, siblings eventually separate and choose their own course in life. With time and geographical distance, residual childhood irritants and resentments are less likely to flare up. But when siblings join the family firm, resolution is much more difficult. The continuing closeness of all parties, including the parents, aggravates the situation: old feelings of envy and jealousy cannot be put to rest because all the actors in the play are still present. Family members can end up in a vicious circle of endlessly repeating conflicts—a continuation of the old emotional childhood patterns.

The web of unresolved childhood entanglements becomes denser in adulthood as succeeding generations and in-laws join the family drama. When love has been a scarce commodity and an object of competition during the developmental years, the stage is set for later internecine strife. Because family and business disputes tend to become confused, decision making in family firms corroded by envy is done on an emotional rather than a sound business basis. And because these disputes have their origin in early childhood, they can be extremely messy—far more difficult to disentangle than would be the case in publicly held corporations.

This factional infighting can become Byzantine in family firms that have survived a number of generations and are run by large families. Obviously, maintaining a cohesive family unit becomes more difficult as the generations spread out and entanglements become progressively complex. As indicated in the Gucci family story that follows (see Figure 5.1), the danger is that too much time and attention will be spent on conspiratorial activities and not enough on the substance of the business.

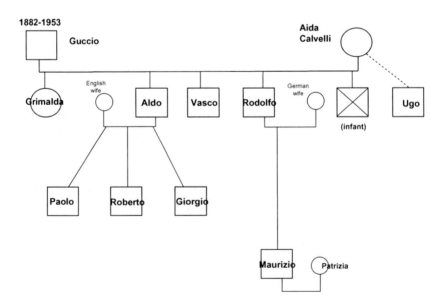

Figure 5.1 The Gucci family tree

A Family Story: Gucci

On March 27 1995, the world was shocked to hear that Maurizio Gucci, former chairman of the Gucci luxury leather goods and fashion dynasty [18], had been shot dead in broad daylight while entering his office in central Milan—a miserable end to the career of one of the scions of the Gucci family. Maurizio Gucci's life had been tainted by family feuding as he struggled with other family members for control of the company. The trials and tribulations of the family firm were a veritable soap opera, in which family members sued each other for breach of contract, misconduct, and even assault and battery.

Two years before his death, Maurizio Gucci had signed away his 50% holding in Gucci and ended his family's ownership of the company that, for three generations, had been a by-word for luxury and glamour. However, during the previous two decades the company had become the turf for a familial civil war, turning brothers against brothers and sons against fathers. Their greed, rivalry, intrigue, and violence were ultimately self-defeating and tore the family and company apart. Although they were well aware of what they were doing, they did not seem able to stop themselves destroying the source of their own wealth and success.

By the early 1990s, Gucci had seen spectacular success: the Gucci name had become synonymous with wealth and fashion and, like Chanel No. 5, had assumed an iconic value of its own. The family had come a long way from the first House of Gucci store in Florence, opened in 1922 to provide a repair service and sell high-quality leather goods and gift items. But relations within the Gucci family were highly strained. The private Gucci story, well hidden for many years behind the glamorous storefronts, was one of envy, suspicion, antagonism, and sibling rivalry, almost from the company's inception.

Guccio Gucci, the company's founder, combined an aggressive temperament with a need for control: it was a brave son who contradicted him or challenged his business decisions. Four of his five children—sons Aldo, Rodolfo, and Vasco and only daughter, Grimalda—worked in the company, but while Guccio insisted that all his sons should have shares of equal value in the business, his daughter, allegedly his favorite child, was blatantly excluded. The company was to be run only by Gucci men.

Guccio's albeit partisan even-handedness ignored the fact that his sons did not put an equal amount of work and commitment into the company. Aldo and Vasco had been involved in the company throughout their adult life but their attitudes were very different. Vasco was easy-going to the point of laziness, and although he had inherited his fair share of Gucci creativity he was happiest in the country, indulging his passion for hunting. Aldo, however, was his father's right-hand man, totally committed to the company, although his relationship with his father was stressful, as Guccio consistently blocked his son's attempts to move the company into different directions. Rodolfo joined the company in his late 30s, after a failed career as a film star, but his father, despite Rodolfo's lack of experience, immediately installed him in a position equivalent to Aldo's.

In the circumstances, it seems inevitable that perceived—and real—unfairness should fuel the competitiveness and jealousy of the Gucci sons' relationships with one another, particularly that between Aldo and Rodolfo. The family dynamics—rivalry, volatility, fragmentation, and suspicion—were mirrored in the business, resulting in disorganization, secrecy, and caution.

Guccio died suddenly in the summer of 1953, of heart failure. He did not live to see the glory days of his company's success. His death released his sons' ambitions and removed the major obstacle to their plans for expansion. The initial period following Guccio's death was one of uneasy strategic alliances: Rodolfo and Aldo against Vasco; and all three against their sister Grimalda, whose petition to gain an equal share in her father's estate was ruthlessly squashed by her brothers in court.

By the time Vasco died in 1975, a third generation of Gucci sons had moved into the company. Uniting to retain their brother's share in the company by buying out Vasco's widow, Aldo and Rodolfo became joint owners of Gucci, Rodolfo retaining 50% of the shares, while Aldo allocated 10% jointly to his three sons. As the third generation moved into increasingly responsible positions, and despite the fact that Gucci was doing better than ever, the gaps between cousins, uncles, and brothers widened.

By the late 1970s, Gucci was everywhere yet the ubiquity of the mark was not matched by the company's prosperity. In 1978, the year Gucci announced a record turnover of $48 million, they also announced a profit of precisely zero. There should have been far more money around than there was. An enquiry, assisted by Aldo's oldest son Paolo, who had been fired by his father, revealed that Aldo was implicated in tax evasion. By this stage, the fratricidal and patricidal dynamics within the family were becoming increasingly overt.

In 1983, Rodolfo died. In 1985, Aldo, at the age of 81, was imprisoned for tax fraud, convicted largely on the testimony of his son. Between those dates, Maurizio, stepping into his father's half-share of the company, maneuvered both Aldo and Paolo off the board and out of Gucci. The rest of the family soon followed them. For the first time since his grandfather had opened his store in Florence, one man was back in charge of the company, and he was the only Gucci.

Paradoxically, as the Gucci family disintegrated, the company itself grew stronger. Once the damaging aftershocks of Aldo's conviction and the media frenzy over the family meltdown had subsided, it became clear that the company was in good health, if under-active.

Despite his commitment to the company, Maurizio's business judgment was highly questionable. A series of poor decisions, taken in opposition to his advisers, put Gucci on the verge of bankruptcy. His ill-fated tenure at Gucci was not the only upheaval in his life at that time. When the death of Rodolfo released the final bond in their difficult relationship, Maurizio's response had been disproportionate. The teenager whose enormously wealthy father had bought him a modest car, while his friends drove Porsches, and only allowed him out on his bike if the chauffeur went with him, now got himself a private plane and several luxury properties, filled his garages with fast cars and motorbikes and bought ocean-going yachts. The indulgence in forbidden treats was understandable. However, it also seemed that his freedom from one controlling relationship prompted him to lay waste to everything he perceived as a constriction, including his marriage.

On May 22, 1985, Maurizio told his wife Patrizia that he was going on a short business trip, packed a case, and left their Milan apartment. The following day, he sent a friend to tell her that he would not be returning: the marriage was over.

Maurizio was generous, if implacable, and after their protracted divorce in 1991 Patrizia was awarded the equivalent of $500 000 annual alimony. Maurizio continued to support their two daughters. However, he could maintain neither his family nor himself in the way they were all used to. The excesses of his lifestyle meant that his personal debts increased to more than $40 million as Gucci faltered.

Patrizia's response to the divorce—'I want to see him dead'—was taken no more seriously by her friends than the recriminations that follow the break-up of any marriage are usually taken. An explanation for her bitterness and spite seemed to have been found when she was diagnosed with a brain tumor in 1992. The tumor was successfully removed without any apparent ill effects.

In 1993, Maurizio was voted off the board of Gucci and sold all his shares in the business. Forty years after the death of its founder, the last member of the Gucci family, and the only third-generation survivor, signed the company away.

Epilogue

Maurizio Gucci gradually began to rebuild his life, starting a new business venture and settling down with a new partner, Paola Franchi. He remained in Milan, to be near his children. Then on September 23, 1995, he was shot and killed on the steps outside his office as he arrived at the start of the day's business. Eighteen months later Patrizia was arrested and charged with his murder. At her subsequent trial, she was found guilty of having hired a hit man to kill her ex-husband, and sentenced to life imprisonment. Her appeal to have her conviction overturned, on the grounds that her brain surgery had affected her personality, was dismissed in a ruling by the European Court of Human Rights in June 2005. On January 25, 2006, Italy's highest court of appeal rejected a motion to release her on medical grounds and confirmed that she is to complete her 26-year sentence in jail.

Newspaper accounts of the fights between Guccio Gucci's children and grandchildren reveal only the surface of this multigenerational drama—a drama whose origins lay with its founder. Guccio made a habit of playing his three sons against each other, stirring up intense feelings of envy and sibling rivalry. These emotions then echoed among *their* children as the fathers used their sons as proxies to resolve old battles, trying to spite one another. Like spoiled children, the family members became obsessed by greed and devoted themselves to seeking ways to double-cross each other until their vengeful activities resulted in self-destruction.

GAMES FAMILIES PLAY: THE ROLE OF FAMILY MYTHS

Over time, the fallout from the kind of interrelationships described above can become hardened into family myths. Similarly to the notion of 'texts' (described in Chapter 1), family myths are beliefs and assumptions shared by members of the family to explain the way things are done within the family. These myths can take on a powerful, navigating function, but usually create mutually agreed roles and rigidly prescribed behavior, which determine how family members function together. Like cultural myths that are used to explain the nature of the universe and humankind, they give structure to the family's experiences, create continuity between past and present, act as a guide for future actions, contribute to equilibrium in the family, and are buffers against the forces of change. As we have seen, generational envy, jealousy, and sibling rivalry have a major influence in the genesis of family myths, to which traumatic life events (death, birth, desertion, and illness) can also contribute. These family myths will have an impact on the various roles family members assume in the business.

Taking both a psychodynamic and family systemic perspective helps us to understand the degree to which myths play important defensive and protective roles in families [19]. They can help people to cope with stress and anxiety and, by prescribing specific ritualistic behavior patterns, enable the family to establish a common front against the outside world. Although they can be useful in this way, family myths also often enable a family to cover up unpleasant real-life situations with idealized self-images. In this sense, the myths can be considered a kind of family compromise: because the myths that contribute to certain behavior patterns within the family must be endorsed by everyone, all the family members will be affected by these myths.

However, this is not necessarily healthy cooperation and can be a form of collusion, whereby unwanted aspects of one family member's behavior are repudiated, split off, and transferred to another family member. Perceptions of transferred behavior harden over time until the reality of who actually did what becomes permanently distorted.

Family myths are often mobilized in times of crisis. The defensive system is activated and family members start to operate on automatic pilot. As A.J. Ferreira puts it, 'the family myth is to the relationship what the defense is to the individual' [20]. These myths create an unchallenged defensive posture within the family, and their power can be enhanced by the fact that the rules that govern each family myth are not explicitly defined. Much of what makes up a family myth lies deep beneath the surface. So, while family myths offer a rationale for behavior within the family, they also conceal the true issues, problems, and conflicts.

THE IMPACT OF FAMILY MYTHS ON THE FAMILY BUSINESS

Family myths become a blueprint for family action, but they can also turn into a straitjacket, reducing a family's flexibility and capacity to respond to new situations. If the family is also involved in a family business, the impact of these myths can become considerable, hampering the company's ability to deal with changes in the environment. Family myths orchestrate the unspoken dos and don'ts within a company and structure company behavior. They have an influence on the kind of people who are brought into the company, the kind of people who are identified as having high potential, and the kind of socialization methods used in developing these individuals.

Family myths also determine taboo issues within the organization, and because they are such good social defense mechanisms (with their unspoken objective of keeping the family together), they are not easily challenged. In corporate culture, employees question the myths at their peril. Certain common myths develop across the spectrum of family firms and we will now consider some of these in detail [21].

The Myth of Harmony

In spite of evidence to the contrary, and notwithstanding an enormous amount of evident conflict and tension within the family, the principal members of some family businesses often buy into the myth that harmony reigns in their business, ignoring the reality of the situation through denial and idealization. For example, Peter, the patriarch of one family enterprise, tells one of the partners of a consulting firm how well all the members of the family are working together—a statement that the consultant is trying to reconcile with his perception of the disastrous interface between the sales and manufacturing departments run by two of Peter's sons.

This family firm functions in a state of pseudo-mutuality; they all pretend that all interactions within the family are harmonious, whereas in fact, they are not. They try to exclude any open recognition that there is in fact no mutuality in the firm. Obviously, Peter intensely wants mutuality, but taking this position also implies an actual intolerance of differences. For the sake of his peace of mind, he needs to hang on to the fantasy of family togetherness. When the myth of harmony reigns, children are caught in a dilemma: every attempt to differentiate, to find their own way, disturbs this carefully established equilibrium and can lead to disaster [22]. Reality is ignored as they are asked to live a lie. This method of dealing—or rather, not dealing—with reality originates in the belief that the world is basically a dangerous place. Families seek to believe that they are in harmony in order to secure a sense of control in a dangerous world. Only through togetherness will survival be possible. Naturally, such an unrealistic outlook toward what is happening in the family does not augur well for the future of the family-run enterprise.

The Myth of Stereotyping

Stereotyping, in which everyone in the family has a specific assigned role, is another common myth. Stereotyping is based on the expectation that if certain behavioral boundaries are crossed, catastrophe will follow. This expectation means that there will be no flexibility, no possibility of trying something new. Preconceptions dating from childhood may predetermine adult opportunities. For example, Jan, who was a sickly child, is not put in charge of sales, even though (given the demonstration of his talents in another company) he might be rather good at it. According to the myth, Jan is not strong and should not travel. Another example would be the myth that certain information must be kept from father 'because he has a weak heart.' Family members live under the assumption that catastrophe will follow if father becomes upset. And so on. These inaccurate role definitions hamper organizational creativity and adaptability.

The Myth of Martyrdom

Martyrs create their identity around the idea that they are constantly obliged to do things against their will. Despite the power they hold, they maintain that they have no choice or control. A good example of this is the owner of a company who protests that he does not really like working long hours but is obliged to do so in order to provide for his family. He will not admit that there are other ways to do his job; that he does not have to put in such long hours; that he could delegate more. People who subscribe to this myth are unable to acknowledge the fact that they act the way they do simply because they enjoy it. They like being at the office; they like to exert control. As Sam Steinberg (mentioned in the Introduction) used to say, 'I don't have ulcers; I give ulcers.' He liked what he was doing. The martyrdom myth, like the others, leads other people in the company, consciously or unconsciously, to buy into it, and perpetuate dysfunctional behavior.

The Myth of the Scapegoat

In the myth of the scapegoat, the blame for all the company's problems is put on a single family member: 'If only Salima knew how to behave, how to pull her own weight, everything would be all right.' However, the real source of the problem, and others' shared responsibility for it, are not recognized.

In this example, we can see triangulation in action, implying situations whereby two people in conflict, rather than resolving their disagreement, involve or entangle a third person in an attempt to avoid or diffuse their own problems. Through scapegoating, where one family member plays the role of the 'bad' or 'deviant' one, the rest of the family will be held tightly together. The scapegoat will deal with the prevailing conflict by expressing emotional or behavior problems. At the same time, unfortunately, the real issues are not dealt with.

As with other common family myths, scapegoating originates with tensions within the family that need an outlet. Rather than addressing those tensions appropriately, the myth-driven family finds an appropriate family member—a vulnerable victim—and assigns him or her the scapegoat role. But the choice of a scapegoat is not a random process; specific factors determine why a particular person is chosen. Often the shortcomings of the scapegoat symbolize other family members' weaknesses.

For example, if there is conflict in the family because of the father's lack of success in leading the business, a child who was a poor student at school may become a natural scapegoat, allowing the father's failure to remain unacknowledged. The mother who cannot expose her dissatisfaction with her husband's lack of success can then also blame the child instead. The child then becomes the appointed incompetent, the black sheep, the klutz. And to maintain family harmony, everyone in the family, including the scapegoat, institutionalizes the role.

Unfortunately, a scapegoated child finds it hard to change roles later in life. Often designated the problem child, he or she remains the bearer of all the family's ills. Eventually, problem children no longer merely tolerate the role they are handed but begin to actively play the part, as long as it serves the purpose of reducing tension in the family. These children may even know, at some unconscious level, the critical importance of their role in keeping the family together. And these attributions flow over to the family business. The same black sheep is blamed over and over again for all that is going wrong in the family business, while the blunders of others are repeatedly overlooked.

The Myth of the Messiah

The myth of the messiah is fed by the fantasy that redemption and salvation for a business's problems will come from some omnipotent source. The unfortunate person anointed as the messiah walks into an environment overburdened with expectations. He or she is supposed to put right everything that is wrong in the organization. Usually, messiahs are outsiders—for example, a consultant, an executive coach, a newly hired senior executive, or a highly praised, recently hired (non-family) president.

The messiah myth is grounded in the expectation that here, finally, is someone who can change things, someone who will transform the situation the company finds itself in. Of course, no one can live up to such grandiose expectations, and the messiah figure is bound to fail. Indeed, failure is covertly expected: tripping up the messiah strengthens the family's belief that they were right after all, that they do not really have to change. Furthermore, aligning against the messiah does good things for family cohesion, creating a sense of belonging and a feeling of righteousness

The messiah may have different feelings, however, as he or she recognizes the trap. The high turnover in family firms among both consultants and much-praised, newly hired senior executives is symptomatic of this process in action.

SUMMARY

In this chapter, we have seen that the driving forces of narcissism, sibling rivalry, envy, and family myths can be very powerful indeed. If these are not properly harnessed early in life and given constructive outlets, dysfunctional entanglements may occur, with devastating results—particularly if the people in question are running a business together.

Having considered how narcissism in family business leaders can powerfully affect that business, in the next chapter we go on to look at some other common personality characteristics in founder–entrepreneurs that make them particularly brilliant at founding companies and, on occasion, particularly difficult to work with.

ENDNOTES

1. Bowlby, J. (1969). *Attachment and Loss*. New York, Basic Books; Lichtenberg, J.D. (1991). *Psychoanalysis and Infant Research*. New York: Lawrence Erlbaum; Heatherton, T. and Weinberger, J.L. (eds) (1994). *Can Personality Change?* Washington, DC: American Psychological Association; Kagan, J. and Moss, H.A. (1983). *Birth to Maturity: A Study in Psychological Development*. New Haven: Yale University Press.
2. Freud, S. (1917). A Childhood Recollection from '*Dichtung und Wahrheit*,' Vol. 17, p. 156.
3. Kohut, H. (1971). *The Analysis of the Self*. New York: International Universities Press; Kohut, H. (1977). *The Restoration of the Self*. New York: International Universities Press; Kohut, H. and Wolf, E.S. (1978). 'The disorders of the self and their treatment: an outline,' *International Journal of Psychoanalysis*, **59**: 413–426; Kernberg, O. (1985). *Internal World and External Reality*. New York: Jason Aronson.
4. Kets de Vries, M.F.R. and Miller, D. (1984). *The Neurotic Organization*. San Francisco: Jossey-Bass; Kets de Vries, M.F.R. (2006). *The Leader on the Couch*. London: John Wiley & Sons Ltd.

5. American Psychiatric Association (2000). *Diagnostic and Statistical Manual of the Mental Disorders, DSM IV* (4th edn). Washington, DC: American Psychiatric Association; Millon, T. (1996). *Disorders of Personality: DSM IV and Beyond.* New York: John Wiley & Sons Ltd.

6. Kets de Vries, M.F.R. (2006). *The Leader on the Couch.* London: John Wiley & Sons Ltd.

7. Name disguised.

8. Kernberg, O. (1975). *Internal World and External Reality.* New York: Jason Aronsen.

9. Kets de Vries, M.F.R. (2006).

10. Kets de Vries, M.F.R. and Miller, D. (1984). *The Neurotic Organization.* San Francisco: Jossey-Bass.

11. Mahler, M., Pine, F. and Bergman, A. (1975). *The Psychological Birth of the Human Infant.* New York: Basic Books.

12. A term from psychoanalysis describing the objective evaluation of the external world performed by the ego, which allows a person to distinguish between fact and fantasy (Sutherland, S. *The Macmillan Dictionary of Psychology* (2nd edn, p. 386). Basingstoke: Macmillan Press.

13. Winnicott, D.W. (1971). *Playing and Reality.* New York: Basic Books; Winnicott, D.W. (1975). *Through Paediatrics to Psychoanalysis.* New York: Basic Books.

14. Details of the Samuel Johnson story are taken from the case study 'Succession and Continuity for Johnson Family Enterprises,' by Carol Adler Zsolnay and John L. Ward, of the Kellogg School of Management, Northwestern University (2004).

15. Samuel Johnson's comments are taken from the film 'Carnauba: A Son's Memoir,' by Alex Albanese and Landon Parvin, Raposa Productions.

16. Klein, M. (1975). *Envy and Gratitude and Other Works, 1946–1963.* New York: Delta.

17. Schoeck, H. (1969). *Envy: A Theory of Social Behavior.* Orlando, Fla: Harcourt Brace Jovanovich; Davies, A.F. (1980). *Skills, Outlooks, and Passions.* Cambridge, UK: Cambridge University Press; Kets de Vries, M.F.R (1992). 'The motivating role of envy: A forgotten factor in management theory,' *Administration & Society,* **24** (1): 41–60.

18. Adapted from an INSEAD case study written by Sally Simmons, of the Cambridge Editorial Partnership, Cambridge, UK, under the supervision of Manfred Kets de Vries.

19. Wynne, L.C., Ryckoff, I.M., Day, J. and Hirsch, S.I. (1958). 'Pseudomutuality in the Family Relations of Schizophrenics.' *Psychiatry,* **21**: 205–220; Ferreira, A.J. (1963). 'Family Myths and Homeostasis.' *Archives of General Psychiatry,* **9**: 55–61; Kepner, E. (1991). 'The Family and the Firm: A Coevolutionary Perspective.' *Family Business Review,* **4** (4): 445–461.

20. Ferreira, A.J. (1963), p. 60.

21. Stierlin, H. (1973). 'Group fantasies and family myths: Some theoretical and practical aspects,' *Family Process,* **12** (2): 111–125; Pillari, V. (1986). *Pathways to Family Myths.* New York: Brunner/Mazel.

22. Wynne, L.C. et al. (1958).

CHAPTER 6

THE ENTREPRENEUR: ALONE AT THE TOP

Most people do not have the high need for achievement or the extreme need for control that are critical functions in creating new businesses. Entrepreneurs are unusual in that they typically demonstrate four specific behaviors: they identify opportunity for innovation; they manage risk; they secure resources; and they create value [1]. A few entrepreneurial start-ups go on to become publicly listed firms, but the majority is transferred to the entrepreneur's family, typically his or her children. In either case the values and motivation of these powerful entrepreneurs are reflected in their families and shape the cultures of the ventures they create. These *residual values* in both the family and business are important to our thinking as we explore the psychology of family businesses. In this chapter, we explore an archetypal entrepreneur to demonstrate the powerful motivations and personalities that create new firms.

COMMON PERSONALITY CHARACTERISTICS OF FOUNDER–ENTREPRENEURS

Character consists of enduring, pervasive behavior patterns that are derived from complex, deeply embedded psychological characteristics [2]. And founder–entrepreneurs have very specific behavior patterns. To understand their behavior, and the effect they can have on those around them, it makes sense to disentangle some of these patterns [3]. Broadly speaking, founder–entrepreneurs tend to be people who are achievement-oriented: they like taking responsibility for decisions, and they dislike repetitive, routine work. They are creative and imaginative, with high levels of energy and great perseverance, and they are willing to take calculated risks. These personal strengths enable them to transform a simple, even ill-defined, idea into something viable and real. Because of their high energy levels, entrepreneurs can instill contagious enthusiasm in others in their organization [4]. By conveying a sense of conviction and purpose, they persuade others to follow them. Whatever it is—seductiveness, gamesmanship, theatre, or charisma—entrepreneurs know how to build an organization and give it momentum.

However, entrepreneurs often have particular personality quirks, deriving from their developmental histories, that make them difficult to work with. Many aspiring entrepreneurs have had to deal with dislocation, poverty, death, illness, and desertion during childhood and, unsurprisingly, these experiences have colored their outlook later in life [5].

A closer look at the inner theater of the entrepreneur often reveals a shaky sense of self-esteem and identity. Although they present themselves as confident and self-assured, appearances can be deceptive: entrepreneurial behavior is often more counter-phobic (reactive) than proactive. Many entrepreneurial individuals counteract feelings of low self-esteem, inferiority, and helplessness through excessive control and activity. Most want to take charge of everything themselves—especially those who found it hard to follow orders as employees—and have great difficulty taking direction from others. They do not like to be subjected to control and they dislike structures. They like to be independent, and be in control.

The bias of these individuals toward action can also create problems. Rapid rather than thoughtful responses can have dire consequences for an organization. These people may have skills that are perfectly suited to the wild ride of the start-up phase, but they may not have the experience to run a large, stable company on a more professional basis. Most importantly, they may have trouble letting go: appointing a competent CEO or

COO, allowing divisions to spin off or be sold, developing potential successors, retiring, and handing over the reins to the next
generation.

Entrepreneur Derek du Toit [6] admits:

> The entrepreneur who starts his own business generally does so
> because he is a difficult employee. He does not take kindly to
> suggestions or orders from other people and aspires most of all to
> run his own shop . . . His idiosyncrasies do not hurt anybody
> so long as the business is small, but once the business gets larger,
> requiring the support and active cooperation of more people, he
> is at risk if he does not change his approach. It has been correctly
> stated that the biggest burden a growing company faces is having
> a full-blooded entrepreneur as its owner!

LARRY ELLISON AND ORACLE

In order to explore more deeply some of the themes commonly
active in the intrapsychic world theater of founder–entrepreneurs,
we have selected for study one extraordinarily accomplished individual, Larry Ellison, the founder of Oracle. Ellison is an archetypal entrepreneur, in that his failures and successes have been
larger than life and well chronicled. He is an interesting example
of a tremendously successful entrepreneur whose personality has
contributed to his well-publicized accomplishments—and out-
sized failures.

Although this chapter is not meant to be an armchair, wild
psychological analysis of Larry Ellison, a discussion of his personal
characteristics (at least, those we have discovered from reading
public sources) will serve to illustrate some, but by no means all,
of the themes we will explore [7]. We are sharing the story of
Larry Ellison because his exceptional business performance is
driven, we believe, by personality traits commonly found in
many founder–entrepreneurs.

Now in its third decade, Oracle is nearly as ubiquitous as
Microsoft in the way it affects the daily lives of ordinary people.
Oracle, for example, provides the software for payrolls, inventory
control, and automatic teller and credit card transactions, among
many other things. And yet the tremendous technological impact

of Oracle has been somewhat obscured by the flamboyant behavior of the man at the top.

Ellison has been accused of exaggerating the performance of Oracle products (although less often now than in the early days). He has apparently created a hard-knocks family background for himself, and at the same time has gilded his adoptive father's curriculum vitae significantly, not to mention his own. He has often been called a liar. And yet such accusations do not seem to bother him.

If there is one thing that both his critics and his friends agree on, it is that Larry is larger than life both as a leader and as a man. As one observer described him, 'He typifies the extremes of the technology industry: its wealth, brilliance and speed as well as its ego, hype and ruthlessness' [8]. Ellison has referred to his media image as 'Larry the Character.' 'It's strange, like I am an actor in a soap opera who plays himself' [9].

Pseudologia Fantastica

If Larry Ellison is a myth of his own making, as he has been widely described, the myth begins with his birth in 1944 to a young unmarried woman. He was adopted as an infant by an aunt and uncle of his birth mother and raised in a south-side Chicago neighborhood that locals would later describe as a cozy, predominantly Jewish, working-class area, and that Ellison has called a 'ghetto' and 'the projects.' Louis and Lillian Ellison (whom Ellison always refers to as his mother and father) lived in a two-bedroom apartment. Louis was an auditor and accountant (Ellison sometimes tells people that his father was in the FBI); Lillian was a bookkeeper. Ellison remembers his mother as loving and committed, but his father was 'the ultimate conformist.' At various times Ellison has also claimed that Louis was a millionaire, championship tennis player, and candidate for Congress, although little evidence exists for any of these claims [10].

Louis frequently told Ellison what he thought of him: that the youngster would never amount to anything. 'That was his form of greeting, as opposed to "Hi" or "Good morning",'

Ellison has said [11]. When Ellison was 12, Louis announced to him, in mid-conversation (or in mid-argument—Ellison does not recall the exact circumstances), that he was adopted.

In 1966, after dropping out of university for a second time, Ellison headed for California in his Thunderbird convertible. Arriving in the San Francisco Bay area he survived for a time on the money he made working odd technical jobs in banks, insurance companies, and small businesses. He also married and divorced during this period.

In 1977, after working for two software development companies, Ellison founded his own company with two former colleagues. Ellison and his team decided to build a commercially viable relational database for businesses, using IBM's academic research, which was in the public domain. They wanted to build it better and to build it first—with the emphasis on first.

The early story of Oracle features a succession of luck, competitors' mistakes, and bold entrepreneurship. The Oracle database first went on the market in 1979, three years ahead of IBM's similar product. Within five years, Oracle Corporation had reached $12.7 million in sales. From the beginning, Oracle was a sales-driven, win-at-all costs 'pirate-ship of a company' [12].

Larry Ellison was on a quest for dominance. This was reflected not only in a push for technical superiority, but also, dramatically, in the way he put together a remarkably aggressive salesforce. 'Growth at any cost' was a favorite company saying at the time.

By 1989, Oracle had become a Silicon Valley icon, with over 4000 employees. Oracle created more millionaires during that time than any other company in the valley, and the parking lots were full of expensive cars (of which Ellison's Ferrari was the flashiest).

Larry Ellison not only dominated the market during this period, he also dominated his employees. 'You would spend a lot of time anticipating what Larry would do next,' according to one long-time executive. A search consultant said, 'He made many millionaires, but most of them ended up hating him' [13].

Ellison also went through two more marriages during this period. His second marriage lasted only 18 months. On the night the divorce became final, Ellison called his first wife and spent hours talking with her about what prevented him from having a successful relationship.

The Oracle culture was Larry Ellison. As one former employee put it, 'Larry is one of the smartest guys in the software industry. He's also one of the most arrogant. He has a mountain-size ego. And that cockiness became the model for the entire Oracle organization' [14]. The sales at any cost culture had reached a frenzy by 1990, fed by a super-incentivized and largely unsupervised salesforce. Some sales commissions were paid out in real gold coins. The corporate culture was described as Darwinian. As one executive said, Ellison established no common direction or guidelines; growth was all that mattered.

In 1985 a memo was issued by Oracle's treasurer expressing his concerns about receivables, special payment deals, and inaccurate billing information to the COO. However, no one took much notice of this memo. Ellison's goal was to double the size of the company every year, and nothing was to get in the way of that.

In addition, the company was getting a reputation for selling 'claimware'—that is, promising features in its software that did not exist. What was more, customers were noticing that Oracle often ignored their complaints. One analyst said, 'Oracle was growing so rapidly during the late 1980s that it was able to scoff at things like customer support and having a product that worked' [15]. Finally, by 1990, some customers had stopped paying their licensing fees.

Oracle was forced to restate revenues in September of 1990. These revelations surprised Wall Street, and within weeks the company's market cap fell from $3.7 billion to $700 million. Accusations were soon flying. Oracle's overheated culture, and Ellison in particular, were blamed. Ellison later repeatedly blamed other Oracle executives.

Several executives and top managers fled; Ellison fired others. The SEC (Securities and Exchange Commission) later fined Oracle, and the board discussed Ellison's removal. The company was near bankruptcy. On October 31, 1990, its shares bottomed out at (split-adjusted) 13 cents.

For the first time, Ellison loosened his grip and brought in two experienced outsiders to run the daily operations and restructure the company. (However, he retained enough stock that his power and authority could never have been seriously challenged.) In 1992, the company earned $61.5 million on sales of $1.2 billion. In 1993, Oracle released the vastly improved Oracle 7. Things were going right for Ellison again—he had a superior product to sell, a good executive team to run the shop, and enough free time to brainstorm.

From 1992 to 1999 Ellison led Oracle with what was described as messianic zeal. He could see that, with the growth of the Internet, there were not only tremendous opportunities for Oracle's software business, but also a pretext (and a huge incentive) to recreate Oracle itself, transforming the organization into the ultimate e-corporation.

Through the 2000s, Ellison has remained as much in the news as ever. He has reached an age when many executives start thinking about retirement. He burned through 10 top executives in 10 years, some of whom are now competitors. He has yet to have a strongly identifiable successor. And people wonder, who else besides Larry could keep Oracle moving?

DECIPHERING THE INNER THEATER OF THE ENTREPRENEUR

This brief review of the facts (and myths) of Larry Ellison's background and leadership style raises some intriguing questions. What should you look out for if you work with, or for, a founder–entrepreneur? What is likely to cause problems? What are the probable pitfalls? What options are there in difficult situations? What provisions can be made to accommodate an entrepreneur? Do founder–entrepreneurs have more personal problems than other people? In short, what are the essential things we need to know about what makes entrepreneurs tick? To make them more understandable, it is helpful to decode some of the themes prevalent in their intrapsychic theater.

Magnificent Obsession and Need for Control

Many founder–entrepreneurs seem to be driven by a magnificent obsession—an idea, concept, or theme that haunts them and eventually determines the kind of business they choose to be in. Larry Ellison had a natural affinity for computer programming, one of the few things he did well as a young man.

Like Ellison, many founder–entrepreneurs seem to some degree to be misfits. They need to create and control their own environment far more than most people do. They often have trouble working in an organization where they have to report to a manager, finding deference insupportable. Many of the entrepreneurs we have studied are preoccupied with the threat of subjection to some external control or infringement of their will. When such people are suddenly placed in a subordinate position, power conflicts are inevitable. They cannot bear feeling at the mercy of others. Even when they move away from old controlling influences, these concerns linger on.

Conversely, because they are driven by their own magnificent obsession, founder–entrepreneurs may have less tolerance for subordinates who think for themselves. In entrepreneurial organizations, this desire for control can lead to extreme behavior: a founder–entrepreneur might ask, for example, to be kept informed about even the most minute operational details. On the other hand, the founder might consciously or unconsciously ignore important advice from subordinates if he fears it might prevent him from achieving his goals.

For many reasons—one of which arose perhaps from a need to differentiate himself from his adoptive father, whom Ellison described as having an automatic and unthinking deference to authority figures and rules—Ellison has always been the 'oracle of Oracle,' the one person with the vision and the hyper-drive for maximum market share. Nevertheless, through inexperience, as he claims, or a disregard for facts, as some former colleagues believe, he cultivated a corporate culture that allowed Oracle to run right into a wall in 1990. But by 1999, Ellison had become a different kind of leader [16]:

Ellison has been getting his biggest kicks from, of all things, running Oracle. The man who used to brag about how much tennis he played on company time has been logging 50-hour-plus workweeks. He is personally supervising, with messianic zeal, everything from a revamping of Oracle's notoriously aggressive sales organization to an overhauling of the company's operations and information systems to a strategic rethinking of what Oracle's business really is. . . . So why is Ellison acting like a real boss? As he would say, 'It's the Internet, stupid.'

What had brought about this change of heart? Ellison himself offered one explanation [17]:

The way businesses worked changed. Suddenly computers are central to the way we do marketing, selling, the way we do support. Hold it, hold it! I'm good at this computer stuff. I can help. I'm suddenly competent. An e-business, oh, I can run one of those. I'm good at that. A conventional business, I'm not very good at that.

Ellison had rediscovered his magnificent obsession. From 1999 on, he has remained firmly in control of Oracle. One consequence of this is that several top executives have left the company, including Ray Lane, once considered Ellison's heir apparent. Lane apparently quit in frustration, saying at the time, 'The relationship with Larry changed. Now, he's running everything' [18].

As Ray Lane's comment illustrates, the need to retain control may affect entrepreneurs' ability to work with others. Some entrepreneurs are strikingly ambivalent when an issue of control surfaces: they are filled with fantasies of grandiosity, influence, power, and authority, yet they also feel helpless. They seem to fear that their grandiose desires will grow out of control and thereby put them at the mercy of others.

Suspicion of Authority

Founder–entrepreneurs often have serious difficulty addressing issues of dominance and submission and are suspicious of authority. This attitude contrasts greatly with that of hired executives. While executives seem able to identify in a positive and constructive way with authority figures (using them as role models), many of the entrepreneurs we have observed lack an executive's fluidity in operating between superiors and subordinates. Instead, they experience structure as stifling. They find it very difficult to work with others in structured situations—unless, of course, they create the structure and the work is done on their terms.

In the mid-1970s, the young Larry Ellison briefly worked at Ampex, an audio and video equipment company in Sunnyvale that did work for the federal government, where his attitude toward management quickly became apparent. He worked for Bob Miner, a boss he chose for himself. 'I thought that my manager, the manager they had assigned me to, was not technically competent. So, I refused to work for him . . . I said, "I'll work for Bob. He's the best guy".'

When Ampex's memory system project failed to meet requirements, Ellison, Bob Miner, and their colleague Ed Oates were quick to criticize management and its ill-advised decisions, taking an 'If we had been in charge . . .' attitude to the failure. Ellison saw a wide-open window of opportunity for software development outside Ampex. He called Bob Miner and Ed Oates; it was time, he said, for them to create their own company. 'I think I was driven to do this because I knew I could never really survive inside a conventional corporation,' Ellison later said. 'If people asked me to do things that didn't make sense, I just couldn't!' [19].

This strong preference for self-direction in entrepreneurs may originate in a family constellation in which a child did not properly identify with parental authority and failed to find dealing with authority figures a positive experience. In these situations, authority figures are perceived as dangerous because they are viewed as being inconsistent, unpredictable, and overcontrolling. Consequently, the child (and later the adult) becomes a rebel. Every authority figure (real or fantasized) triggers misplaced transference reactions, complicating relationships and creating an irresistible urge to fight authority.

Larry Ellison had ambivalent feelings for his adopted father. He does not remember much about how he learned he was adopted, only that Louis announced it out of the blue. Ellison clearly recalls that his father frequently told him that he would never amount to anything. And yet, after fleeing Chicago to make a new life for himself in California, Ellison brought his ailing father out to live with him, and cared for the older man until his death. Their relationship did not improve much; Larry always felt that his father disapproved of him. It would seem that Ellison continued to hear his father's criticism long after the man's death. Perhaps he needed a father figure (or a 'father-in-the-mind') as a motivator. He once said, 'I can't imagine anything worse than failing.' According to a former Oracle executive, 'There's this idea in Silicon Valley that everyone should be playing like it's a friendly chess match. Ellison doesn't think this for a second. He thinks of himself as a samurai warrior' [20].

Distrust and Paranoia

Although among many entrepreneurs, suspicion of others is closely related to the need for control, some stand out as extreme examples in terms of their distrust of the world around them. Because of the perception (real or imagined) of victimization during their early life, they live in fear of being victimized again. Their childhood experience left them with a paranoid streak: they are always on guard against authority figures, and always ready should disaster strike.

Paradoxically, many of these individuals feel at their best when their fortunes are at their lowest. There may be a cyclothymic pattern to their behavior. (Cyclothymia is a term describing a condition with cyclical change between exhilaration to depression.) When they are riding high, they imagine themselves incurring the envy of others, a legacy of dysfunctional parental or sibling relationships. To avoid tempting fate, when people ask them how things are, they respond by saying that business is 'only so-so' or 'not too bad.' But at a low ebb, if their luck changes, they feel as if they have paid the price, or done penance for their success. This produces a sense of relief, so that their predicament can have a positive effect on them. With the alleviation of anxiety, they have the energy to start again—which they do with enthusiasm and a sense of purpose.

Larry Ellison's behavior does not seem particularly cyclical, but it is significant that after the near-loss of his company in 1990, he took time out for reflection and came back stronger and more driven than ever. By the mid-1990s Ellison was ready to launch Oracle on an epic quest. Oracle sales were around $5 billion per year, and its database business was flourishing but showing signs of maturing. Competitors such as Siebel, PeopleSoft, and SAP were creating applications that threatened Oracle's business. Ellison took a hard look at the future. What was the next big thing for Oracle? The answer was not long in coming: Oracle would create Internet-based business application software that would work perfectly with Oracle's databases, an unbeatable combination. Concretely, the quest would require a transformation from a client–server approach to a focus on Internet computing. As Ellison correctly foresaw, it would also eventually lead to a face-off with Microsoft. (This would become a battle that Ellison took very seriously, but also appeared to enjoy tremendously.)

Returning to the distrust and paranoia that surrounds many founder–entrepreneurs, we have seen that they continually scan the environment for something to confirm their vague suspicions. But while this degree of vigilance may protect entrepreneurs from being taken unaware, it can also lead them to lose all sense of proportion. Focusing on certain trouble spots and ignoring others means that they overreact to trivial things and lose sight of reality.

When a strong sense of distrust, assisted by a need for control, takes over, the consequences for the organization can be serious: sycophants may set the tone, people may stop acting independently, and political gamesmanship can become rampant. In these situations, entrepreneurs may interpret harmless acts as threats and counteract destructively.

Some entrepreneurs are hypersensitive to threats from the outside. This can sometimes be constructive, alerting them to competitor, supplier, customer, or government moves that affect the industry. Ellison rightly perceived Microsoft as a threat in the late 1990s. Microsoft had tried to erode Oracle's database business, but by the end of the decade, Microsoft was distracted by the success of Netscape. Oracle was flying under Microsoft's radar—for the moment. 'An opportunity to get Oracle big and strong enough to stand toe-to-toe with Microsoft. . . . Oracle was in a very strong position' [21]. It looked as if Oracle could pass Microsoft as the world's dominant software company, and Larry Ellison could become the richest man in the world.

In 2000 news broke that Oracle had hired investigators to sift through the garbage of lobbyists defending Microsoft during its US antitrust case. Ellison was unrepentant: 'Some of the things our investigator did may have been unsavory. Certainly from a personal hygiene point they were. I mean, garbage, yuck' [22]. Silicon Valley was back to its favorite sport: Larry-and-Bill-watching. 'Gonad vs Brain; Satyr vs Geek!' [23]. Who could resist? According to one report [24],

> This latest escapade incorporated all the traits that make him so watchable: ruthless competitiveness; love of the spotlight; a preternatural obsession with Microsoft and Gates; and a management style that sometimes has an inmates-running-the-asylum feel. This is precisely the kind of goofy thing Larry might dream up. It's rather out of character for the company. Ray Lane must have been on vacation.

Other entrepreneurs are paranoid about threats from within. The turnover in entrepreneurial organizations can be very high, as the founder–entrepreneur may act from instinct rather than reason when judging his people.

Larry Ellison has many admirers, but he also has some very vocal detractors. For many Oracle employees, 'There are only a certain number of years they can take. It's not like Larry's necessarily a bad guy. He's just very, very intense,' noted one former executive [25]. Working for Ellison has been compared to riding a tiger: you have to stay on, or the tiger will eat you. As another executive said, 'There are only two kinds of people in the world to Larry: those who are on his team and those who are his enemies. There isn't any middle ground' [26].

It can be difficult to counter distorted reasoning and action, because if you look hard enough, you can always find something to confirm the founder–entrepreneur's suspicions—someone might steal something, or, more prosaically, there may be employees who are less than enthusiastic about the founder's vision and strategy.

Unfortunately, the entrepreneur who manages in this particular way often loses sight of the price the company pays when employees are exposed to constant distrust: deteriorating morale, low employee satisfaction, and declining productivity.

Fear of Betrayal

A deep-seated sense of distrust leads many founder–entrepreneurs to set up their company with old friends and/or family members. This can work well in the early start-up stages: the small group communicates honestly and openly; there are clear, common goals; and everyone trusts everyone else implicitly. This organizational structure may create problems later, however. The old friends and family members (not to mention the entrepreneur) may not develop the necessary skills to run daily operations in a larger company. There may be a culture of cronyism, with people hired later than others being kept out of the inner circle. On a more personal level, the founder–entrepreneur may feel a sense of betrayal if one of his old friends, or children, decides to leave the organization.

Tom Siebel left Oracle in 1990 to start his own company, producing customer relationship management (CRM) software, an idea that Ellison had initially rejected at Oracle. By 2000, Siebel Systems had 21% of that market, and Oracle, who had entered the market later, had only 6%. Ellison started an aggressive program to beat Tom Siebel at his own game by giving Oracle's CRM product to customers over the Internet, for free. Siebel has said about his former boss, 'Larry doesn't foster a lot of loyalty. People stay at Oracle because they are well paid and fear recrimination. But Larry is a control freak. He has a knack for taking the best and the brightest—and then he tries to destroy them' [27]. On January 31, 2006, Oracle announced that they had acquired Siebel Systems—after a long and bitter battle.

There are other anecdotes that show Ellison reacting strongly to what might be considered betrayal on the part of former employees. In particular, Siebel condemned Ellison's treatment of Gary Kennedy after the 1990 crash. 'Larry engaged in a systematic personality and character assassination process [of Kennedy] that went on for three years. He was just brutal' [28]. Joe Costello, a former board member, also felt that Ellison was unreasonably vindictive. After Costello left the Oracle board (a departure fueled by an explosive argument with Ellison), he said that Ellison had 'said some really nasty things about me, things he was going to do to destroy me and ruin my personal life and destroy my career in the future' [29].

On January 13, 1997, Larry Ellison testified in court for the second time in two years about whether or not he had had sex, on a certain Friday night in 1993, with Adelyne Lee, his former girlfriend and former Oracle employee. Adelyne had sued Oracle and Larry Ellison for 'wrongful termination, failure to prevent discrimination, and mental distress,' arguing that she had been fired for refusing to have sex with Larry. Their lawyers had finally agreed on a settlement of $100 000 out of court. Although the settlement seemed to be a victory for Adelyne, it turned out that she had won only a battle, not the war.

Ellison had been convinced from the start of the suit that Adelyne had forged an e-mail to make it look as if her boss had sent it to Ellison. The damning message read, 'Adelyne Lee has been terminated per your request. . . .' After losing the first case, Ellison would not let the matter drop. Eventually he uncovered phone records showing that Adelyne's boss had been making a phone call from his car at the precise time the e-mail had been sent. With the evidence of her misconduct finally in his hands, Larry sued Adelyne in the criminal court. He demanded only $100 000—pocket change. This time Larry won. Adelyne not only had to pay out, she also went to jail. She was escorted out of the courtroom in handcuffs to begin her one-year sentence—to the great delight of the Oracle staff. 'Don't mess with Larry!' said the thought-bubble over Adelyne's picture on the mugs in the offices at Oracle Parkway, California. Was this really about sex, or was there more to it than that?

There have been defections that Ellison accepted more graciously, although they were particularly hard for him. In 1996, Jenny Overstreet, who had been Ellison's trusted ally and executive assistant since 1983, decided to resign from the company and focus on her personal life, which had been close to non-existent during her years with Oracle. One morning, after going through the daily business with Ellison, she informed him abruptly of her decision. She had no idea how he would react, although she had taken the precaution of asking her team to clear her desk, in case Larry prevented her from returning to her office. Ellison reacted calmly, however, and after trying to talk her into staying, he gave up quietly, saying at the time, 'Well, everything in my life just changed forever.'

However, in an interview two months later, Ellison changed his tack, saying [30]:

> I think she did the right thing. She was so devoted to her profession that it was distracting from other things in her life. . . . I didn't feel betrayed. . . . I thought it was good for her to leave, and I thought it was good for me that she left. The job was overwhelming her, and things were not getting done.

Desire for Attention

The classic heroic myth begins with the story of the hero's humble birth, describes his rapid rise to prominence and power, and then tells how he conquers the forces of evil, becomes vulnerable to the sin of pride, and finally falls from grace through betrayal or heroic sacrifice. The basic themes—birth, conquest, pride, betrayal, and death—are relevant to all of us. However, with the symbolic Greek chorus of the employees (not to mention the consultants and other outsiders in the background) applauding the entrepreneur's achievements but warning him about the pitfalls he has to negotiate, these themes are particularly important to some founder–entrepreneurs. It could be said that such people are attempting to act out a heroic myth in reality, and many of them live with a great deal of resultant tension.

The origin of the need in such people to play a quasi-mythological role may be related to their lack of recognition while they were growing up. Perhaps the entrepreneur's parents were not sufficiently encouraging to the developing child; perhaps something went wrong while the child was developing as a person. As discussed in Chapter 5, this can leave the child with an insecure sense of self-esteem and a strong need to show the world that they cannot be ignored, that they matter. Consequently, besides feeling that they are living on the edge, or that their success will not last, many of these people also have an overriding concern to be recognized, to be seen as heroes.

Ellison and his first girlfriend Karen owned three pairs of matching shirts between them. They were together for five years, until Karen ended the relationship. Ellison later said [31]:

> The fact that I stayed with Karen for five years is one of the worst things anyone can say about me. You know, I was named one of *Playboy*'s top 10 best-dressed people. I think my journey from those stupid matching shirts with Karen to *Playboy*'s best-dressed list is a more heroic journey than going from the south-side of Chicago to running Oracle.

As further evidence of his need for attention, Larry Ellison often indulges in adolescent pranks, and he is certainly not camera-shy. There are many Larry stories that illustrate this. In August 2000, Ellison, then the world's second-richest man, was entertaining on his 243-foot yacht off Capri when a smaller yacht—measuring a mere 200 feet—caught his eye. It belonged to the world's third-richest man, Microsoft co-founder Paul Allen. Paul and his friends were setting out for a twilight cruise on that warm summer evening. Within minutes, Ellison was at the helm of his own yacht, urging his captain into hot pursuit of Allen's unsuspecting crew. Gunned up to 40 mph, the larger yacht overtook Paul's and left a huge and unexpected wake that sent Paul and his guests falling to the decks. Ellison returned to the harbor, greatly amused. 'It was an adolescent prank,' he said. 'I highly recommend it' [32].

Andy Grove, former Intel CEO, once claimed that his friend Larry works very hard at his bad-boy image [33]—chasing women, racing Ferraris and expensive sailboats, engaging in dog-fights over the California desert in his fighter jet (a de-fanged Italian Marchetti that he had to settle for after attempting unsuccessfully to buy a MiG), and spending millions to recreate a Japanese manor at his estate in the Silicon Valley hills. In fact, it is hard to talk about Larry Ellison without ending each sentence with an exclamation point.

Again, one can interpret the founder–entrepreneur's need for attention as a reaction against feelings of insignificance. Some founder–entrepreneurs have a well-internalized inner voice that tells them they will never amount to anything. But, regardless of who put this idea into their minds, these people are not the sort of retiring types who will take this kind of rebuke passively. They will struggle to defy it through their actions. They possess enough inner strength to prove the voice wrong and show the world that they do amount to something. They fight their way to the top in spite of all the dangers; they get the applause; they find a way to master their fears.

A manifestation of this need for attention is seen in entrepreneurs who feel compelled to build monuments as symbols of their achievements. The term 'edifice complex' is sometimes used to describe such people. The monument may be an imposing office building or production facility; sometimes it is a product that takes on symbolic significance. In late 2000, rumors of Ellison's death caused Oracle's share price to drop temporarily. He reportedly commented that he later dreamed that he was flying his jet and crashed in the Oracle parking lot. He said he thought that would be a cool way to go. In this dream, we see an interesting juxtaposition of a very public and dramatic death scene, and, one would imagine, the symbolic destruction of an edifice, both in the literal and figurative sense.

COMMON DEFENSIVE STRUCTURES IN FOUNDER–ENTREPRENEURS

As discussed in Chapter 1, one of the influences on people's character style is the kinds of defenses that they habitually use, and these will color that person's relationships.

Splitting

A defense commonly found in founder–entrepreneurs is that of 'splitting' (see Chapter 1), the tendency to see everything as being either ideal (all good) or persecutory (all bad). This particular defense is associated with the other defense mechanisms of denial and projection, all of which enable people to reject aspects of themselves they find unacceptable. A result of using this defense is that the person using it develops a world view that is dramatically oversimplified and means that they can no longer appreciate the complexity of human beings and the consequent ambiguity inherent in most human relationships. Instead, they tend to see other people and themselves in extremes, idealizing some and vilifying others. Their attitudinal pendulum shifts very easily. Larry Ellison is no stranger to this pattern.

Projection

We all have a tendency to externalize internal problems: we project our discomforts and fears onto others. The reason projection is useful psychically is because we can disown the emotions that we find uncomfortable by identifying these emotions in other people (and thus feel better about ourselves). When we can attribute a threat to another person, or to an event, the threat becomes more manageable; but projection becomes problematic when it is exaggerated and becomes the predominant reaction to stressful circumstances. It is a method that people commonly adopt in an effort to see themselves as blameless: they project on the outside world what they fear in themselves. Larry Ellison did a fair amount of blame-shifting in the wake of the Oracle meltdown in 1990.

People who rely on this defense a lot (albeit unconsciously) can also end up with a limited sense of personal responsibility. They distance themselves from problems and deny or rationalize away whatever responsibility they have. They refuse to see what they do not want to see and blame others. In an organization, this kind of thinking contributes to political infighting, denial of responsibility, insularity, and the creation of warring factions.

Other entrepreneurs deal with the difficulty they experience in managing anxiety and depression by using the defense commonly described as 'a flight into action.' They try to manage anxiety by taking action, often impulsively and thoughtlessly. This has less to do with their impatience at having to wait out events than a fear of passivity, which they associate with loss of control and vulnerability to others. The only option they see is to act pre-emptively.

As suggested before, some founder–entrepreneurs also have a tough time maintaining a stable image of themselves as competent and can be prone to deep mood swings. When things are going well, they are pleased with themselves, but also worried about whether their success will last. But when the bubble bursts and something goes wrong, the pendulum shifts completely in the other direction. Then everything is terrible, the situation is hopeless, and bankruptcy is just around the corner.

MAINTAINING THE BALANCE

The behavioral and personality characteristics commonly found in entrepreneurs make for individuals armed with two-edged swords. Larry Ellison has undeniably made the best of his drive, intelligence, and unique vision of the world to create a superb organization. However, he has also put the existence of the organization at risk more than once. By the mid-2000s, Oracle was facing another potential challenge: who would be Ellison's successor. At the risk of oversimplifying, we could speculate that some of the personality characteristics we have examined here— fear of betrayal, distrust, a desire for constant attention—may have directly influenced Ellison's willingness to prepare a successor.

Entrepreneurs do not necessarily have more personal problems (or personality disorders) than other people, although many of them may be somewhat narcissistic. Not all entrepreneurs self-destruct and neither do very many accomplish as much as Larry Ellison has. Entrepreneurs tend to demonstrate similar behavior patterns when dealing with the stresses and strains of daily life (as do executives in publicly traded companies). In certain instances they will be actually swept away by those stresses, in other situations they manage to maintain their balance.

The influence of certain countervailing forces (such as the government, banks, labor unions, the press, trusted and forthcoming friends and partners, health, and good judgment) can all help in preventing excesses. But all too often, entrepreneurs are alone at the top—either because they have alienated their partners and friends, or because their paranoid outlook prevents them from trusting the people who could help them.

In the next chapter we look at the particular problems faced by the next generation in families where they are expected to step into the shoes of their parents as leaders of the family business—parents who may well display the very characteristics we have just been considering in this chapter. We will look at the effect this can have on the subsequent behavior of the new generation once in power themselves.

ENDNOTES

1. Carlock, R.S. (1994). *The Need for Organization Development in Successful Entrepreneurial Firms*. New York and London: Garland.
2. Kets de Vries, M.F.R. and Perzow, S. (1991). *Handbook of Character Studies*. Madison, Conn.: International Universities Press.
3. Kets de Vries, M.F.R. (1996) 'The anatomy of the entrepreneur: Clinical observations,' *Human Relations*, **49** (7): 853–883.
4. Kent, C.A., Sexton, L. and Vesper, K.H. (eds) (1982). *Encyclopedia of Entrepreneurship*. Englewood Cliffs, NJ: Prentice-Hall; Sexton, D. and Smilor, R. (eds) (1986). *The Art and Science of Entrepreneurship*. New York: Ballinger; Dyer, W.G. (1992). *The Entrepreneurial Experience: Confronting Career Dilemmas of the Start-Up Executive*. San Francisco: Jossey-Bass.
5. Collins, O.F. and Moore, D.G. (1970). *The Organization Makers: A Study of Independent Entrepreneurs*. New York: Meredith; Kets de Vries, M.F.R. (1977) 'The Entrepreneurial Personality: A Person at the Crossroads,' *Journal of Management Studies*, **14**: 34–58; Kets de Vries, M.F.R. (1996).
6. du Toit, D.F. (1980). 'Confessions of a successful entrepreneur,' *Harvard Business Review*, Nov.–Dec., pp. 44–48.
7. See also, Kets de Vries, M.F.R. and Florent-Treacy, E. (2003). 'Larry Ellison: A samurai warrior in Silicon Valley,' INSEAD Case Study, www.ecch.com.
8. Leibovich, M. (2000). 'The outsider, his business, and his billions,' *The Washington Post*, Washington, DC. A1.

9. Anonymous (2002). '"Win" over SAP makes Oracle happy as Larry,' *The Sunday Times*, London, January 27.
10. Wilson, M. (1997). *The Difference Between God and Larry Ellison* (p. 18). New York: William Morrow.
11. Leibovich, M. (2000).
12. Serwer, A. (2000). 'The next richest man in the world,' *Fortune*, **142** (11; November 13): 98–124.
13. Serwer, A. (2000).
14. Montgomery, L. (1993). 'The comeback kid,' *Financial World*, **162** (7; March 30): 38.
15. Montgomery, L. (1993).
16. Schlender, B. (1999). 'Larry Ellison Oracle at web speed,' *Fortune*, **139** (10; May 24): 128–136.
17. Serwer, A. (2000).
18. Hamm, S. and McNatt, R. (2000). 'There's life after Larry Ellison,' *Business Week*, 3697, (September 4): 10.
19. Hamm, S. and McNatt, R. (2000).
20. Leibovich, M. (2000).
21. Schlender, B. (1999).
22. Cohen, A. (2000). 'Peeping Larry,' *Time*, **156** (2; July 10): 94.
23. Serwer, A. (2000).
24. Cohen, A. (2000).
25. Cohen, A. (2000).
26. Wilson, M. (1997). p. 214.
27. Hawn, C. (2001). 'Oracle on the Edge.' *Forbes*, **168** (4; August 20): 82–88.
28. Wilson, M. (1997). p. 215.
29. Wilson, M. (1997). p. 285.
30. Wilson, M. (1997). p. 326.
31. Wilson, M. (1997).
32. Leibovich, M. (2000).
33. Serwer, A. (2000).

CHAPTER 7

LEADERSHIP TRANSITION: REPLACING A PARENT AS CEO

As we have just seen in the previous chapter, what makes entre-preneurs tick is generally a rich mix of the creative and the ir-rational. Unfortunately, it is precisely this high-octane mix that can make it difficult for next-generation family members to join (or decide not to join) an organization run by a parent or other family member. Conflicts between family and business practices inevitably become greater in times of transition. This is because the family members are facing significant changes in roles and responsibilities requiring them to negotiate new interpersonal relationships. The parent who is passing the company leadership role to their son or daughter often feels a sense of loss in terms of their personal role within the firm. The younger adult also struggles with doubt and uncertainty as he or she attempts to fill the shoes of the all-powerful parent/CEO.

In this chapter we will be looking at the difficulties faced in family businesses at the time of succession, as well as the problems a son or daughter can experience when it falls to them to run the family business while either or both of their parents are still very much involved in it.

OPTIONS FOR TACKLING THE SUCCESSION PROBLEM

When a powerful parent who is also the head of the family company decides to move on to other business challenges, or to retire, he or she has four options:

- Sell the company
- Take it public
- Liquidate assets
- Pass ownership on to other family members.

The first two options are straightforward, but may be limited by economic constraints. If the business is performing badly or is in a mature industry with limited new opportunities it is unlikely that it can go public or be sold to another buyer at a fair price. This leaves liquidation or transfer to the family as possible harvest strategies, with liquidation often seen as the action of last resort.

Other factors may also act to weigh the family CEO's decision in favor of the fourth option; for example, he or she may want to continue the family legacy by bringing in a son or daughter. All too often the fourth option becomes the default action when the founder–entrepreneur or family CEO dies without having clearly expressed, or planned for, succession. An organization that finds itself with a reluctant or unprepared chief executive, who has been pressed into service through the death or coercive tactics of a parent, is an organization that faces specific challenges. Dysfunctional behavior at the senior level can have serious repercussions, impacting on organizational structure and strategy and creating a company culture that mirrors the personality defects of the man or woman at the top [1].

In organizations it is the leader, more than other participants, who has the possibility of making his or her fantasies a reality. It is therefore interesting to examine what happens when there is a transfer of power from an entrepreneur–founder to the next generation. Two important questions that need to be asked are:

- How do the mantel of power, and possibly the stereotype of gender, affect a family member who is thrust to the fore, particularly if that individual is someone already struggling with a low sense of self-esteem (of which he or she may be unaware until pushed into this position of prominence)?
- Why does the behavior of that person, who hitherto has seemed bright, likable and well-adjusted, suddenly change when he or she becomes the person in charge?

In order to address such issues we will explore them in this chapter by using a case study that features a fictional family from a recent film in which art mirrors life in a particularly illuminating way.

THE INHERITANCE

In the opening minutes of the Danish film *Arvet* (*The Inheritance*) [2] we are introduced to the privileged life of Christoffer Borch-Muller. This confident and happy man, somewhere in his late thirties, is the owner of a popular restaurant in Stockholm. He is married to Maria, a lovely and accomplished stage actress. One day, Christoffer's father stops by unexpectedly on his way home from a business trip to Finland; Christoffer and Maria are delighted to see him. Over wine, father and son banter about the past. The father tells Maria, 'Christoffer and I once worked together.' Christoffer adds, 'It was a catastrophe. I was thrown out of the family firm.' Christoffer's father replies, 'Just wait until you have a son of your own.'

This is to be the last conversation Christoffer would have with his father. The older man returned to Denmark and hanged himself, leaving no explanation for his actions—although his family would soon discover that the family firm was deeply in debt.

Borch-Muller Stal, a steel manufacturer that has been in Christoffer's family for four generations, now faces bankruptcy. Returning to Denmark for his father's funeral, Christoffer is immediately confronted by his mother's non-negotiable demand that he return to run the company. She informs him that although Christoffer's brother-in-law Ulrik has been seen by everyone as the heir apparent, in reality Christoffer was his father's chosen successor, and Christoffer is the only one who can save the family organization.

Christoffer is clearly in a terrible position. That afternoon, he must announce the news of his father's death to the company's 900 employees. His forceful and convincing mother also wants him to announce that he, not his brother-in-law, will become the new CEO. At the same time, his wife Maria reminds him how desperately unhappy he was when he worked for his father several years before, and he agrees with her that he should not take over. Later, however, standing before the gathered factory workers, Christoffer tells them that he is the new leader of the steelworks. His wife and brother-in-law are silenced in anger and disbelief.

The die is cast. Torn between loyalties, Christoffer eventually becomes his mother's pawn but the company is saved as Christoffer leads it into a brilliant merger, at the cost of his own integrity and happiness.

PSYCHOLOGICAL PRESSURES ON NEW LEADERS

So what pressured Christoffer Borch-Muller into behaving so apparently uncharacteristically and becoming the kind of leader he did? Clearly this change was as much due to internal pressures he experienced as to outside events. We now, therefore, consider what might have been happening in Christoffer's inner theatre.

Unmet Dependency Needs

Employees of a family firm always view the sons and daughters of the owners working in the business as being different. This attitude is accentuated when a son or daughter then becomes the top executive, particularly in a family like Christoffer's in which employees eventually discover that the younger man does not have the same talent as his father had. The network of complex mutual dependencies that the predecessor has built up over the years is now changed completely, and is not available to the new leader, who may therefore experience a sense of isolation. Being the successor of a formidable parent can be a difficult burden to bear.

One of the tasks of organizational leaders is to take care of their company's existing strategic and structural needs. They are also expected to articulate a vision of the future, show others how to achieve it, set performance expectations, and manage the corporate culture. However, there are a number of other, subtler aspects to leadership—one of which is taking care of the dependency needs of the employees: playing the role of a container and providing a holding environment [3] (as discussed in Chapter 1). However, this may be difficult for the leader because, due to the inherent isolation of that person's role, his or her own dependency needs are not being met.

As distance grows between the new leader and those who now directly report to him or her, the person at the top is often left without peers. As a result, the leader's normal human dependency needs for contact, support, and reassurance can increase until they become overwhelming, making the leader especially vulnerable to manipulation. In addition, the new leader of a family firm may feel a certain us–against–them mentality—himself (as a representative of the family) versus the employees. In the film, Christoffer's first mistake is a brutal lay-off of 200 employees in an attempt to appease the bank. He realizes too late that he has fired some of his father's oldest and most trusted workers.

Cut off from the support of employees like these, Christoffer becomes ever more susceptible to his mother's well-meaning but ruthless strategies. She coldly pushes Christoffer to renounce his brother-in-law, sister, and wife. Her fantasy—and her own frustrated wish for power—becomes clear when she finally tells Christoffer: 'You've got the talent. You were born to this responsibility. Your sister is weak like your father was, but *you are most like me.*'

Being Out of Touch with Reality

The problem with leaders being isolated is that it can cause them to lose touch with reality. In his first few months on the job, Christoffer loses the trust, and thus the honest advice, of the employees and managers who had served his father well. At the same time, he consciously sets up barriers to prevent his wife from being a part of his business life, telling her, 'I don't want to mix the two things. Work is outside; our life is here.' This leads to a reduction in Christoffer's reality-testing ability.

In order to keep in touch with what is really happening in the world (rather than seeing it in terms of one's own inner world) leaders need to create a corporate culture in which employees have a healthy disrespect for their boss—where the information flow goes both ways. When this is missing, and people become wary and selective about the kind of information sent upward, the decision-making capabilities of the key actors become impaired. Very soon, the organization will turn into a political arena where turf fights become the norm, and the primary task of the organization—to run the business effectively and efficiently—is forgotten. For example, when Christoffer learns that his brother-in-law Ulrik is plotting against him, his mother instigates Ulrik's dismissal. Ulrik's wife, Christoffer's own sister, comes to the family home late that night to confront him about firing Ulrik. She swears never to speak to Christoffer again, telling him that he has ruined the family. Maria only learns about Ulrik's fate as she overhears the argument. Christoffer warns Maria again that his family business 'has nothing to do with us,' but Maria is well aware that this, of course, is not the case. Thus, Christoffer isolates himself from everyone in his family of origin and his marital family and nearly everyone in the company— except his mother, who is the controlling owner of the company and the power behind the throne.

The Burden of Being the Recipient of Projections

Another pressure on new leaders is experiencing the role as bearer of other people's projections about authority. Christoffer's father, judging by his employees' sadness after his sudden death, had been greatly loved and respected. He appears to have been a fair man, with a sense of responsibility toward his employees. Although he obviously had feet of clay, as his hidden debts and suicide revealed, his employees nevertheless expect his son to be the same great man his father was. Added to the idealized memory of his father, Christoffer also suffers the burden of being viewed as a messiah, coming to save the company from disaster. Christoffer's mother also sees him as a replacement for his father and perhaps as a means of controlling a family and business in which we can imagine she had previously held only a supporting role.

In addition to acting as catalysts in the achievement of the organization's objectives, top executives are frequently subject to the projections (or transference) of their employees' ideals, wishes, feelings, and fantasies. When transference kicks in, memories of relationships with significant figures from the past may be triggered. Employees may then endow their leaders with the same omniscience (and faults) that they attributed in childhood to parents or other significant figures. The problem in this is that such a burden can begin to affect the mental health of the leader concerned. This 'transference trap' may be acted out in several ways and can affect both leaders and their employees [4].

Sometimes employees idealize their leaders in an attempt to recreate the sense of security they felt in childhood when they were cared for by apparently omnipotent parents. Because leaders, as authority figures, fit easily into employees' subconscious definition of the parent role, employees often endow their leaders with unrealistic powers and attributes—which, in turn, can inflate the leaders' self-esteem. During periods of organizational upheaval (such as cutbacks or expansions), when employees are particularly anxious to believe in their leadership as a way of maintaining their own sense of security and identity, employees will go a long way to please or charm their leaders—including giving in to extravagant whims.

Thus in times of organizational crisis, leaders can become surrounded by 'yes-men and women.' If leaders receive too much uncritical admiration from their employees—as recipients of their projections—they can begin to believe that they really are as perfect, intelligent, or powerful as others think or want them to be. Losing one's grasp on reality in this way is a common human failing, but it can be particularly dangerous for entrepreneurs and leaders of family firms because they often have the power to act on such delusions of grandeur.

History provides innumerable examples of those whose mental health was affected by being the recipient of their followers' fantasies, ranging from political leaders such as King Saul, Caligula, Nero, Hitler, Colonel Gaddafi, and Saddam Hussein to business leaders such as Howard Hughes, Robert Maxwell, and Bernie Ebbers. This is not to say that every founder–entrepreneur or leader of a family firm will develop pathological behavior upon reaching the top of the organization. What differentiates those who crash from those who do not is the latter's ability to stay in touch with reality and to deal with the psychological pressures that the position of leadership entails. These are the kinds of people that stay sane in insane places. Many leaders are very good at handling the pressures that leadership brings; indeed, some individuals who may previously have been rather colorless turn into great leaders when they attain positions of power and influence. However, some individuals who create or run a family business cannot tolerate the pressures; the regressive pulls simply become too strong. It is these dynamics that we will now consider in detail.

Blame and Paranoia

It is not difficult to imagine the atmosphere in Christoffer's company as family members and employees experience lay-offs and the subsequent merger. Such an atmosphere is common in family firms and the transference trap may contribute to leaders assuming rather grandiose strategies: they may become callous about employees' needs, or exploit employees and then drop them when they no longer serve their purpose. Some employees who were not previously prone to transference reactions react with legitimate anger to this type of behavior in a leader. Others, with a more dependent disposition, subconsciously blame the leader for failing to live up to the exaggerated expectations that they had themselves created. These employees may quickly turn from admiration to hostility and rebellion.

Like children, dependent employees are prone to splitting when perceiving those on whom they depend. The new CEO of a family firm who was initially welcomed as a messiah can be surprised at how suddenly the mood of the owners or the employees can shift. After just one setback, employees may view the leader as responsible for all the company's evils—even problems that developed long before his or her arrival. Faced with this change in employee attitudes from admiration to rebellion and anger, leaders can become irritated and even develop feelings of persecution. They may be tempted to retaliate—possibly by firing their critics—if they do not receive the expected dose of admiration. They may fly into rages, creating a climate of fear.

Leaders also split by mentally dividing their employees into those who are for them and those who are against them—which then breeds an organizational culture of fear and suspicion. Employees who are for their leaders support them even if they engage in unrealistic, grandiose schemes or imagine malicious plots, sabotage, and enemies.

Christoffer, before his father's death, was happy and successful in the life he had made for himself in Stockholm. When he was subjected to the pressures of taking his father's place, however, he began to behave irrationally. The excessively high expectations that the company employees had of him as his father's son contributed to his problems. Unable to withstand the psychological pressures of idealization, he began to assume that some of the qualities ascribed to him were actually true, and behaved accordingly. However, when his grandiose actions were not accepted wholeheartedly by his family, he began to show signs of paranoid behavior and to retaliate by blaming others—a pattern we have already discussed in Chapter 6.

Unresolved Issues with Parental Authority

Some narcissistic parents may be able to convince those of their children working in the firm that their parents' grandiose behavior is for the children's own good. In many instances, these adult children give in, trusting in the supposed wisdom of the parent. When Christoffer tells his mother, 'I am losing Maria,' his mother answers, 'Forget her.' Christoffer immediately changes the subject, as if Maria has already gone from his mind.

Because of the strength of unresolved problems from their childhood, some children never make a break with the fantasized parental figure of the past and so never go on to develop an adult perception of their parent as a human being like themselves, with strengths and weaknesses. The opposite may also be true: sons and daughters in family firms may continue their childhood rebellion against a parent's authority, sometimes in a passive-resistant manner, unconsciously undermining the parent in subtle ways. Other times this rebellion actually breaks out into the open, resulting in symbolic parricide.

After a scene in which Christoffer and his father discuss their differing perspectives on the time when Christoffer worked in the family firm, we are left with the impression that the father deeply regrets not having been able to work with his son. Later, Christoffer's mother pushes her son to transform the company completely through a merger in which the company's name and national identity is changed—a strategy with which Christoffer completely agrees—thereby removing all trace of her husband both within the company in the form of its culture, and in the outside world.

The Fear of Success

George Bernard Shaw famously wrote in one of his plays 'There are two tragedies in life. One is not to get your heart's desire. The other is to get it' [5]. In our success-oriented society, failure is looked upon as a catastrophe, something we all fear, and so we can probably easily understand the first part of Shaw's statement. But while fear of failure is understandable, fear of success is more of a puzzle. Sigmund Freud tried to demystify some of the dynamics behind this seemingly unreasonable emotion in an article entitled 'Those Wrecked by Success,' in which he noted that some people become ill when a deeply-rooted and longed-for desire comes to fulfillment [6]. He gave an example of a professor who cherished a wish to succeed his teacher—a wish to over-throw an authority figure that reminded him of unresolved child-hood conflicts with his father. When his wish eventually came true, the professor was plagued by feelings of depression and self-deprecation and found that he was unable to work.

Some entrepreneurs or owners of family firms fall victim to the fear of success. Christoffer initially rejected his mother's plea to take his father's place, but quickly let himself be convinced.

However, Christoffer soon appears to be ill at ease. He torments himself by wondering whether his actions are justified. He acts like an impostor, someone lucky to get the job. To make matters worse, he also develops a fully-fledged drinking problem. After the merger, and after Christoffer breaks his promise to his wife to leave the company within two years, Maria returns to Stockholm, taking their son with her. Christoffer spends the next few days drinking himself into a stupor. Unable to deal with Maria's desire to share his life in another context, he divorces her.

Christoffer's experience exemplifies the belief—sometimes conscious, sometimes not—that success can be attained only by displacing someone else. People who behave this way, especially those with unresolved sibling rivalry, subconsciously view success as a symbolic victory over one of their parents (an Oedipal victory)* or siblings. However, gaining success and tangible accomplishments in adulthood can be a pyrrhic victory for such people. Success in the Oedipal struggle is symbolically equated with betrayal—a provocative, hostile act that not only leads to feelings of guilt but also invites retribution. People in the grip of these beliefs fear their competitors, and their unresolved competitive feelings become confused with present-day reality. Because success is feared as an invitation to negative consequences, these successful individuals downgrade their accomplishments or view themselves as impostors rather than as people who achieved success through their own abilities. They are ashamed of themselves, and therefore they must rupture all contact with the people they love and respect most.

In management situations, these irrational thoughts and behavior patterns may not become evident as long as the execu-

---

* The Oedipus complex refers to a stage of psychosexual development in childhood where a child of either gender regards the parent of the same gender as an adversary and competitor for the exclusive love of the parent of the opposite gender. (The name is derived from a Greek myth of Oedipus, who kills his father and marries his own mother.) Resolution of the Oedipus complex is believed to occur by identification with the parent of the same sex and by the renunciation of sexual interest in the parent of the opposite sex. Most people outgrow the Oedipal phase, but there are individuals who retain a strong Oedipus complex as adults.

tives experiencing them are in a society of equals, where their problems may be subdued. But as soon as these executives reach a leadership position, they are likely to become anxious, deprecate their accomplishments, and even engage in self-defeating behavior.

The last scenes in *The Inheritance* are quite sad, as Christoffer, now remarried to a woman to whom his mother introduced him (and strongly encouraged him to marry), looks up from a park bench and sees Maria at the window of the apartment where they once lived together. She is playing with their young son, and she appears to him more beautiful than ever. Christoffer now realizes that he tried to redress feelings of guilt and loss at the expense of his own happiness with his young son—thereby ironically fulfilling his father's last prediction.

STAYING ON COURSE

The story played out in *The Inheritance* illustrates what can happen when family business leaders are isolated and no real parallel family and business strategic planning is taking place. Both Christoffer and his father fall into the same trap, and one is left hoping that Christoffer will not meet the same fate as his father.

However, to end this chapter on a more positive note, we will now look at the kind of questions family business leaders can ask themselves in order to build safeguards into their organizations—safeguards that will help them to avoid the dysfunctional family and business behavior that *The Inheritance* illustrates so well.

Publicly held companies tend to have a number of safeguards, built into in a system of checks and balances that help to prevent their organizations suffering from a CEO's dysfunctional behavior. For example, key policy decisions, made by a number of stakeholders such as the government, unions, banks, and customers, often act as a countervailing power, helping to keep leaders in touch with reality. Moreover, organizational processes in large publicly held companies tend to find their own momentum and are resistant to dramatic change. Unfortunately, because of their concentration of ownership, entrepreneurial and family firms do not always have similar safeguards.

Family business leaders often need the help of advisers to make them aware of the sorts of psychological forces we have been discussing in this chapter, and to learn how to identify potential signs of trouble. They need to be taught to engage in a regular process of self-evaluation, and how to use family and business governance structures to strengthen their own account-ability. A board of directors with independent members, and an empowered family council (which we look at later in Chapter 12) can be powerful tools for helping executives to improve their performance.

An adviser can help by posing the following questions, both to the leaders themselves and to the owners, board members, and family council:

- Does the leader exercise a form of parental authority by hoarding all decision-making power and information?
- Does the leader have a short-term, fire-fighting mentality? In other words, does he or she feel that the company should act according to the leader's whims? Are priorities unclear? Is there a lack of long-term planning?
- Is the leader resistant to change, believing that, as the chosen representative of the family, he or she always know best?
- Is morale deteriorating in the company, as evidenced by politicking and infighting? Is there a lack of trust?
- Is the leader equally accessible to family and non-family members?
- How does the leader react to bad news or criticism?
- Does the leader think of employees in terms of those who are for and those who are against him or her? Do only yes-men and women survive?
- How realistic is the leader's vision of the company's future? Does the company exist primarily to provide employment for family members? Is there a large discrepancy between the leader's own and others' points of view?
- Is the leader willing to accept responsibility if things go wrong, or does he or she blame others?

- Is the leader quick to take offense and prone to feeling unfairly treated?
- Is the leader's relationship with individual family members the overriding factor in the way the business is run?
- Does the leader have a great need to blow his or her own trumpet?
- Does the leader feel anxious and guilty when successful and have difficulty believing that professional success is caused by his or her own accomplishments rather than by sheer luck?
- Is there any planning for succession?

Having now looked at family businesses in terms of various important psychodynamic ideas, in the next chapter we will move on to explore the family systems model in more depth and demonstrate how this also sheds light on processes in family businesses.

ENDNOTES

1. Kets de Vries, M.F.R. and Miller, D. (1984). *The Neurotic Organization*. San Francisco: Jossey-Bass; Kets de Vries, M.F.R. and Miller, D. (1987). *Unstable at the Top*. New York: New American Library.
2. 2002, directed by Per Fly, Zenatropa Entertainment, Denmark.
3. Bion, W.R. (1961). *Experiences in Groups*, London: Tavistock; Bion, W.R. (1962). *Learning from Experience*. London: William Heinemann; Winnicott, D.W. (1958). *Collected Papers. Through Paediatrics to Psycho-Analysis*. London: Tavistock Publications; Winnicott, D.W. (1965). *The Maturational Process and the Facilitating Environment*. New York: International Universities Press.
4. Kohut, H. (1971). *The Analysis of the Self*. New York: International Universities Press; Kohut, H. (1977). *The Restoration of the Self*. New York: International Universities Press; Langs, R. (1976). *Bipersonal Field*. New York; Kets de Vries, M.F.R. (1989). *Prisoners of Leadership*, New York: John Wiley & Sons, Inc.; Kets de Vries, M.F.R. (1993). *Leaders, Fools, and Impostors*, San Francisco: Jossey-Bass.
5. Shaw, G.B. (1903). *Man and Superman*, Act IV. Cambridge, MA: The University Press.
6. Freud, S. (1916). 'Some character-types met within psychoanalytic work,' *The Standard Edition of the Complete Psychological Works of Sigmund Freud*, Vol. 21 (trans. and ed. J. Strachey). London: The Hogarth Press and the Institute of Psychoanalysis.

CHAPTER 8

A SYSTEMIC VIEW OF THE BUSINESS FAMILY

Our families of origin (our own parents and siblings) are our first experience of what organizational life is all about. What we learn there about important lessons and skills—including communication, persuasion, planning, decision-making, and conflict management—remains indelible. This early exposure to interpersonal and group relationships influences how we react later in organizational settings.

In this chapter, we first explore the origins of systems theory in general and then see how this is applied in the field of family therapy. We then consider how these ideas can be used to help to explain the events in family businesses.

A TWO-WAY RELATIONSHIP

By now it should be clear that when a family leads or controls a firm, it is their shared values and experiences that shape the firm's goals and social interactions, including, for example, attitudes toward succession, leadership, and governance. Furthermore, the family's influence is often a critical factor in decisions about concrete business issues, such as finance and strategy.

However, this interchange is a two-way street. Business relationships, particularly between parents and their children, also lead to intense and often emotionally charged family interactions. Parents want their business to succeed, but they also see as their ultimate responsibility the raising of children who feel good about themselves. Moreover, the parents' own sense of self is also at risk when their children work in the family business, because they often feel their children's performance reflects on them and their own accomplishments. In addition, it is not very gratifying if the business they have created, and which they have planned to pass to their offspring, turns out to be a burden or a threat to the children's personal and professional success in life.

As growing children gradually begin to realize the importance of the family business to their parents, it can become an ideal arena in which to compete for their parents' recognition and affection and to seek redress for hurts or slights from family members. It can be easier to compete against more powerful family members in the business sphere, where business performance becomes the measures of achievement, rather than the activities in the home [1]. The family systems approach has much to offer in examining these kinds of problems. However, before we consider this in particular we will briefly consider the origins of the systems approach as it developed in other contexts.

THE EVOLUTION OF SYSTEMS THEORY

Systems theory came to the fore as a specific discipline in the 1950s introduced by researchers like Ludwig von Bertalanffy, Anatol Rapoport, Kenneth Boulding, Margaret Mead, Gregory Bateson, and others [2]. The systems perspective brings together theoretical principles and concepts from a number of disciplines—the philosophy of science, physics, biology, and engineering. Applications of the systems approach can now be found in numerous domains such as sociology, political science, organizational theory, health administration, management, economics, and psychotherapy—in particular, family systems theory.

The understanding of systems has now evolved to the point where we all incorporate many of these concepts into our everyday language without even being aware of it (as we often do with psychoanalytic concepts). For example, we speak of a health care system, a body system, an information system, a banking system, a political system, and a family system.

Systems theoreticians emphasize the notion of interdependence of relationships. Their focus is to foster a better understanding of how all parts of a system interact with one another, and take on a holistic shape. Students of systems theory point out that when we only look at the component parts of a system, we miss important information that can only be discovered by looking at the overall system. In many instances, the whole has properties that cannot be found in its constituent elements.

Homeostasis, the capacity to self-sustain, is an important concept in systems theory. Over time, despite fluctuations, systems will always seek to return to a stable, constant condition—and due to a system's ability to self-correct and self-regulate, it is able to return to its homeostatic state. To enable that process to take place, however, the various parts and people in an organizational system need to be connected through positive and negative feedback loops. Through these feedback systems, a change in one part of the system will affect the other parts—which, in turn, will affect its original condition.

To illustrate how a feedback loop works, imagine that you are holding your hand too close to a fire. As your skin is burned you experience pain, which acts as a warning signal (feedback). You then react to this information by moving your hand away from the fire. As time goes by, the burned area begins the process of healing itself in order to return to its usual stable state: a well-functioning hand. You are left, however, with a vivid memory associated with fire and pain. Next time you are close to a fire, you will take this information into consideration.

THE DEVELOPMENT OF FAMILY SYSTEMS THEORY

An important name associated with the adoption of general systems theory in psychology was that of Gregory Bateson, an early pioneer in this domain [3]. An anthropologist by training, Bateson emphasized the importance of the relationships between people rather than merely focusing on the individual, and thus emphasized communication patterns above an individual's private wishes and fantasies. To him, communication meant forms and rules of interaction; meaningful words and gestures that concerned both a sender and a receiver. Communication was intelligible not just from the point of view of the individual but specifically in the context of a relationship between people.

Double-Bind Communication

In applying these ideas about communication to mental disorders (for example, schizophrenia), Bateson and other thinkers suggested that the problem of psychological disturbances lay not only with the individual patient but also with the nature of the interaction patterns in the patient's family network. For Bateson and a number of his associates, schizophrenia was the outcome of distorted communication patterns in the family.

Although the ascribing of schizophrenia solely to distorted communication patterns in relationships may be an oversimplification, some forms of communication can indeed have a very disturbing effect on people. Bateson demonstrated how certain communications patterns embody logical errors, thus preventing a message from being received correctly—creating what he described as 'double binds.'

A double bind is a communicative situation where a person receives different or contradictory messages. There will be two conflicting messages: one at a verbal level, one at a more covert level. The overt/covert implication of the message creates a psychological impasse as contradictory demands are made on the individual. No matter what kind of directive is followed, the response will be construed as incorrect as the person must choose between equally unsatisfactory alternatives. Naturally, a relationship where an individual is dependent on another for physical and emotional survival—as is the case in family situations—the effect of double bind, paradoxical communications can be devastating. And unfortunately, as our experience confirms, double-bind communications are all too common in family situations [4].

The definition of the double bind becomes clear in one of Bateson's examples [5]. A schizophrenic patient, well on his way to recovery, was visited in the hospital by his mother. He greeted her with great enthusiasm, putting his arms around her in an embrace. Instead of reacting congruently, she stiffened in response, making him withdraw his arms. Then, as a reaction to this response the mother asked him if he did not love her anymore. The patient blushed, and the mother responded that he should not be so easily embarrassed and afraid of his feelings. Given the nature of these several instances of double-bind communication, the patient then regressed into another schizophrenic episode. We notice in this example that the patient, if he interprets his mother's messages correctly, cannot but conclude that to keep his mother's love he must not show that he loves her (by embracing her) but if he does not show that he loves her (withdrawing his arms and blushing) he will also lose her love. Whatever he does, he ends up as a loser.

As this example dramatically illustrates, individuals with difficulties cannot be understood without examining their relationships with their families, which are more than a composite of discrete individuals, representing a matrix of relationships. The ties between members are powerful and deeply rooted because these recursive relations are composed of patterns of mutual expectation. The double bind illustrates how families create dysfunctional communication feedback loops, whereby members of the family get stuck in vicious circles (as happens with family myths, as discussed in Chapter 5).

To take another example, a CEO/owner of a family business blames his son, VP Sales, for not following up on many of his sales inquiries. The father makes it very clear that this is bad for customer relations. When listening to his tirade, his son becomes withdrawn, demonstrating a passive–aggressive way of dealing with the situation. The consultant working with the family asks who is supposed to do the follow-up to sales inquiries. The father replies that he has no choice but to do it himself. It is clear that he thinks that he is very good at it—after all, it was his sales capability that got the company off the ground. As a matter of fact, he may be so good at it that his son feels it is a waste of energy to get in his father's way. The son's dilemma is having a choice between being nagged for not doing something (i.e.

dealing with clients) or being blamed for not doing it perfectly. Whatever he does, it is going to be a no-win situation. The father feels good, however, because he will be able to save the day. In the meantime, both parties have become embroiled in a mutually reinforcing, dysfunctional communication dance.

In the seminal book *Pragmatics of Human Communication*, Paul Watzlawick and his associates make an attempt to formalize more specifically Bateson's double-bind theory [6]. According to Watzlawick, every communication has content and a relationship aspect: the latter classifies the former and can be considered a meta-communication. Watzlawick implies that all forms of communication include more information than just the plain meaning of the words—i.e. information on how the communicator wants to be understood and perceived.

In emphasizing the role of meta-communication, Watzlawick and his colleagues expanded the double-bind theory into a general theory of pragmatic paradoxes. This approach has been made more operational by strategic family therapy and techniques like paradoxical intervention. Like Bateson, adherents of this point of view look at the pathological situations as a product of distorted communication patterns. To deal with these incidents, they use paradoxical ways to intervene in knotty family situations by attempting to break established and non-productive family patterns.

Paradoxical Interventions

Based on their conviction that family members are caught in paradoxes that they cannot escape, practitioners of strategic psychotherapy suggest that the therapist, executive coach, or consultant should move up one level. For example, the coach can compound the family's paradox by ordering the family not to change at all. They may discuss extreme scenarios, with the family members imagining the worst thing that could happen. They may even go so far as to prescribe the symptom in the hope that the client will defy them [7].

An example of a paradoxical intervention might be as follows. The only son of the owner of a family business complained to his executive coach about his father's tendency to intrude in his private life. This was usually done under the pretext of bringing gifts for his children and wife. His father's extreme helpfulness was also acted out in the office. The son told the coach that his father's interventions were driving him crazy. To get away from it all, and to get more emotional space from his father, he had gone as far as to join one of the regional offices based in another country. But even that move to a distant place was not far enough. His father continued to check up on him by phone and e-mail. And to add insult to injury, his parents made it a habit to stay with them each summer for an extended period of time. Having his parents with them was one thing, but his father taking over the household was another matter all together. According to the son, his father was unstoppable. In spite of all his son's protestations, once he arrived the father would do all the food shopping and give instructions for the management of the household. The son noted that his father's behavior was causing friction in his marriage. After listening to his tale, the coach advised the son not to protest the next time his father tried to take over. On the contrary, he suggested that the son should invite his father to take charge of the household. The son's challenge would be deliberately to behave childishly.

The outcome of this intervention appeared to be successful. Some time later, the son reported to the coach that when his parents arrived that summer he did not discourage them from doing the shopping. He made sure there was very little food in the house and arranged no activities or projects for the family during his parents' stay. When his father insisted on going shopping—unlike previous occasions—he encouraged him to buy more, especially expensive items. But the straw that broke the camel's back was when he asked his father, as they passed a car dealership, whether he could help him finance a Ferrari that was for sale. With glee, the son recounted that his father had become quite irritated and had told him in no uncertain terms that it was time for him to grow up and take responsibility for his life. Ferraris were not a priority. He should be saving money to send the children to college. His father told him in no uncertain words that he was no longer a child; he was an adult. The son also mentioned that his parents had cut short their stay, making an excuse to go home earlier.

By introducing this paradoxical intervention, the coach had broken the usual dance between the father and son, a dance that had the father trying to keep the son in a one-down, childish, immature position. The intervention became the first step in a rearrangement of the existing rituals in the family system.

THE FAMILY SYSTEMS PROPOSITION

Broadly speaking, the family systems perspective argues that the behavior patterns in each family are unique—that each family develops what the family systems approach calls myths, scripts, and rituals—all of which provide a shared view of the outside world and mutual definitions of each other. These elements effectively individualize the family. Through these interaction patterns the family defines itself as a coherent whole with more or less clear boundaries. And since (according to systems theory) change in one part of a system brings about change in the entire system, each individual family member becomes a potential leverage point for positive or negative change. The implication of this is that a person's behavior will both be influenced by and influence an environmental context—which includes, of course, the person's family. The actions of one family member will have an effect on the others, and the functioning of one member cannot be completely understood if taken out of the context of the functioning of the people closely involved with him or her.

Family systems theory refutes any suggestion that the behavior of a given family member is unrelated to the behavior of the others. A family system functions because it is a unit in which every family member plays a critical, unique role in the system. It assumes that the family as a whole is larger than the sum of its parts. Family systems theory attempts to move beyond simple cause-and-effect thinking toward a more comprehensive understanding of the multiple factors that interact across time to produce problems or symptoms. The family systems approach dramatizes that frequently the person exhibiting symptoms of distress is, in fact, reflecting the troubles of the whole system. When using a systems perspective, rather than assuming that one family member—the one with the symptoms—is the problem, it is assumed that the responsibility for both the problem and the solution lies within the whole family system [8].

That brings us to one of the very positive aspects about family systems theory: it shifts the focus from the problematic individual seeking treatment to the family, where clearly interactions are not as effective and as satisfactory as the family members might believe them to be. Family problems are redefined as an emergent property of systemic interactions, rather than an issue to be blamed on individual members.

According to this systemic outlook, one member of the system cannot change without causing a ripple effect throughout the family system. However, in order for a family systems intervention to succeed, the whole family must acknowledge the problem and the whole family must work on the solution. Intervention implies reordering the family system in order to remove the dysfunctional elements that produce or maintain the symptoms.

The Family System as a Client

Another pioneer offering a comprehensive view of how to intervene in family settings by using family systems theory was Murray Bowen [9]. His technique of intervention is a direct outgrowth of psychoanalytic theory. In his work, Bowen goes to great lengths to conceptualize the family and its functioning as an integrated system. Like other students of systems dynamics, he argues that in order to understand the dynamics of a family system one must look at what goes on between individuals, not simply within them. By using a multigenerational approach, with history and insight as engines of change, he views both the individual *and* the family as the client. Bowen's emphasis on theory and insight, as opposed to action and technique, distinguish his work from more behaviorally oriented family therapists, such as Salvador Minuchin and Carl Whitaker and his associates [10].

FAMILY SCRIPTS AND RULES

Much family behavior is aimed at maximizing intimacy, accumulating resources, raising children to independence, and interacting with other human systems. Families develop their own particular scripts—using family systems terminology—about how the family members need to behave and interact in order to achieve these things successfully. (The 'family scripts' are quite similar to the psychodynamic concept of text and myth, discussed in Chapters 1 and 5.) These scripts are guidelines that prescribe what is expected, allowed, and prohibited in a given set of circumstances. They may be based on historic, and possibly outdated, views from earlier generations of that particular family. They include rules of interaction, which may well be unspoken but come to be understood by family members and are very important in maintaining homeostasis within a family system. By supporting effective family functioning, even if flawed, the family's rules or scripts provide a pattern of consistent behavior or expectations that the family will understand.

Family scripts are deeply rooted in a family's culture and social values and are transmitted across generations by the senior generation. In many cases, a family will not consciously recognize the particular script that governs their behavior, and so an important role for an adviser or coach using the family systems (and psychodynamic) approach is to help families to identify the components of this script and understand its implications clearly. For example, when the children were little a family rule may have been that nobody at the dinner table could speak until being spoken to. This might have been an effective rule for managing an unruly group of children during mealtimes, but it is unlikely to foster fruitful discussions when the children grow up and become members of the family business executive team. However, this kind of habit may be so engrained in family members that it needs to be brought to their consciousness before it can be adjusted.

A family's operating rules govern the degree to which family members are emotionally connected. It is this connectedness that makes the functioning of family members interdependent, and the result of it is that family members profoundly affect one another's thoughts, feelings, and actions. They solicit one another's attention, approval, and support, and react to one another's needs, expectations, and distress. A change in one person's functioning is predictably followed by reciprocal changes in the functioning of others.

As a family moves through its life cycle, the relationships of each member with others in the family will inevitably change. A young child who is initially dependent upon her parents for all forms of nourishment and protection may grow up to be increasingly rebellious before leaving home in order to establish independence. Clearly, the script that determines the relationship between this child and the parents will need to be renegotiated in good time if the relationship is to remain helpful and healthy.

At certain moments in the life cycle, the script needs to allow high levels of connectedness and at other times it will have to be adjusted to allow greater separateness. Both separateness and connectedness can be helpful or harmful depending on their context. (The concepts of separateness and connection are discussed further in Chapter 9.) Our previous example of the too-helpful father and his irritated son illustrates the enacting of a script that is no longer appropriate.

FAMILY SCRIPTS IN THE FAMILY BUSINESS

Unfortunately, in many families established scripts continue to be enacted even after they have become ineffective. This is a particular problem when the script also affects the family business. For example, a family with a strong parental hierarchy (the family scripts says that the parents are always in charge) will have a difficult time with a business management structure that is based on competence and job descriptions—as, logically, it should be. No matter how capable a son or daughter may be, it is written into this family's script that the parent will always be the boss. Family scripts like these create particular tensions during periods of life cycle transition or new business circumstances.

Various aspects of the family script will be particularly relevant in the business situation—especially those that assist the family in organizing itself. Most families have rules about:

- roles at different ages and for different genders;
- power and decision making;
- communications and conflict;
- connectedness and autonomy.

These rules are significant in the business environment because they will affect which members of an extended family will enjoy employment, ownership, and governance opportunities in the family business. For example, some families are very open and allow anyone to participate in the business, including in-laws and partners; other families clearly limit family membership to the nuclear family, the marriage family, or the extended family (which may or may not include in-laws or partners). Gender also has significant implications in many families where ownership or career opportunities are limited to male descendants.

The relative amount of power different family members wield is also sometimes influenced as much by cultural norms as by family rules. For example, in Chinese families there are clear rules of hierarchy based on the Confucian culture. These rules would give a grandfather in a family business a very significant role as the head of the family, even when he no longer has any operating or ownership responsibility in the family business.

Rules on Communication

All family members have an intimate knowledge of the ways in which their particular family listens (or fails to), speaks (or remains silent), discloses information, expresses feelings, cooperates, and negotiates among themselves, as well as the level of respect and regard they show toward other family members during this communication.

Communication can be a useful mediating activity to enable families to explore new ideas and options. However, family communication is clearly governed by the family's rules, while that same communication is needed to help a family to develop new agreements about their rules. Rigid families that are unwilling, or unable, to try new behaviors often lack the communications skills required to consider new ways of operating. Therefore, families with rigid rules need some type of intervention to allow a source of new information into the system. Outside board members, or an executive coach who ask questions about how the family operates and what works well can be a simple but significant intervention for an inflexible family, because it opens a door to new topics for a future agenda.

Some families even have rules on how to keep a conflict alive, maintaining the family in a state of equilibrium [11]. Such families are more likely to deny, avoid, blame, or confront each other about a conflict than collaborate on a workable long-term win–win solution. This is because, as mentioned earlier, the automatic tendency of any family system is to maintain equilibrium, or the status quo—even if that status quo creates distress or ongoing conflict. Collaborating on a solution will mean change, and, consequently, loss for individuals or the larger family system. Problems can therefore serve to stabilize the family, and this is often the case in business families. Careful analysis of family business conflicts sometimes reveals that a father's reluctance to discuss his own retirement stems from his unwillingness to address his son or daughter's inadequacies as a successor. It is easier for him to fight against retirement than to tell his child that he or she is not capable of being the next CEO. In conflicted families, as family members side against each other, relationships harden and other people (both insiders and outsiders) are frequently drawn into these conflicts [12]. Family activities turn into plays in which everyone has a well-defined script but the drama never ends [13].

Given the existence of these overt and covert scripts, change is not easy to achieve within a family system. The patterns that a family uses to function satisfactorily are often passed on from generation to generation. Although many of these rules can be very functional in helping to maintain homeostasis, they can also become very problematic. When an ineffective process in the family shapes the lives and future relationships of younger members, it contributes to the creation of cross–generational entanglements. These are often demonstrated in the form of triangulation, which we consider next.

Triangulation

An important part of therapeutic interventions in a family system involves looking at how two-person relationships become unstable under stress, thus increasing the likelihood that a third person will be drawn in to stabilize the system—the process introduced in Chapter 5 as triangulation [14]. Any intentional attempt to effect change within a family system needs to start with the identification of triangles, as this can often clarify exactly how a family system is dysfunctional. Viewing the families of clients as triangulated (as opposed to the vaguer term dysfunctional) assists family advisers not only in understanding the context within which a family's unwanted behavior has developed, but also in deciding on a strategy for intervention.

As mentioned in Chapter 5, in family systems theory, triangulation refers to a situation in which, rather than resolving their disagreement, two people in conflict involve or entangle a third person in an attempt to diffuse or avoid confronting their conflict. The triangle, a three-person emotional configuration, is the basic building block of many emotional situations, in a family or any other group—a situation of jealousy being the prime example.

A good illustration of three-party relationships in families is what happens when parents experience crises in their relationship for which they have no adequate coping mechanisms. They will tend to look for ways to discharge some of the tension between them. The more uncomfortable person will attempt to reduce anxiety by bringing a third person into the equation. When the third person is their child, parents often jointly project their problems onto the child [15]. They triangulate, because triangles are more flexible and stable than two-person relationship systems. Triangulation enables the parents to avoid looking for solutions to their own problems by bonding together to control their child [16]. By adopting this tactic, they often succeed in shifting 'badness' from themselves onto their children.

We can distinguish various forms of family triangles [17]. A very typical one is the detouring or scapegoating triangle that we have just described. Another cross-generational form of triangulation occurs when one of the parents demands that a child side with her or him against the other parent. For example, a husband and wife are estranged. The husband is disengaged and hurtful. The wife is enmeshed and vengeful. The mother builds an alliance with the son, pitting mother and son against father, transgressing and blurring generational boundaries.

Then there is a form of triangulation in which the child initiates an alliance with one parent against the other parent. This differs from the previous example because here it is the child who initiates the coalition, and the attachment between parent and child exceeds that between the two parents.

As suggested, triangles have both a functional and a dysfunctional element. The positive element of triangles is that they can provide stability by maintaining a family's homeostasis. The negative aspects of triangles, however, are that they do not allow the family to address the real problems at hand. They try to circumvent the problem by focusing on someone or something else.

All these family triangles are likely to have negative developmental consequences for any child involved in them. They all create a false sense of attachment and security and do not give the child the opportunity to develop a healthy separate identity.

The behavior of rigidly triangulated families can often become deeply pathological. In these families, the rules dictating the apparently irrational behavior of the third person in a triangle are often hidden. Therapeutic attempts to deal with the third party's apparent problem or symptom in isolation are therefore rarely effective. However, if one person in the triangle finally has enough and refuses to participate any longer, the family will be forced to take some form of action to address the underlying problem. Only then, by making the unconscious conscious, will the adviser be able to help not only the individual who is being victimized but also the other two family members who are using the third as a subconscious means of maintaining closeness or distance. When family members in a family business view one family member as the problem, and devote their attention to fixing that problem, the triad has a tendency to shift from the family system to the business environment, where dysfunctional relationships are re-enacted in the business setting.

For example, where triangulation is a pattern in the family, normal cross-generational boundaries can often become blurred when the issue of succession in the family business arises. Sons line up with mothers against fathers; fathers line up with sons against daughters; parents line up against their children in sibling disputes—there are many such unhappy combinations and all of these come at a high emotional price in terms of anger, resentment, guilt, and depression (and a high cost to the functioning of the family business). Furthermore, advisers to family firms need to be on the lookout for triangulation patterns because it is all too easy to be drawn into such alliances. It is essential for the adviser to be able to decipher triangulation patterns in order to avoid this from happening. Individuals in triangulation mode have a knack for drawing a third party into the dispute for social support rather than allowing him or her to attempt to solve the core problem.

A PRACTICAL EXAMPLE OF FAMILY SYSTEMS THINKING

To illustrate the application of systems thinking in a family business setting, let's briefly consider a typical situation: a rigid and controlling entrepreneurial father is constantly at odds with his highly motivated son. Although the son loves his father, he resents the older man's inflexible leadership style. The son continually tells his father that the company requires a new style of leadership. The father appears to listen, but in the end, nothing changes. Even worse, each direct challenge to the father's authority stimulates the father to tighten his control.

Taking a family systems approach, instead of pushing his father, the son should apply some systems thinking to the situation. His current behavior seems to be contributing to his father's refusal to budge, so the son needs to change his own behavior because (according to systems theory) if any one element in a system changes, the rest will change. The son should work carefully within the boundaries established by the father—whether or not he agrees with them—and focus his talent and energy on *exceeding* his father's expectations. If the son redirects his energy and efforts from changing his father to changing himself, he will influence the total family system, which in turn may trigger change in his father. A high-performing son is in a very different position with his father, and may ultimately be given more authority and greater responsibilities.

This approach could be criticized on the grounds that, although the son may change, it is unlikely that a father with a strong-willed entrepreneur's leadership style will respond to the change in him. However, if the ultimate goal is to expand the son's influence and responsibilities (trying to change the father's behavior might be an intermediate stage in this process) this will not necessarily matter. The son's enhanced capabilities are likely to influence the father in some way and, more importantly, the son is likely to feel better about himself, and therefore better about his working relationship with his father.

This example demonstrates how systems thinking looks at all the associations between elements in the system, rather than attempting to describe a problem or to establish causality or pathology. It does not matter (for our purposes) if the father is too rigid about sharing authority with his son. What matters is for the son to focus on his own behavior because when he changes this, he will create a difference in his family system that stimulates his father's thinking and create more options for new behavior.

In the next chapter we will be considering two tools from the family systems field that can be extremely useful in understanding systems in business families.

ENDNOTES

1. Kay, K. (1991). 'Penetrating the psychosustained conflict,' *Family Business Review*, **4** (1): 21–44; Kay, K. (1992). 'The kid brother,' *Family Business Review*, **5** (3): 237–256; Kay, K. (1996). 'When a family business is a sickness,' *Family Business Review*, **9** (4): 347–368.
2. Von Bertalanffy, L. (1969). *Perspectives of General Systems Theory*. New York: G. Braziller; Churchman, C.W. (1968) *The Systems Approach*. New York: Laurel.

3. Bateson, G. (1972). *Steps to an Ecology of Mind: Collected Essays in Anthropology, Psychiatry, Evolution, and Epistemology.* University of Chicago Press.

4. Bateson, G., Jackson, D.D., Haley, J. and Weakland, J. (1956). 'Toward a theory of schizophrenia,' *Behavioral Science*, **1**: 251–264.

5. Bateson, G. (1972).—as note (3).

6. Watzlawick, P., Jackson, D.D. and Bavelas, J.B. (1968). *Pragmatics of Human Communication: A Study of Interactional Patterns, Pathologies, and Paradoxes.* London: Faber; Watzlawick, P. (1976). *How Real Is Real?: Confusion, Disinformation, Communication.* New York: Random House.

7. Fisch, R., Weakland, J. and Segal, L. (1982). *The Tactics of Change: Doing Therapy Briefly.* San Francisco: Jossey-Bass.

8. Heilveil, I. (1998). *When Families Feud.* New York: Penguin/Putnam.

9. Bowen, M. (1966). *The Use of Family Theory in Clinical Practice.* New York: Jason Aronson; Bowen, M. (1974). *Toward the Differentiation of Self in One's Family of Origin*, New York: Jason Aronson; Bowen, M. (1978). *Family Therapy in Clinical Practice.* New York: Basic Books; Kerr, M.E. and Bowen, M. (1988). *Family Evaluation.* New York: Norton.

10. Minuchin, S. (1977). *Families and Family Therapy.* Cambridge, MA; Harvard University Press; Minuchin, S. and Fishman, C.H. (1981) *Family Therapy Technique.* Cambridge, MA: Harvard University Press; Minuchin, S., Rosman, B.L. and Baker, L. (1978). *Psychosomatic Families.* Cambridge, MA: Harvard University Press; Napier, A.Y. and Whitaker, C.A. (1988). *The Family Crucible.* New York: HarperCollins.

11. Jackson, D. (1957). 'The Question of Family Homeostasis.' *Psychiatric Quarterly Supplement*, **31**: 79–90, (Part 1); Jackson, D. (1968). *Human Communication, Vol 2, Therapy, Communication and Change.* Palo Alto: Science and behavior.

12. Selvini Palazzoli, M., Boscolo, L., Cecchin, G.F. and Prata, G. (1978). *Paradox and Counterparadox.* New York: Jason Aronson; Bowen, M. (1978). *Family Therapy in Clinical Practice.* New York: Aronson; Hoffman, L. (1981). *Foundations of Family Therapy.* New York: Basic Books; Berg, I. (1994). *Family Based Services: A Solution-Focused Approach.* New York: Norton.

13. Byng-Hall, J. (1995). *Rewriting Family Scripts: Improvisation and Change.* New York: Guilford.

14. Bowen, M. (1976). 'Theory in the practice of psychotherapy,' In Guerin, P.J. Jr (ed.) *Family Therapy: Theory and Practice* (pp. 42–90). New York: Gardner Press.

15. Vogel, E.F. and Bell, N.W. (1968). 'The emotionally disturbed child as the family scapegoat,' in Bell, N.W. and Vogel, E.F. (eds) *A Modern Introduction to The Family* (pp. 412–447). New York: Free Press.

16. Minuchin, S. (1974). *Families and Family Therapy.* Cambridge, MA: Harvard Press.

17. West, J.D., Zarski, J.J. and Harvill, R. (1986). 'The influence of the family triangle on intimacy,' *American Mental Health Counselors Association Journal*, **8**: 166–174.

CHAPTER 9

DIAGNOSING FAMILY ENTANGLEMENTS

The challenge for many family members is how to stay connected to their family while, at the same time, creating sufficient space for themselves as individuals. Understanding this dance of distance and closeness is important in making sense of the nature of the family dynamics. To help to sort out family entanglements in the diagnostic process, we will introduce in this chapter two conceptual instruments that can be used to explore entanglements that often occur within family systems. (It is important to keep in mind that these psychological concepts need to be considered within the family's cultural and social context.)

Central to family systemic thinking is the idea of psychological boundaries in defining relationships. Boundaries define who we are as individuals and who is a part of our family system. Exploring boundaries helps the family systemic therapist to describe who is connected and the nature of their relationship. Examples of typical relationship include the couple and the nuclear family (the parents and children). The boundary between parents and children mean that parents will share a relationship that is different than the one they share with their children. Psychological problems or conflicts are often created when boundaries are not clear or ineffective in defining relationships.

We start by explaining the genogram, a diagrammatic record of a family's history and relationships. We then look at the Circumplex Model, a conceptual framework that provides information about degrees of family entanglement. In addition to the Circumplex Model, we will also make a number of observations about differentiation and dependency patterns to better understand the kinds of problem that may emerge in family businesses. Finally, to illustrate our way of making sense of family businesses, we will consider Circumplex theory in relation to two families in particular. (A more detailed look at the genogram and the Circumplex Model can be found, respectively, in Appendix 1 and Appendix 2.)

THE FAMILY GENOGRAM

The concept of the genogram was developed in the 1970s by Murray Bowen as a tool to help to unravel relationships between family members by showing family affiliations and relational patterns in diagrammatic form [1]. It is a multigenerational, pictorial display of a family's history and relationships and, as such, can be very useful in drawing attention to possibly unexplored patterns of behavior and events within a family. Bowen mainly used the genogram in a clinical setting, but the tool was later popularized by Monica McGoldrick and Randy Gerson, who recognized its potential for wider application [2]. Family advisers and therapists working with families often begin their intervention by creating a genogram during a family meeting where all the members present contribute to the process.

A genogram is organized by generation and families of origin, with simple symbols used to represent gender and different types of lines illustrating family relationships. Often a family will create their genogram with an outside professional. Genograms begin with demographic information about marriages and divorces, number of children of each marriage, birth and birth order, and deaths. Some genograms also include information on disorders running in the family (e.g. alcoholism, depression, and heart problems), alliances (close supportive relationships in the family), and specific living situations (children raised outside the parental home, step-children, blended families). Family business events might also be listed.

Males are identified on a genogram with a square, females with a circle. Deaths are indicated by an X through that individual's marker. Spouses or partners are linked with lines, and separations and divorces are indicated by slash lines running through those lines. Birth, marriage, divorce, and death dates are indicated by initials and date. Circles can be used to include and indicate members outside the nuclear family living together. Cut-offs, alliances, enmeshments, and stressful relationships can all be indicated using different kinds of lines to connect individuals. Figure 9.1 below shows some of the conventional symbols normally used in a genogram.

Genograms are useful for bringing to light interesting information about family history, such as naming patterns, sibling rivalry, or significant events like immigration. The genogram may also signal underlying emotional issues (including conflicts in the family) that need further exploration.

By completing a genogram with their adviser or consultant, family members can arrive at powerful shared insights about their

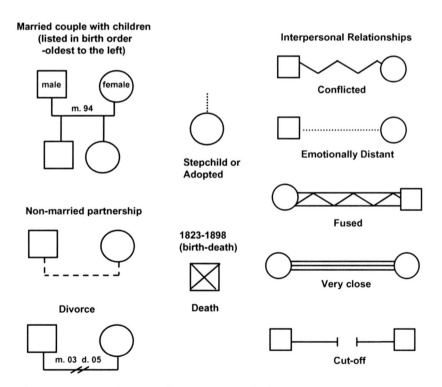

Figure 9.1   A selection of genogram symbols

family experience. The discussions that occur as a result of engaging in this process not only assist the family in filling in the blanks in their history but also make them much more aware of how each one views the family. Identifying intergenerational patterns within their family can also be the beginning of a journey into their own inner world.

In addition, from the consultant or coach's point of view, the genogram can be very helpful in an initial interview. This is because it can act as a record of the facts and characteristics of a family, as well as helping highlight problem areas in the family—thereby enabling the coach to reach early decisions about which treatment strategies to pursue and when. We will now look at a specific family, the Baldinis, and illustrate their shared history with a genogram that we've created. As you read the case vignette, you should ask yourself: What is Julietta's problem in her relationship with her younger sister?

Our analysis of the genogram in Figure 9.2 will follow the case story and help you better understand Julietta's behavior.

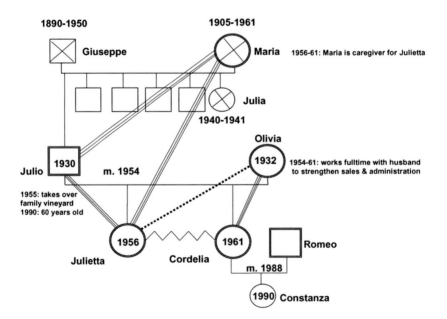

Figure 9.2   The Baldini family genogram

A Family Story: The Baldinis

The Baldini family [3] have nurtured their olive orchards near the Tuscan–Umbrian border in Italy for nearly a century, earning an international reputation for their olive oil. Founder Giuseppe and his fields had survived—and even thrived—despite the rise of the Fascists, the Second World War, and personal tragedy. In 1940, Giuseppe's wife, Maria, gave birth to a little girl after five boys. The family was ecstatic, but their joy was cut short when the child died a year later.

By the time of his death in 1950, Giuseppe's obsessive devotion to quality had paid off nicely—most notably with the Pure Gold olive oil brand. Having confidence in all of his five sons, Giuseppe had encouraged the eldest, Julio, to follow in his footsteps, and the others to pursue careers of their own choosing. Happily, this arrangement suited everyone, with clearly defined delineations between personal and business lives. Serious troubles only surfaced for the family business within the following generation.

Julio married Olivia shortly after his father's death. His father-in-law, a successful winemaker, advised Julio to buy out the rest of his family. The latter were quite willing, retaining only minor stakes for mainly sentimental reasons. This new corporate structure freed Julio and Olivia to enact their own production and marketing policies, which soon proved very fruitful. Olivia's concept of distributing Baldini olive oil as a premium product across the continent became especially profitable.

The seeds of eventual discord were only really sown in the third generation, in the form of Julio and Olivia's daughter Julietta. Joining the operation at her parents' urging, she gradually took on more responsibilities in administration and marketing. Her younger sister, Cordelia, became an accountant for a multinational firm. Cordelia's husband, Romeo, who had managed his family's thriving dairy, soon joined Julio and became the 'son' he never had.

Julio urged Julietta and Romeo to form an executive team to manage Baldini. While Julio's and Olivia's relationship with their son-in-law was quite positive, the same could not be said of their dealings with the increasingly demanding and alienated Julietta.

In 1990, familial tensions came to a head. Julietta stayed away from the christening of Cordelia's and Romeo's daughter. Julio and Olivia, wishing to step aside as Baldini's chief executives in the near future, were soon faced with a dilemma. How could they hope to propose Julietta and Romeo as co-managing directors of a business that, if things went according to plan, would eventually be owned by both their daughters?

Julietta soon grew more openly impatient. She wanted the more senior management duties that her father had long promised would be hers 'at some point.' Her parents were facing a confrontation all too common in family firms where blood ties, emotions and issues of succession combine in a mixture that proves unpalatable for all concerned.

In this family enterprise, we see that ongoing success, subsequent changes in business practices and philosophy, and different (sometimes clashing) priorities among family members/shareholders have apparently generated a gradual, but potent atmosphere of disharmony.

The additional information in the genogram tells us quite a bit about this family. First of all, we see that in 1990, grandfather Julio turned 60—the age at which his own father had died. In an 'anniversary reaction' to his father's death, Julio could be consciously or unconsciously worrying that his own death might be approaching, making him push his children to take over the business. This explains some of the pressure in the system, but to find the roots of the conflict between the sisters, one has to go further back into the history of earlier generations in the family.

When Maria's first grandchild, Julietta, was born, the gap in Maria's life (from the time of her own baby's death) was finally filled. Maria became the primary caretaker for the new baby, while Olivia helped to run the family business. Julietta thrived in her grandmother's care, but in 1961, when Julietta was 5, Maria died suddenly, at a relatively young age. The genogram shows us another significant event that occurred that same year: Cordelia, Julietta's sister, was born. Julietta's world was turned upside down. The only 'mother' she had truly known, Maria, was gone. Olivia now had to care for a baby and a 5-year-old, with the baby receiving most of her attention. The sense of sadness and abandonment Julietta felt after her grandmother's death was directly related to a significant upheaval in her own life—something that she might have unconsciously blamed on her sister.

As Julietta grew older, she became increasingly close to her father; she was his namesake and in many ways he treated her as the son he never had. She did well at university and returned to work in the family business after graduating. Julio asked Romeo, Cordelia's husband, to join the family business, and Romeo proved to be quite good at the job. Romeo's relationship with Julietta, however, steadily worsened, because of his marriage to Julietta's sister, and his role as a rival for her father's attention.

The genogram shows several very close relationships, and two that are distant or conflicted. In addition, we see two triangles. The triple lines indicate the strong attachments between Maria, Julio, and Julietta. The dotted line reflects the distant relationship between Olivia and Julietta, and the jagged line tells us that there is real conflict between Julietta and her sister.

When we studied this family's genogram (a real family situation with all identifying facts disguised) it became apparent that the problems between the sisters, and between Julietta and her mother, were rooted in the period when Julietta's beloved grandmother died. It is natural for a child to make associations between events, and for Julietta, her anger at her mother (for making her grandmother 'disappear' and a new baby 'appear') became displaced onto her sister. After reviewing her family's genogram, Julietta herself recognized many of the patterns discussed above. She remembered the period of her sister's birth as a very unhappy time, and she could see that she was now treating her sister unfairly. She recognized how these early experiences had contributed to the present conflicted situation. She also realized that she was no longer the sad little girl who had lost the major care-taker in her life. Circumstances had changed. She was now an adult. Coming to this realization made Julietta willing to try to work out her relationship with her sister and parents. Doing so, she also recognized that she might need help in working through her feelings with the members of her family. It made her decide to see a therapist. In addition, the Baldini family continued to work with a family adviser to develop a succession plan and a family constitution to support better working relationships and warmer family interactions.

THE CIRCUMPLEX MODEL OF MARRIAGE AND FAMILY SYSTEMS

The Circumplex Model was originally developed as a tool for clinical diagnosis and for specifying treatment goals with couples and families [4]. Part of the model involves the use of two dif-ferent clinical rating scales that measure two significant dimen-sions of family behavior: cohesion and flexibility. (Individuals are asked to fill out a questionnaire that asks about their behavior in the family.) The creators of this model believe that balanced levels of cohesion and flexibility are associated with healthy family functioning; and that extreme levels of either can create problems within the family.

For a family to do well in terms of cohesion or emotional bonding, there needs to be a balance between too much closeness (which leads to enmeshed systems) and too little closeness (which leads to disengaged systems). Families need to balance separate-ness and togetherness. There also needs to be a balance on the flexibility dimension between too much change (which leads to chaotic systems) and too little change (which leads to rigid systems).

Although circumplex research and thinking was originally developed for use with families and couples, it also has direct application to business families, where the ability to address and manage change effectively is fundamental to organizational success. A basic concept of the Circumplex Model is that effective communication skills are the tools by which families can balance their levels of cohesion and flexibility. (There is more information about the clinical rating scales and the Circumplex Model in Appendix 2.)

Family Cohesion

The central measurement of the cohesion scale is the family's emotional connection: how the family system balances togetherness as a family with their separateness as individuals. The cohesion scale can be measured along five positions ranging from *disconnected* (very low level of closeness), *somewhat connected* (low to moderate), *connected* (moderate), *very connected* (moderate to high closeness) to *overly connected* (very high connection). The model suggests that the three more balanced levels of cohesion (somewhat connected, connected, and very connected) make for the most effective family functioning [5].

Either of the two extremes, *disconnected* and *overly connected*, can be problematic for business families because they can create an exaggerated focus on the needs of either the business or the family system. Disengaged families have no emotional reason to be together and cannot count on each other in times of trouble. In disengaged families there is a total focus on the business and its needs, with little concern for the family, and family members are valued primarily for their economic contribution and business performance, creating a strong 'business first' philosophy.

At the other extreme are enmeshed families who are overly connected emotionally. These families place family needs ahead of business concerns, often threatening the viability of the business. These 'family first' businesses often promote a family member to a high-level position based on family membership alone. These families may alienate non-family employees and develop inbred and ineffective leadership [6]. In contrast, other business families negotiate and adopt written family agreements clearly describing the qualifications for employment in advance to prevent family emotions from influencing employment decisions.

Family Flexibility

The second variable in the Circumplex Model is *flexibility*, which considers how well the family system retains stability when facing lifecycle changes and external influences. Some of the concepts measured here include leadership (control), negotiation style, family roles, and family rules.

The flexibility scale follows the same structure as the cohesion scale, with five behaviors ranging from *inflexible* (very low flexibility), *somewhat flexible* (low to moderate flexibility), *flexible* (moderate flexibility), *very flexible* (moderate to high flexibility) and *overly flexible* (very high flexibility). The Circumplex Model argues here, once again, that flexibility in the middle positions is more conducive to family effectiveness than the two extremes [7]. A critical success factor for businesses is the ability to adapt to changing business or market conditions. A flexible family can negotiate transitions and encourage younger family members to take leadership roles in the business.

Decisionmaking in the family business is another area in which the more balanced family has an advantage because their style allows them to recognize and adapt to the environmental force the firm faces—for example, 'We don't have to continue producing buggy whips just because that is what our great-grand-father did 100 years ago.'

At the overly flexible extreme, the family functions in a chaotic state of too much change, with no clear leadership, and erratic discipline. There is no consistency in how the family functions or in what is expected from family members. There are also often ongoing conflicts and struggles because of a lack of an ownership structure that would positively influence the direction or account-ability of the business. The decision-making style of a chaotic family system is a possible threat to the family's business.

At the other extreme, we find families that are overly rigid, with no systems or procedures to allow them to adapt to life cycle transitions. An inflexible family will have difficulty recog-nizing that the family may need to change their business prac-tices, such as including more non-family members who can bring new perspectives to senior leadership roles. Some business families

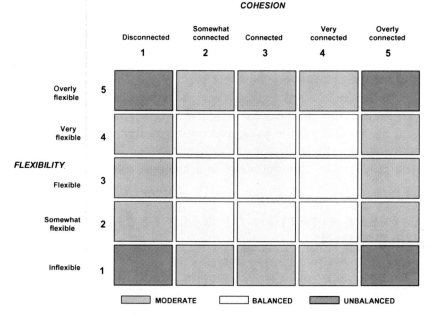

Figure 9.3   The Circumplex Model family map

never learn to change their traditional business or organizational practices and the business suffers—in extreme cases being sold or going out of business altogether.

Figure 9.3 shows a Circumplex family map, which advisers use, based on their observations or the family's questionnaires, to help families to identify their own level of cohesion and flexibility. A well-balanced family will fall somewhere in the center. Of course, it is also possible that different individuals in the family will describe their family in opposing ways; for example, a son might describe the family as rigid, while the mother feels that the family is quite flexible. These differences of perspective are also informative and worth exploring.

The Importance of Communication in the Circumplex Model

Communication is identified as a 'facilitating variable' in the Circumplex Model, meaning that it can assist the family's ability to move to a more balanced position on the cohesion or flexibility scales. Positive communication skills in the Circumplex context include listening, showing empathy for others' points of view, having a capacity to speak out, self-disclosure, sharing feelings, and staying focused on the topic [8].

In family business settings there is frequently a breakdown in communication because the original parent–child roles complicate the boss-employee roles, and cross-communication develops. Inevitably conflicts arise if one family member is communicating in a family role, and the other in a business role.

DIFFERENTIATION OF SELF FROM FAMILY OF ORIGIN

The genogram and the Circumplex Model help us to better understand the degree of differentiation of the individual within the family. As mentioned in earlier chapters, it is useful to understand how family influence can affect a young person's ability to become an autonomous—or differentiated—adult during his or her life cycle. Table 9.1 shows various factors that distinguish the dependent self from the more differentiated self.

In order to live a satisfying life, all young adults need to move from dependence on their parents to a position of autonomy, differentiation, and interdependence [9]. (It's important to be

Table 9.1   Differentiation versus immaturity

Immature self (dependent)	Adult self (differentiated)
Connected to parents	Separate from parents
Wants rewards now	Works towards future goals
Has no patience	Has patience
Has no self-control	Has self-control
Irresponsible	Takes responsibility
No self-awareness	Is self-aware
Does not care what adults think	Concerned about what adults think
Makes demands	Respectfully expresses needs

sensitive to social and cultural differences when applying concepts such as differentiation. For example, differentiation in an Anglo-Saxon culture represents different behaviors and values than differentiation in more traditional Asian societies.) In family businesses, this process is often complicated by the strong connections that the family's legacy creates on both emotional and financial levels. In some business families, members of the older generation structure the business and its assets in such a way that the children never have any real control over their own lives. Constricted by trusts and other inheritance plans, the next generation is forced to stay dependent on their parents (or their parents' bankers or other legal advisers) and thus to live their lives in a continual state of frustration. Such behavior on the part of the older generation is one of the factors that can impede young family members' differentiation from their parents.

Individuals who never learn to differentiate will have trouble separating their thoughts and feelings from those of the family as a whole, with serious consequences in all areas of their lives. An adult who is not differentiated from his or her family of origin is also likely, later, to have confused or conflicted marital or parenting relationships.

Some business families emphasize their strong family values precisely in order to limit differentiation, because they want to keep the family involved in the company. Next-generation members who want to do their own thing or go their own way are pressured by the rest of the family to conform. Faced with constant criticism of any 'deviant' behavior both in the family and at work, the individual often capitulates. Such families are characterized by strict rules, responsibilities and obligations, and often overt or disguised governing behavior. Not surprisingly, business families of this type damage their own business, as such rigid patterns of behavior stifle creativity and original thinking.

Young adults who never work outside their family business are often handicapped in their developmental passage to adulthood. Both generations remain locked in the original, early family dynamics, reinforced by the fact that these young adults are working in a business where their parents write their job descriptions, sign their paychecks, and monitor their career progress. These undifferentiated individuals are often unable to develop their own capabilities or ever view themselves as capable adults. The undifferentiated adult will thus often act like a child, and be unable to function independently in challenging situations. The story of Sam Johnson, described in Chapter 5, is a good illustration of how someone made efforts to complete his developmental process by repeating a defining experience in his own father's life and coming to an understanding of his relationship with his father's legacy.

To illustrate these points further, let's consider two starkly different family stories.

TWO FAMILY STORIES

In both of the following stories, you will see how the family of origin, its structures, and rules about power, conflict, and communications significantly influence both family members and the family business. You will see how two aging fathers face the growing independence of their children, whom they each love in different ways: one father is critical and controlling, the other is caring and supportive. Their children's behavior is also culture-bound. As you read these stories, look for commonalities and contrasts, and reflect on the key roles that gender and culture play in each family, while considering how the issue of succession is treated (or is likely to be treated) in each family.

A Family Story: Zhi's Dilemma

Liu Zhi was 35 and appeared to have the best of several worlds. For the last three years he had been living in London, a city he loved. He had a new job in which his talent and connections in Asia had rapidly made him an important player.

However, Zhi had brought a bit of his past with him to England. His apartment was full of valuable Oriental furniture and rich rugs from his home in Thailand. He served his dinner guests unusual Asian delicacies. He made no secret of his background as a member of an extremely wealthy overseas

Chinese business family. He had obviously enjoyed a privileged upbringing: he was someone for whom doors always opened before he had to knock.

Zhi's past had also left less obvious but painful marks on him. Zhi considered himself to be in voluntary exile in London. Years ago, he had turned his back on tradition, on his family's business empire, and on his family, and fled to the West. His father, Liu Hong, had been his mentor but also, in Zhi's eyes, his tormentor. He had had no option but to free himself from his father's influence and from the family business.

Zhi had earned his MBA in the USA and was now working for Tate & Lyle, a company that competed directly with his father's sugar-trading company in South East Asia. He was beginning to feel safe and successful in his new life in London.

Unfortunately, Zhi's behavior—living an independent life far from home—was unacceptable to his family, who felt that he had disgraced himself and, to a far greater degree, the family by doing so. For an overseas Chinese family, having a son who turned his back to his filial duties was worse than having a child who had died. Zhi had been disinherited, and the family closed ranks around his father, Hong, as they always had. Zhi had not spoken to his father in five years.

And then, out of the blue, Hong telephoned Zhi in London.

He began by reminding his son that after several years of declining profits, Plantation Sugar Trading, the family company founded by Zhi's great grandfather, was struggling. It was in a maturing industry, and the Southeast Asian economic crisis had been a terrible setback. Hong told Zhi that he had no desire to see the family firm swallowed up in an acquisition—but he was old, and no longer wanted to run the company by himself. As Hong had no other sons, responsibility for the family enterprise fell on Zhi. He would have to return to Thailand, or Hong would sell the company as quickly as possible, even if that meant selling at a loss. This, he reminded Zhi, would disgrace not only his father, but the memories of his grandfather and great-grandfather.

Zhi said he needed to think about what he wanted to do before giving Hong an answer. He promised to make his decision within two weeks.

From Zhi's perspective, the decision was extremely complicated. He had worked for his father 10 years earlier, but had felt underpaid, exploited, and subject to his father's irrational and extreme criticism. He left the company, and Thailand, after two years. If he returned, the struggle for power would be dramatic. He felt that unless he could outwit his father, he would be destroyed.

Everyone in the family recognized Hong as an intense individual with a strong personality. Zhi described his father as a critical and unreasonable parent. Zhi's mother, Yi, performed as a dutiful and powerless wife, devoting much of her time to her interest in chamber music.

Zhi's childhood was a tapestry of luxury, privilege, and regular abuse. He and his three sisters were either mistreated or ignored for weeks on end. Family problems were never spoken of openly; there was a sharp divide between the public and private faces of the Liu family. As far as Yi's own family was concerned, the expectation (an expectation she fulfilled) was that she should quietly bear the situation as a proper Chinese wife, never revealing the extent of the problem to outsiders.

Although Hong had often talked about turning the company over to Zhi one day, it was apparent to Zhi that it would not be any time in the near future. Hong's behavior toward Zhi seemed particularly manipulative. When Zhi finally decided he had had enough, it was not only because succession would be a long time coming, but also because he felt that Hong's leadership of the company was endangering the future of the business. Zhi said, 'He was extremely controlling, autocratic and mistrustful. It was hard for him to keep good people in the company.'

Zhi's decision to leave caused a great uproar. When he told his father he was leaving, 'at first he thought it was a joke, and then considered it an act of war when he realized I was serious. He then told me I would never find another job, because all potential employers were either competitors or suppliers of his company.' To add insult to injury, Yi said Zhi's decision was unfair to his father.

After joining Tate & Lyle in London, Zhi felt as if he had finally found a home, even though he had been excommunicated from his family. He moved into his own apartment, with no financial support. Hong had made it clear to Zhi that he would never inherit anything if he did not rejoin the family firm, but Zhi was perfectly satisfied with his new life, and did not really care about his inheritance.

Then came Hong's call. What should Zhi do?

Applying the Circumplex Model

In considering this case study and the one that follows our goal is not to assess whether one family is better—or more effective—than the other. The family members we present here care deeply about one another, but have different ways of interacting. In fact the point of this book is to point out that any family, whatever their cultural background and current situation, can use psychological tools to help them to understand better how to improve their own particular family style, in order to support both family harmony and the next generation's performance.

At the point in time described in the case vignette above, in Circumplex terms the Liu family would be described as emotionally enmeshed, despite the physical distance between them inflexible, and unable to communicate their individual wishes and needs (see Figure 9.4). The family is obviously not functioning well, and the business—which has been in the family for four generations—is now at risk as a result.

It is important, in addition, to make some attempt to appreciate the cultural context because, although extreme in this case, the situation described is typical of Chinese families where two generations have very different values based on differing education and experiences. For an older man raised with traditional Confucian values and with vivid memories of his ancestors' struggle for survival, the family name, legacy, and hard-won wealth, are

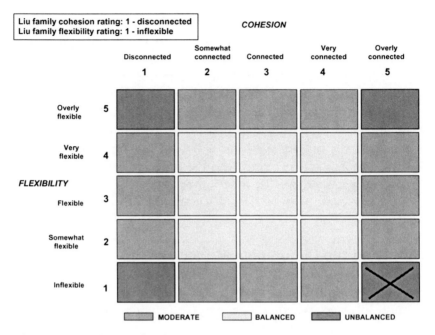

Figure 9.4   The Liu family map

precious family assets to be protected at all costs. Zhi, on the other hand, with his Western MBA, wants to be treated as an experienced international executive, not a misbehaving child.

What can be done? First, we must recognize that although culture plays a strong role here, it does not have to become a wall that separates the two men. Zhi and his father need to renegotiate their relationship, rather than continue in a stubborn battle of wills. There are other options that an adviser could point out to them, including:

- Zhi could return to the company under the protection of a mentor, for example, a trusted senior Chinese executive who could help him to understand better and build upon the importance of both professional management and Asian family traditions.
- A non-family CEO could be hired to run the business during a transition as Hong begins to reduce the time he spends on operations.

- Zhi could be encouraged to recognize that he needs to demonstrate his leadership without asking his father to compromise too much, because his father is not going to change.
- Finally, Zhi's parents could be shown that if they could learn
  to accept Zhi's need for autonomy, he would probably be
  willing to spend more time with them. As a grown man
  living in his own home, Zhi could then participate in family
  traditions, without being at the mercy of his parents'
  whims.

A trusted adviser or executive coach could help Zhi's family by
examining the family dynamics and helping the family to renegotiate their existing structure to develop new and more effective
patterns of interaction. It is clear that the family's rigid patterns
of interaction and strong hierarchy will make this a tough assignment. If the family does not change, however, it is quite likely
that Zhi's parents will be unable to keep the family and business
together. Unless they can reach a new understanding with their
son about his role and their relationships to one another, there
will no longer be a family business, and the family itself my be
under threat. We now go on to look at a second, very different,
family story.

A Family Story: Sophia Coppola

If film-making can be considered a skill to be handed down
through generations, then Sofia Coppola [10] is poised to be
a successor worthy of her father's legacy. Daughter of iconic
film director Francis Ford Coppola (*The Godfather*, *Apocalypse
Now*), Sofia has directed a string of quirky but critically
acclaimed films, including one for which she won an Oscar
for best screenplay (*Lost in Translation*).

Sofia, who turned 35 in 2006, grew up with her two
brothers on a vineyard in Napa Valley, California, as a part of
an extended group of Italian–American families and friends
who gathered regularly around the dinner table to talk about
filmmaking. Francis regularly involved his children in his
work, taking the family with him to his movie sets around

the world, and sometimes using them in his films. He encouraged them to film their required projects for school, rather than writing papers. Sofia later contributed to screenplays and wardrobe design on her father's films.

In her twenties, Sofia dabbled in photography and art school, and designed clothes, but without great conviction. She recalled saying to her father at one point, 'Dad, am I just a dilettante?' Francis replied:

'I thought just the opposite was happening now. I said to her, "No, you don't have to specialize—do everything you love, and then, at some time, the future will come together for you in some form".'

He was right. About his daughter's 2006 film *Marie Antoinette*, Francis commented, 'It has Sofia's personality throughout, which is what I hope as filmmakers my kids would do. In the wine business we call it *terroir*, when you know it comes from the land.'

Although the Coppolas are not really owners of a family business in the purest sense, their family enterprise is filmmaking and their relationships provide a useful example of a successful family in Circumplex terms. The Circumplex Model would see the Coppola family, as described here, as connected, flexible, and able to communicate their individual wishes and needs. The family appears to be functioning well and the father is supporting his daughter's success in a typically male sphere of activity.

Some fathers might see the success of their offspring as a threat to their accomplishments and legacy, and might even work to discourage their daughter's ambitions. However, Sofia's father is demonstrating what Erik Erikson described as 'generativity' (see Chapter 4): he is helping the next generation to explore their talents and interests around the family business of filmmaking. Francis encouraged his daughter to do what she loved in her own way, even when she was still a student. One can imagine Francis Ford Coppola, despite his reputedly larger than life persona, some day being proud to introduce himself as 'Sofia Coppola's father.'

Sofia Coppola clearly grew up in a different cultural and familial context from Zhi. A relaxed, informal Californian lifestyle fostered a greater flexibility for the Coppolas, despite the close-knit Italian–American heritage that was so apparent in their large family gatherings. Francis seems to have been able to pass on his passion for filmmaking to his daughter. Even more importantly, when she was ready to try her hand at it, he stood out of her way and let her work independently.

Although most of us would probably prefer to grow up as Francis Ford Coppola's child, it is important to remember that Liu Hong also loves his son deeply, and only wants the best for him—within the context of Liu family values and legacy. Guided by his family's traditions, Hong is trying to pass on his sense of filial duty and responsibility, and probably feels that he is doing Zhi a great honor by naming the younger man as his successor. If Zhi returns to Thailand and finds a feasible way of working with his father, they might be able to develop an evolved, adult relationship that would be rewarding to both of them.

In the next chapter we move on from considering the ways in which business families and their leaders tend to operate to look at the question of how individuals, families, and organizations deal with change—which is often what brings many family business problems to a head.

ENDNOTES

1. Bowen, M. (1978). *Family Therapy in Clinical Practice*. New York: Basic Books.
2. McGoldrick, M., Gerson, R. and Shellenberger, S. (1999) *Genograms: Assessment and Intervention*, (2nd edn). New York: Norton; McGoldrick, M. and Gerson, R. (1985). *Genograms: Assessment and Intervention*. New York: Norton.
3. This vignette is taken from INSEAD Case Study 04/2005-5279, 'Trouble in Tuscany: exploring business family relationships,' by Prof. Randel S. Carlock and Prof. Ludo van der Heyden.
4. Olson, D.H., Sprengkle, D.H. and Russell, C.S. (1979). 'Circumplex model of marital and family systems: I. Cohesion and adaptability dimensions, family types, and clinical applications,' *Family Process*, **18** (1): 3–28; Olson, D.H., Russell, C.S. and Sprengkle, D.H. (1984). 'Circumplex model of marital and

   family systems: Vl. Theoretical update,' in: Olson, D.H. and Miller, P.M.
   (eds) *Family Studies Review Yearbook*, Vol 2. New Delhi: Sage Publications.
5. Olson, D.H. and Gorall, D.M. (2003). 'Circumplex model of marital and
   family systems,' in Walsh, F. (ed.) *Normal Family Processes* (3rd edn). New
   York: Guilford.
6. Carlock, R.S. and Ward, J.L. (2001). *Strategic Planning for the Family Business:
   Parallel Planning to Unify the Family and Business.* London: Palgrave/
   Macmillan.
7. Olson, D.H. and Gorall, D.M. (2003).
8. Olson, D.H. and Gorall, D.M. (2003).
9. Bowen, M. (1978). *Family Therapy in Clinical Practice*. Northvale, NJ: Jason
   Aronson.
10. Source for this case vignette: Peretz, E. (2006). 'Something about Sofia,'
    Vanity Fair, September: 237.

PART III

INTEGRATION AND ACTION

CHAPTER 10

ADDRESSING TRANSITIONS AND CHANGE

Whether they like it or not, families and businesses are systems that change continuously, so change management is a skill all family businesses will have to learn at some point, regardless of ethnic or cultural background, leadership style, size, or the number of generations involved. However, advisers, family systems therapists, or executive coaches working with entrepreneurs and families have long recognized that transition in these particular organizations requires specialized interventions, techniques, and frameworks—to take account not only of organizational behavior and business issues, but also of the multiple roles and complex interpersonal relationships within the families who own these firms [1]. In this chapter we will consider various models that describe the change process as it typically occurs in individuals, business organizations, and families. We then go on to look further at the role of the family systems therapist in enabling change in family businesses.

LEWIN'S IDEAS ON CHANGE

In 1946, the social scientist Kurt Lewin launched the Research Center for Group Dynamics at the Massachusetts Institute of Technology. His contributions to change theory, action research, and action learning would earn him the title of 'father of organization development' [2]. He became particularly known for his work in the field of organizational behavior and the study of group dynamics, through arguing that people's behavior is related both to their personal characteristics and to the social situations in which they find themselves.

By paying attention to both personal characteristics and the social situation—taking a systems approach—Lewin helped to shape the field of family psychology. Many of the problem-driven models of family therapy use his basic model of identifying ineffective behavior in the system, considering and testing new behaviors, and then accepting new behaviors as a part of daily family routines. In his research Lewin made several important observations on change that help us to think about the challenges that arise during transitions in family firms:

- The success of any organizational change depends on that organization's ability to manage the conflicting forces that both restrain and drive the process.
- Engaging a group in a discussion (rather than providing specific instructions) helps that group to accept the need for change more readily.
- The way in which a group learns and works together (their 'process') is a significant factor in supporting and implementing any changes in behavior.
- An organizational system will resist change when the people in that system are not involved in developing plans and making decisions.
- Change is more likely to occur when management engages the entire organization in the process, because agreement on the need for change is even more important than the change itself.
- For change to occur (that is, for new behaviors to be identified and applied) a group must first 'unfreeze' its current behaviors and then work through a process of communicating and learning, eventually identifying new behaviors before finally 'refreezing' (or making the new behavior a part of the group's norm) (see Figure 10.1).

It was previously thought that if a company's management team decided on a course of action for their company, their employees would simply accept and comply with the management directives. We now know that, to be effective, new organization structures and decentralized decision-making processes require the support, contribution, and energy of people at all levels of the organization.

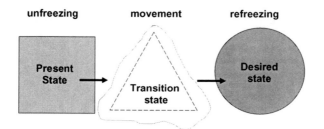

Figure 10.1 Lewin's three-step process of change

For effective change to occur it must take place both within individuals and within the larger group to which they belong.

In order to understand how the change process works, we will look more closely at the way change occurs in individuals, before returning to a discussion of the change process within organizations and families. An important difference when working with family businesses is addressing change that occurs within the family system at both the individual and systemic level. It is equally important when developing plans or strategies for either the family or the business that we consider the parallel needs of both to ensure that the change process is aligned.

A MODEL OF INDIVIDUAL CHANGE

As we all know from our personal experience, change is not an easy process: people resist change [3]. There are forces within every one of us that oppose change, and our social and psychological investment in the status quo makes it very difficult to weaken that internal opposition. Anxiety associated with the uncertainty of engaging in something new, or being exposed to old dangers and risks, often prompts us to allow avoidance behaviors (little tricks for keeping ourselves out of frightening situations) to become deeply ingrained [4]. People also strive to preserve dysfunctional patterns of operating, often willingly accepting situations that do not work, rather than taking steps into the unknown to improve their situation.

Building on the work of Lewin, and through his work with the Challenge of Leadership senior executive program at

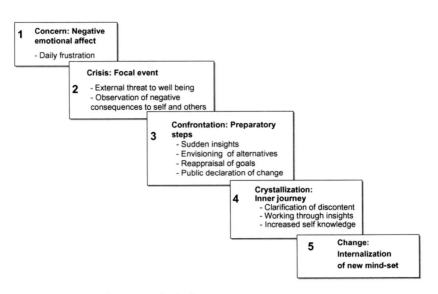

Figure 10.2   The individual change process

INSEAD,★ Manfred Kets de Vries has developed a new model for change.

In Figure 10.2, we see five critical phases in the change process developed by Kets de Vries: *concern, crisis, confrontation, crystallization,* and *change,* which have similarities with Lewin's concept of unfreezing, movement, and refreezing. We will now look at each these five Cs in turn.

Concern

If the human tendency is to resist change, how does the process of making change in our lives ever get underway? Why does a

---

★ The *Challenge of Leadership* program improves senior executives' understanding of how their behavior, and that of others, affects the functioning of their organization by dealing with processes outside the recommended models. The program creates a learning community in which executives feel uninhibited to discuss personal motivations, ambitions, values, and emotions. Participants learn how to make more effective decisions by paying attention to the emotional side of management.

person's resistance start to weaken? Given the relative stability of individual personality, getting the process of change into motion usually requires a strong inducement in the form of pain or distress—discomfort that outweighs the pleasure of secondary gains (psychological benefits such as sympathy and attention) that create in the current situation an immunity to change.

People must experience a sense of concern about their present situation, whether the trigger is family tensions, health problems, negative social sanctions, an accident, feelings of isolation leading to a sense of helplessness and insecurity, problem behavior, distressing incidents happening to someone close, or simply daily hassles and frustrations. Many executives in the Challenge of Leadership program have reported a high level of negative affect (emotions) in the period just prior to change, generally precipitated by triggers like those described above. Experiencing these emotions brings into awareness the serious negative consequences that will occur from continuing current dysfunctional behavior. It sets the stage for a tipping point, a preparedness to finally break the immunity system that is responsible for maintaining the status quo. Individuals who later reported major change said that they had found the status quo increasingly difficult to maintain. Their situation increasingly unsettled their psychological well-being.

Crisis

When people realize that their bad days are turning into a bad year—in other words, that the isolated occurrence of occasional discontent has become a steady pattern of unhappiness—they are no longer able to deny that something has to be done. From this point on, every new disturbance is recognized as part of the general pattern of dissatisfaction. Complaints coalesce into a coherent entity. Many people have what is commonly referred to in therapy circles as an 'Aha! experience' at this stage, a moment when they are finally able to see that neither the passage of time nor minor changes in behavior will improve the situation—indeed, the situation is likely to become even worse if nothing drastic is done about it.

However, even the insight that drastic measures are required does not automatically compel people to take action. Nonetheless, it typically sets into motion a mental process whereby they start to consider alternatives to the adverse situation. Having made the transition from denying to realizing that all is not well, they are then able to move on from a situation in which every alternative appears more frightening than the status quo to a position where they can undertake a reappraisal process. They are starting to play with their ambivalence, having an inner dialogue about the advantages and disadvantages of taking some sort of action.

Confrontation

Beginning to accept the need for change is a necessary first step, but on its own is no guarantee of action. People need to be confronted by some kind of focal event, a trigger for change that is not necessarily obvious and is sometimes so undramatic that it is only retrospectively interpreted as a milestone. In hindsight, this focal event will be seen as the tipping point.

The focal event is often a minor occurrence that is seen as focal simply because it enables a discontented person to take that long-delayed first step toward change. It becomes the catalyst in the change process, whether it is perceived as major or minor to an outside observer.

A focal event often involves someone important to the distressed person. For one particular CEO/owner it was a major event—divorce from a husband of many years—that became her focal event. The divorce made this woman's relatively comfortable life fall apart and served as a wake-up call for her to re-evaluate her lifestyle. She made changes at home, for example, deciding to spend more time with her children, and to becoming involved in leisure activities that she really enjoyed. But the divorce triggered work changes as well. She realized, as various repressed feelings came to the surface, that she was unhappy at work. The company was stagnating. She had been on automatic pilot, suppressing her creativity. The divorce crystallized her discontent and provided the impetus for change, taking her organization in new directions.

Although a focal event may seem trivial at first glance, it can be an indicator of a whole range of incidents that are symbolic of the problem being experienced. Although objectively perceived as minor, subjectively it is significant, because it calls attention to a problem that has existed for a long time. It precipitates a moment of insight and leads to a reinterpretation of a person's life. Of course, some focal events—such as divorce, or illness—are objectively as well as subjectively significant events of a very serious nature.

It is at this point in the process that people start to become prepared to take action. Their resistance to change is breaking down. Their immunity system, which has been resisting change, begins to break down. They acquire new insights about their situation and see new possibilities, whereas before they knew only helplessness and hopelessness. Their emotional energy has been transferred from concerns of the past (such as dysfunctional behaviors) to aspects of the present and the future. They feel as if a heavy burden has been lifted, and they are mentally ready to tackle a more constructive future.

Change is so difficult that, even with the best of intentions, we can rarely manage it on our own. The third step of the individual change process is the public declaration of intent, which research suggests is a sound indicator of someone having a high degree of commitment to change [5]. Telling others, in a more or less public context, what one plans to do, indicates that the person has reached a certain degree of acceptance of their problem. It shows that traditional defense mechanisms (such as denial, projection, and rationalization) have largely run their course. The person is ready to take new initiatives.

Making a public commitment is crucial because it doubles momentum: it influences not only the person making the commitment, but also that person's environment. A dialog has been set in motion that will lead to further insights. If a person states the intent to give up an addiction to alcohol, for example, acquaintances who approve of that decision are less likely to offer him a drink and will probably comment if he takes one. Furthermore, a public declaration of intent to change the present situation means a willingness to assume a more vulnerable position and to move the problem from a private to a public stage.

Someone making a public declaration is expressing a wish to establish a new identity and a different way of behaving, and to establish a distance from their former, less desirable self [6].

Crystallization

By this point, the toughest challenges of the change process have been met. The personal resolutions of the clarification stage have laid the groundwork for a thoughtful, detailed reappraisal of goals and for experimentation with the new alternatives that have been envisioned. Ideas and plans become clear and definite in form. The destination of this sometimes painful inner journey is increased self-knowledge and a new beginning. As people progress through the various phases of successful personal change they demonstrate a growing ability to give up their old identities and roles and to adopt new ones. They begin to reorganize the world in which they live in a significant way. They re-evaluate their life's goals and meanings, letting go of the old and accepting the new.

Change

We all tend to talk big when it comes to change. But how many of the hundreds of new leaves we promise to turn are ever even touched? The only true sign that change has been achieved is a new mindset. Inner transformation takes place only once a new way of looking at things has been internalized. The final part of the individual change process involves a reshaping of the person's internal world and the acceptance of a new identity. A proactive posture is now taken. Past patterns of thinking, feeling, and acting are discarded as the person begins to turn toward the future. A shift in attitude and behavior has culminated in the redefinition, and even reinvention, of the self.

MAJOR THEMES IN THE INDIVIDUAL JOURNEY TOWARD CHANGE

The journey through the individual change process is not an easy one, whether in one's personal life or in one's work role. Looking back at the hundreds of CEOs and other senior executives who have gone through the leadership change programs, Manfred Kets de Vries has identified a number of common themes with which people struggle as they seek to create new behaviors [7]. These themes are significant enough to create the concern that triggers the change process, and include:

- a sense of loss
- feeling like an impostor
- interpersonal conflict
- diminishing job satisfaction/boredom
- symptomatology/health issues
- developmental imbalance
- lack of life balance.

Let's consider each of these in a little more detail.

A sense of loss

Loss is one of the most difficult things human beings have to deal with during their lives [8]. Regardless of the form loss takes, its consequences can linger for months—or even years—as we try to accept the loss, grieve for what might have been, and possibly bemoan our bad luck [9]. Depressive reactions can distort the grief process if loss is denied or not consciously worked through.

In an organizational context, loss is sometimes difficult to define. When someone loses their job (or even when they leave a company voluntarily) they lose a connection with the organizational community. Career setbacks such as a demotion or retirement are also forms of loss, which if unacknowledged can linger on masked by panic or depression.

Feeling Like an Impostor

Many executives experience growing anxiety as they reach the top of their organization. Will they be able to handle the increasing responsibilities? Will they make the right decisions? They may fear the public exposure of, for example, making speeches, talking to the press, or meeting financial analysts. They may have trouble sleeping, fretting about disasters that might befall the company, and whether they will be capable of handling them. They worry that they might be unmasked as an imposter, someone who never should have been given the job in the first place. This type of anxiety can become a self-fulfilling prophecy, as decision paralysis sets in and prevents them from taking appropriate action [10].

Interpersonal Conflict

Another possible catalyst for change is an intensification of an interpersonal conflict, whether an intimate relationship within the family, with friends, or a dispute between work colleagues. One executive recounted the stress he felt due to an ongoing battle with one of the non-executive members of his family board. Another typical example might be a CEO who is caught up in a merger process, and looking for ways to solve organizational incompatibility problems—because, for example, the two companies involved are not only very different but may not even be operating in the same country.

Diminishing Job Satisfaction/Boredom

Another significant theme is a diminishing return in job satisfaction—people become bored with their job. Once you become head of a business, there are no obvious positions to strive for: the only options are success or failure. Several of the family business owners we interviewed have said, in effect, 'I've finally arrived, and now I'm in for the whole game.' The challenge is how to maintain a sense of freshness, interest, and excitement. Boredom can have negative effects on morale, performance, and quality of work. Monotony, coupled with a need to maintain high levels of alertness, is a combination that generates considerable stress. Boredom is one of the most frequent stressors related to drug abuse and other risk-taking behaviors. This can have dire consequences not only for a person's mental health but also—in the case of family business leaders or other executives—the health of the organization.

Bored people tend to be easily distracted, shift from one uncompleted task to another, and misplace or lose things necessary to complete a task. Behavioral procrastination seems to be related to hyperactivity and other dysfunctional, self-handicapping behavior. For example, one person explained that to fight boredom he had engaged in a disastrous acquisition spree—his way of recreating some excitement in his work. His behavior, however, had also endangered the financial health of his family firm.

Symptomatology/Health Issues

Although rarely discussed openly, many executives experience symptoms of sexual dysfunction, promiscuity, insomnia and a range of phobias, including a fear of flying, public speaking, or social situations. In addition, there are many stress symptoms of a psychosomatic nature such as migraine headaches, stomach complaints, back problems, heart palpitations, skin disorders, and others. Quite a few executives also suffer from alcohol or drug problems. Such symptoms can become a significant source of distress and severe enough to interfere with everyday functioning.

Developmental Imbalance

Another issue that regularly emerges concerns developmental imbalance, when expectations about life remain unfulfilled [11]. People are sometimes faced with life changes that necessitate moving from one social role to another, and they may struggle with assuming this new role. People who fail to cope adequately often experience poor role transition—a form of loss that can contribute to depressive reactions. For example, one woman was functioning as a successful CEO but realized there was very little else in her life: the job was taking all her time. Her friends had moved on a stage, and were enjoying family life and their children. She felt increasingly left out.

Lack of Life Balance

Life balance is a subject that often crops up when senior executives talk about their lives [12]. As life passes and their children grow up, many of these people feel that they are leading a mortgaged life. Finding time for the family becomes an increasingly uphill struggle. They feel they are missing out on important moments in their children's lives and are unable to spend quality time with them. At the same time they are prisoners of their own ambitions. They know they should create a better balance, but they cannot seem to manage it.

THE PROCESS OF CHANGE WITHIN ORGANIZATIONS

A maturing industry, increased competitive pressures on growth or profit margins, financial demands that are difficult to resolve, or a misalignment between shareholder and stakeholder expectations should all act as signals to management and boards of directors that their organization needs to revise its strategic plan for the future.

However, even when there are clear signs that change is required within an organization, it is often resisted because people know it will involve moving into the unknown. In the Steinberg story (see Introduction) people in that organization had to exchange what they knew well—Sam Steinberg's leadership—for an unknown future with a new leader. However, it is not change that people resist so much as the loss of control that results from the change process in organizations.

People may resist organizational initiatives that are clearly required for the organization's survival. This resistance can be unconscious, and lead to self-defeating acts of sabotage: it is socially and psychologically safer to continue as they are, and retain a sense of control. This resistance is understandable when you consider that organizational change also forces employees to question their personal competence, renegotiate long-term working relationships, and examine long-held values and beliefs. They may find the change deeply threatening to their professional identity and financial security. Individuals facing significant organizational change often experience:

- disruption of their work patterns—feeling upset when old ways of doing things cannot be maintained;

- fear of the unknown—not understanding what is happening or what will happen next;
- loss of confidence—feeling incapable of performing well under the new ways of doing things;
- loss of control—feeling that things are being done to you rather than by or with you;
- a lack of control over the speed of the change—feeling overwhelmed by how quickly the situation is changing;
- work overload—not having the physical or psychic energy to commit to the change;
- loss of face—feeling inadequate or humiliated because it appears that the old ways of doing things were not good ways;
- lack of purpose—not seeing a reason for the change and/or not understanding its benefits [13].

Leading the Change Process in Organizations

The organizational change model, as shown in Figure 10.3, provides a roadmap that can help management to overcome organizational resistance by using a participative approach to engage the entire organization in change. The role of management in leading

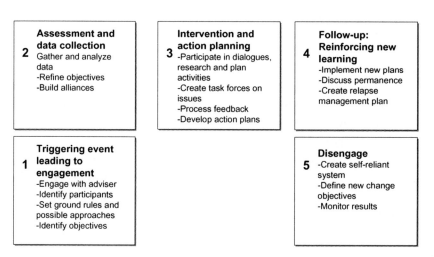

Figure 10.3 Creating an organizational change process

an organizational change process is to provide leadership that fosters a shared mindset and new behaviors, and ensures that the changes are institutionalized in the culture. Balanced leaders who can develop long-term strategies that align their firm's capabilities will be doing their firm an extremely valuable service. As Jim Collins said, in his book *Good to Great*, the best leaders 'never aspired to be put on a pedestal or become unreachable icons. They were seemingly ordinary people, quietly producing extraordinary results' [14].

We will now examine each stage of Figure 10.3 in turn.

Creating a Shared Mindset

The first leadership task involves helping people to recognize the need for change—that the present state of affairs is not viable in the long term and that, despite the unknowns, change is imperative. A critical step here is gathering sufficient data from the organization to make a case for supporting change. Building supportive relationships with people in the organization will help to engage these people in the data collection process. These data will provide a sound basis for allocating resources and for decision making related to new strategies, which then set the stage for new plans and actions. Employees need to be helped to realize that doing nothing will be a significant threat to the organization and the individuals within it. It is also important to demonstrate how new behaviors really can improve performance and reduce potential threats to the organization's viability.

When people are not engaged in the change process, they can develop a sense of helplessness. Furthermore, an organization in which no meaningful action is taken to deal with issues like slow decision making, quality problems, a declining competitive position, or falling market share, is a high-stress environment that diminishes employee performance and commitment. Collecting data and assessing the situation sends a positive message to the organization that the leadership is aware that something needs to be done and is taking action to protect the organization's future.

Once data have been collected and analyzed, it is time to hold an organization-wide event or program through which the CEO and management team can feed back the data collected and begin an action-planning process [15]. This action event can be staged in many different ways:

- an off-site gathering at which members of senior management announce plans for a new organization;
- a series of workshops or seminars;
- a meeting facilitated by an outside consultant.

Whatever form it takes, this event serves several purposes. First, it sets the stage for making changes in the organization's structure and strategy. Second, it engages employees in a dialog about their organization. Third, it clarifies the actions necessary in order to implement appropriate changes in the business's tasks, process, training, and technology. The overriding goal of the event is to ensure broad participation across the organization to support employee engagement and commitment to the new vision and plans [16].

Changing Behavior

The next major leadership task is making sure people at all levels within the organization are committed to the new way of behaving and working together. At every opportunity, leaders need to transmit and articulate the new vision. Employee participation needs to be encouraged to support the changes. Leaders will need to build networks based on task forces and teams to align employees with the new vision. These informal networks can create social pressure to establish new norms and expectations throughout the whole organization.

Employee training and development are effective tools for working beyond initial basic changes toward transforming the entire organization. Most stuck or struggling organizations fail to develop their human capital and talent, resulting in a loss of pride and in mediocre performance. Organization-wide training and development pays immediate dividends by strengthening the organization's skill set and setting small steps that reinforce the change effort through demonstrable progress. Although an extended period of time will be needed to improve sales or profit margins, employee development can be integrated early in the process as part of the data collection activities supporting the change process.

The psychological contract between an organization and its employees to can be enhanced by equipping people with new skills, offering them new work situations or career opportunities. Helping employees to develop their full potential benefits both the organization and the individual, since improved performance increases personal satisfaction, and satisfied employees are more committed.

Institutionalizing Change

The third step involves building attitudes, competencies, and practices. Here leaders work to give employees what they need to make the change effort successful, fostering their development in emotional intelligence as well as in job-specific competencies. They will provide the resources needed to make the change effort successful. They will also use rewards, recognition, and social pressure to obtain the desired results. Moreover, at this point 'small wins' become important for motivational purposes. It is important to attain the final goal, but reaching intermediate goals will keep the momentum going.

Transforming the Organization

In this phase there will be the emotional acceptance and recognition that the new behaviors are working. People may need to be helped to deal with the loss that is part of letting go the old practices and ways of thinking. Making new behaviors part of the organization's culture starts as a cognitive process, which management can support by offering training and other resources. These training programs will help to encourage and internalize an innovation-driven culture. In addition, management must recognize the emotional needs of employees and ensure that they are supported in accepting the loss of their previous situation and are motivated through rewards and recognition. A monitoring process needs to be put into place to give continuous feedback on performance.

If these four phases are successfully completed, employees will accept the need to behave differently and recognize advantages to themselves and the organization, as well as supporting the organization and its new strategies. As the business's performance improves, people are likely to internalize new values and beliefs. Their roles and futures will become clearer, reinforcing their long-term commitment to innovation and organizational renewal.

The word 'transformational' is often used in discussions of organizational change; however, change interventions seldom reach that level of significance. Using life experiences as a parallel for transformation, we can see that individuals will experience only a handful of transformational events that truly change the nature of how they see themselves and interact with the world. Walking for a toddler, giving birth for a woman, or learning to drive a car for a teenager are transformational experiences because the individual's self-image and relationships are changed by developments of this sort. If an organizational change process is going to become transformational in this sense, then change cannot simply be initiated by a seminar or program or even a strategy, but must be a fundamental part of how the organization's employees see themselves and their firm.

Effective leaders are architects who redesign an organization through envisioning a new future, identifying new behavioral options, empowering the organization, and then ensuring that performance is monitored and rewarded. The real challenge for the CEO, senior management team, and employees is crafting an organization committed to human development that continuously regenerates itself, without the need for specifically designed organizational change programs.

THE CHANGE PROCESS IN FAMILIES

The family system, by its very nature, faces change as new events occur throughout its life cycle. Families experience loss through birth (the parents' relationship changes when children come along), death, divorce, and children leaving home. Because of these life events, all members of the family must at one time or another give up their idealization of relationships, dreams, and plans. A first child loses his or her special relationship with its parents when a sibling is born. Parents 'lose' their children when they leave home and begin a life of their own. Each life event challenges the family to create new patterns of interaction in their relationships.

As discussed in Chapter 4, families who run or control businesses also face life cycle transitions in their organizations. An entrepreneur in his sixties must address his own mortality and the impending loss of his role as CEO. Young adults in the next generation must learn to function not as children with strong parental control, but as sibling partners with full ownership responsibilities. The family and firm must accept that their powerful CEO and guiding force will eventually be replaced by a new leader. All this must be faced while also coping with the ever-changing environment in which the business operates. Although every family is unique, families generally cope with change in one of three ways:

- the *strategic* family actively develops new behavior to address anticipated changes;
- the *adaptive* family acts when an imminent change is signaled;
- the *reactive* family only acts when forced to by events.

Once again, succession planning provides a good example for demonstrating these three different approaches. A strategic family will make career plans for the key family and non-family executives and continually monitor performance to ensure that the organization has a pool of qualified succession candidates. Twelve months before the current CEO is due to retire, the board will review the talent pool and nominate a new CEO, who will then work with the current CEO on an orderly transition.

The adaptive family to only begins the succession-planning process during a board meeting after the current CEO has announced his plans for retirement. The reactive family—which is likely to be headed by a seemingly immortal CEO, who has no plans to retire and has not trained a successor—names an acting CEO only after the unplanned exit of the current CEO following a heart attack, or similar dramatic event. Most of the families that we have worked with face change reactively; *post facto*, we are usually helping the family to address a change that was clearly predictable, but which they had been unable to confront without external support.

Whatever their preferred style, the difficulty for all families is that the very forces that help them to function as a family system and maintain stability will also work against change—the recurrent patterns of interaction or homeostasis we described earlier [17]. The family's adherence to the status quo is an attempt to protect the family from separating or becoming less connected. The dilemma with homeostasis is that it maintains both effective and ineffective patterns of interaction, resulting in increasingly dysfunctional behaviors. Parents who are highly controlling of their young children often remain highly controlling of their adolescent children—with predictable conflict as their children strive for more autonomy. Families are often stuck with extremely unsatisfactory relationships because they would rather not risk the uncertainty that could result if they changed their behavior.

Models for Change in the Family

Research on family systems suggests that positive family change occurs when the family learns how to communicate new information that leads to new behavior [18]. Dallos and Aldridge suggest that family change can be described in behavioral terms around four overlapping themes [19]:

- behavioral changes in how the family acts, postures, or gestures to one another;
- structural changes as the family reorganizes hierarchies, coalitions, alliances, and boundaries;
- communication changes, including new topics and new channels;
- experiential changes in the family's shared understanding of its problems and how to solve them.

Our work with family business executives and owners in the Family Enterprise Challenge Program at INSEAD★ has facilitated

★ The *Family Enterprise Challenge program* creates an opportunity to share perspectives with other families and encourages application of new knowledge to each family's real world issues. The program promotes action learning by using the participants' own challenges: in the classroom through exercises, case studies, and personal reflection, and most importantly a concluding, individual 'family meeting' to plan action steps.

the development of a change model that incorporates the application of an action learning model. We find that quite often a certain pattern of change occurs in a family's development when it engages in an educational or therapeutic process. The family's first challenge is to develop new communications skills for sharing ideas and different perspectives; next, they need to move toward negotiating new structures, perhaps allowing younger family members an opportunity to express their views; then they need to practice new communication skills with difficult topics; and, finally, they need to develop action plans that reflect a new understanding of their issues and the possible changes required. The family may not actually make it through *all* these levels of change, but improvements in just *some* areas can still have a positive impact on their family relationships and interactions. We will describe these phases in more detail in Figure 10.4 below. (We also return to the family change model, and describe its application in much greater detail, in Chapter 12.)

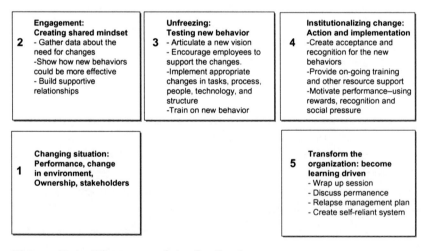

Figure 10.4   The stages of the family change process

Phase 1: Triggering event leading to engagement

Families, like individuals, become willing to change when the stress or loss created by their behavior becomes more uncomfortable than their fear of exploring new options. Often in families an unresolved conflict or a difficult relationship will trigger the agreement to consider new behaviors. As described in Chapter 1, in order to achieve any results in family therapy or consulting interventions, the consultant or therapist needs to develop a therapeutic alliance with that family based on trust and confidence. Often the early meetings between the therapist and the family may be attended by only selected members of the family, and at this point it is critical to identify who should participate and secure their commitment to participate. These early stages should also be used to discuss ground rules and explore possible approaches for the work. It is also useful during this early stage to identify family members who may have a strong interest in blocking any possible changes.

These early working sessions plant the seeds of change as the consultant/therapist tracks the interactions of the family members by identifying the key actors and their positions in the family of origin. This involves capturing information about three generations: relationships with parents, grandparents, siblings, and children. It is here that the genogram can be so useful because the family system is the context in which any change must occur. The extended family is vital in helping to uncover familial patterns over many generations, an understanding of which can assist change.

Phase 2: Assessment and data collection

The second step of the family change process is the family assessment and data collection phase leading to identification of issues or challenges facing the family. The facilitator may interview each family member or selected groups to hear their views on the problems faced. This process should help the family begin to build a shared understanding of family characteristics and difficulties. It is also the first step in helping the family explore new behaviors such as paying attention and listening to all the generations. Family members who are reluctant to recognize or address problems identified by other family members may need coaching from the facilitator. Task forces may be created to help the family explore critical issues in depth; multi-generational task forces often create a new experience whereby all family members listen to each other without having their feelings or views belittled or refuted.

However, it can sometimes be difficult to engage the family's active participation in the assessment process. Some individuals may not want to share their views; others will deny the existence of any problems; and some may choose to leave during the session (possibly slamming the door on the way out). Families reluctant to participate in an assessment dialog might, however, be willing to contribute to completing the family's genogram using purely demographic information as a starting point. The challenge here is simply to establish a safe space in which the family can begin to communicate with each other and identify answers to questions such as 'What problems are affecting our family?' or 'What decisions and plans must our family develop?' In the family business setting, a family business timeline that portrays the challenges and changes the family faces is another tool for eliciting helpful information. Often during these business-focused discussions, issues such as family relationship and family communication will be identified as contributing to the business problems. The ideal outcome of the family assessment is both to identify new areas for planning and decision-making (content), and practicing new patterns of communicating and working together (process).

Phase 3: Intervention and action planning

This phase involves helping the family to address the issues identified in the assessment and goal-setting from Phase 2. It is essential to have completed the previous steps successfully before beginning any such interventions. As in the other phases, attention should be paid to both process and content; here the process is helping the family to learn new and more effective ways of interacting, and the content is the identification of action steps to address the issues revealed in the assessment. This is also the stage at which the management of resistance (see Chapter 1) becomes important. Resistance in this context may take the form of family members not participating with the task forces, or not completing the family homework activities, or not being available for interviews. Some clients may have various transference reactions (see Chapter 1) toward the consultant/therapist/coach, which then may cause resistance to arise [20].

Throughout these family meetings or task force sessions, business issues may be the presenting problems on the agenda, but equally important is improving the family's ability to effectively work together. The goal is improving family functioning around issues such as:

- the parents' ability to communicate about personal issues or conflicts;
- the family's desire for more cohesion or connection;
- learning to think beyond gender or sexual stereotypes;
- sharing power and control of the business;
- addressing different family-members' life cycle transitions;
- renegotiating roles based on life events, especially loss (deaths, divorce);
- managing a specific change such as planned career transition.

In families where there is a lack of differentiation, an exercise like asking the siblings to share how they feel about being a part of the family can create an opening for further discussion. At the same time, we ask the parents only to listen without making any comments. When they behave in such a way, many otherwise 'undiscussables' will get on the table, helping the family to unravel difficult issues.

Phase 4: Follow-up and reinforcing new learning

The final phase in any family change process is reinforcing the new behaviors and processes within the family system. This phase is about confirming the changes the family has internalized, and checking that the process has in fact met the family's needs. It is also important to confirm the family's belief in the *permanence* of the changes. The consultant/therapist/coach should also encourage a degree of celebration of the progress that has been made so far. One important skill that families will need to have learned through the sessions is that of anticipating future challenges, so the outside adviser must at some point discuss with the family how they might go about handling such issues [21].

Phase 5: Disengage

Although the family is now ready to go forward on their own, the consultant/therapist/coach may leave the family with the option of getting back in touch as and when needed, mentioning that this would involve recontracting. It is important to have an end to the change process to ensure that the family does not become dependent on the outside adviser, and takes responsibility for managing the maintenance of the new behaviors. Recontracting should also include observations about relapse management, indicating that some setbacks will be normal parts of the process of disengaging from therapeutic work [22]. The family needs to assign accountability for continued improvement. How they will continue to work together should be a part of the family's agenda for family meetings or the family council. Monitoring the family's performance and communication when engaged in problem solving or planning situations creates the opportunity to seek outside support when required.

FAMILY FOCUS OR ORGANIZATION FOCUS?

Although this chapter has provided guidelines on the predictable phases and outcomes of change processes, each family business is a unique combination of individuals who influence, and are influenced by, their families and the business organization. The first step when working with business families is, therefore, to determine the degree of 'familiness' in the business.

A small organization (about 5 to 100 people), in which most of the people are related, or at least one family member is an executive or director (including firms from start-up size to about the fourth generation), should probably start with a family-focused approach to change. Larger organizations—even though they may still be family owned or controlled—are likely to do best with a more organization-focused change process. But in the final analysis, the keystone in both the old and the new organization—family or non-family—is the willingness and capacity of the individuals to change. The ideal result of any change process is a family business that has empowered individual members, and is able to predict and prepare for transition continually and *strategically* rather than *reactively*.

In the next chapter, we will revisit the story of Steinberg Inc. (described briefly in the Introduction) applying all the concepts raised so far in this book. We will consider how the Steinberg family addressed business leadership, ownership structure, parent–sibling relationships, intersibling relationships and family leadership transitions—all of which were driven by Sam Steinberg's retirement and subsequent early death. These family transitions, coupled with external business threats, required the family, business, and stakeholders to renegotiate relationships, roles, power allocation, beliefs, and rewards. In looking at this case study we'll be taking a road not frequently traveled by business advisers because rather than focusing on the financial and organizational issues that drove Steinberg Inc. to bankruptcy, we will analyze the individuals within the second and third generation of the Steinberg family system to demonstrate the application of psychodynamic-systems thinking to family and business transitions.

ENDNOTES

1. Carlock, R.S., Kets de Vries M.F.R. and Florent-Treacy, E. (2007). 'Family Business' entry in the *International Encyclopedia of Organization Studies*. Thousand Oaks, CA: Sage.
2. See Lewin, K. (1935). *A Dynamic Theory of Personality*. New York: McGraw-Hill; Lewin, K. (1936). *Principles of Topological Psychology*. New York: McGraw-Hill; Lewin, K. (1948). *Resolving Social Conflicts; Selected Papers on Group Dynamics*. Gertrude W. Lewin (ed.). New York: Harper & Row; Lewin, K. (1951). *Field Theory in Social Science: Selected Theoretical Papers*. D. Cartwright (ed.). New York: Harper & Row.
3. Lewin, K. (1951, 1958); Greenson, R.R. (1967). *The Technique and Practice of Psychoanalysis*. New York: International University Press; Watzlawick, P., Weakland, J.H. and Fisch, R. (1974). *Change: Principles of Problem Formation and Problem Resolution*. New York: W.W. Norton; Wachtel, P. (ed.) (1982). *Resistance: Psychodynamic and Behavioral Approaches*. New York, Plenum Press; Argyris, C. (1985). *Strategy, Change and Defensive Routines*. Boston: Pitman; Pervis, L.A. (1994). 'Personality stability, personality change, and the question of process,' in Heatherton, T. and Weinberger, J.L. (eds), *Can Personality Change?* (pp. 315–330). Washington, DC: American Psychological Association.

4. Kets de Vries, M.F.R. (2001). *The Leadership Mystique*. London: FT/Prentice Hall.

5. Maxwell, M. (1984). *The Alcoholics Anonymous Experience*. New York: McGraw-Hill; Stall, R. and Biernacki, P. (1986). 'Spontaneous remission from the problematic use of substances: An inductive model derived from a comparative analysis of the alcohol, tobacco, and food/obesity literatures,' *International Journal of the Addictions*, **21**: 1–23.

6. Kets de Vries, M.F.R. and Balazs, K. (1996). 'Transforming the mind-set of the organization,' *INSEAD Working Paper*, 98/81/ENT.

7. Kets de Vries, M.F.R. (2006).*The Leader on the Couch*. London: John Wiley & Sons Ltd.

8. Bowlby, J. (1969, 1973, 1980). *Attachment and Loss*. New York: Basic Books; Parkes, C.M. (1972). *Bereavement: Studies of Grief in Adult Life*. New York: International Universities Press; Marris, P. (1974). *Loss and Change*. London: Routledge & Kegan Paul; Dietrich, D.R. and Shabad, P. (eds) (1993). *Problem of Loss and Mourning: Psychoanalytic Perspectives*. New York: International Universities Press.

9. Solomon, A. (2001). *The Noonday Demon: An Atlas of Depression*. New York: Simon & Schuster.

10. Kets de Vries, M.F.R. (2005). 'Feeling like a fake: How the fear of success can cripple your career and damage your company,' *Harvard Business Review*, **83** (8): 108–116.

11. Erikson, E.H. (1963). *Childhood and Society*. New York: W.W. Norton; Vaillant, G.E. (1977). *Adaptation to Life*. Boston: Little Brown; Levinson, D. (1978). *The Seasons of Man's Life*. New York: Knopf; Sheehy, G. (1995). *New Passages*. New York: Ballantine Books; Sheehy, G. (1998). *Understanding Men's Passages: Discovering the New Map of Men's Lives*. New York: Random House; Stassen Berger, K. (1998). *The Developing Person through the Life Span*. New York: Worth Publishers.

12. Hochschild, A.R. and Machung, A. (2003). *Second Shift*. New York: Penguin.

13. Kets de Vries, M.F.R. (2001).

14. Collins, J.C. (2001). *Good to Great* (p. 28). New York: HarperCollins.

15. Nanus, B. (1995). *The Vision Retreat*. San Francisco: Jossey-Bass.

16. Lewin, K. (1958).

17. Jackson, D. (1968). 'Human communication,' in *Therapy, Communication and Change*, Vol. 2. Palo Alto: Science and Behavior.

18. Jones, E. (1993). *Family Systems Therapy: Development in the Milan-Systemic Therapies*. Chichester: John Wiley & Sons.

19. Dallos, R. and Aldridge, D. (1986). 'Change: How do we recognize it?' *Journal of Family Therapy*, **8**: 45–59.

20. Karpman, S. (1968). 'Fairy tales and script drama analysis,' *Transactional Analysis Bulletin*, **7** (26): 39–44.

21. Nichols, M.P. and Schwartz, R.C. (1995). *Family Therapy: Concepts and Methods* (3rd edn). Boston: Allyn & Bacon.

22. Carr, A. (2005). *Family Therapy: Concepts, Process and Practices*. Chichester: John Wiley & Sons Ltd.

CHAPTER 11

THE VICISSITUDES OF FAMILY BUSINESS

In this chapter we look in more depth at the Steinbergs, first described in the Introduction, and use their story as a comprehensive illustration of the application of psychological thinking to a family business struggling with conflict—especially that around succession. We will also be applying both the genogram and the Circumplex Model to make further sense of this story.

THE STEINBERGS: A STUDY IN SELF-DESTRUCTION

Snow piled up in drifts outside the Palomino Lodge, the Steinberg corporate retreat in the Laurentian Hills north of Montreal, as the board of directors of Steinberg Inc. began discussions about who would replace 'Mr Sam' as the head of the business empire he had created. Sam Steinberg, the company's founder and driving force, was nearing 65 and would soon be stepping aside as president and moving into the newly created post of chairman.

   As the board began their deliberations, Sam's mind wandered back to another snowy morning over 50 years earlier when he and his mother, Ida, had pulled a wagon full of groceries through the dark, blizzard-clogged streets of Montreal. He could still clearly picture her slight but wiry figure demanding that he move faster because they had shelves to stock and their customers were counting on the Steinbergs to be the first store open for business after two days of blizzard conditions. Dragging his thoughts back into the present, Sam sat half listening to the discussions about the future leadership of one of Canada's most important businesses and couldn't help but wonder what Ida would think of the business empire he had built. He kept thinking to himself, 'Would she be proud of me? Or could I have done more?'

As the discussions became more heated and the atmosphere more charged, Sam's attention returned to the meeting room. The board was debating the selection of Sam's successor, but there was no question where the final decision lay. Sam had built his retailing and real estate empire from a single family grocery store, and, even though his was a publicly-traded company, Sam made the important decisions. In the end, his would be the only vote that mattered.

The tension was high because everyone around the table knew that they were debating not only the company's future but also that of each individual sitting there. Several of the senior family and non-family executives, all present, were competing to take the reins from Sam, and it was almost certain that one of them would be the next president of Steinberg Inc. As they argued over the company strategy for the coming years, they were also jockeying for position in the succession sweepstakes.

Behind the business maneuvering was a much more fundamental question of family values. Ida had always said that the family comes first: take care of the family. The decision was Sam's: would he allow leadership of his company to pass to the most qualified executive available, or would blood ties decide who would be next to hold the top job?

THE IMMIGRANT DREAM

Sam Steinberg was 6 years old when he came to Canada with his family in 1911, penniless immigrants fleeing poverty and anti-Semitism in their native Hungary. It was from the dirt-poor streets of Montreal's old Jewish quarter that he began his incredible climb to riches. Yet the true origin of Sam's empire lay not in Montreal but, rather, back in the old country before Sam was even born, in the difficult life of his mother.

Ida Steinberg was born Ida Roth, the oldest girl in a poor family of one son and seven daughters. Ida's mother ran the family while her father—being a poor provider—concentrated on religious studies. What childhood Ida had was cut short when both her parents died before she was 14 years old. As the eldest daughter, she struggled valiantly to look after her siblings and keep her family together. Ultimately, it was too much for her, however, and the Roth children were separated and sent to live with various relatives.

Ida went to live with her uncle near the town of Debrecen, where he ran a general store. Working in the store gave the industrious Ida her introduction to the retailing business. At age 18, Ida was married to Vilmos Stemberg in an arranged marriage, as was customary in the Jewish community in Hungary. Like Ida's father before, Vilmos was an impractical man, preferring religious studies to his sometime job as a baker. A tiny but hugely energetic woman, Ida managed the household. She gave birth to four children in rapid succession. Sam, the second, was born on Christmas Day in 1905.

By 1911, Ida had decided that a better future for her family lay in the New World. Two of her sisters had already made the voyage to Montreal, and stories of vast opportunities circulated through Hungary's hard-pressed Jewish community. So Ida packed up husband and children and sailed for Canada, selling all the family's possessions to pay for the passage. Ida's brother and two more sisters joined them on the journey. They landed in Quebec City, where an immigration officer somehow changed their family name from Stemberg to Steinberg.

If the new Steinbergs had expected a life of milk and honey in Canada, they were soon to be disappointed. The family lived crammed together in one room of a cold-water house, renting out the other rooms to raise precious pennies. They were always poor, a situation not helped by Vilmos's decided disinterest in work and Ida's considerable fertility (two more Steinberg boys were born during the family's first three years in Canada). It was at least in part Vilmos's troublesome reproductive capacity, and her sisters' dislike of him, that led Ida to decide to separate from her husband shortly after the birth of her last child in 1914. Vilmos left to live alone in a rooming house in Montreal's east end, where he worked as a caretaker in a small synagogue and pursued his religious studies. For the children, their father practically ceased to exist and Ida became the head of the family.

To make ends meet, Ida opened a small grocery store in 1917 on The Main, the strip of St Lawrence Boulevard that was the center of Montreal's immigrant community. All the family worked in the tiny store—Ida, her six children, two of her sisters, and one nephew—and they all slept above it. The children took orders, bought produce, delivered groceries and stocked shelves in the store that operated 16 hours a day, six days a week. Ida did more than anyone, working from dawn to dusk to provide for her family and, above all, keep them together.

Ida's forceful personality dominated all aspects of business and family life. She lived by an ethic of hard work and total honesty. She believed in treating customers well, allowing them to buy on credit when they needed to and always giving them something extra for their money. It was this unwavering belief that was largely responsible for the immensely strong customer loyalty enjoyed by Steinberg Inc. in later years. Ida's rules for life and business also profoundly shaped the outlook of young Sam, who would forever quote his mother's maxims to senior Steinberg executives. Years after her death, Ida's portrait still hung on the wall at the head of the Steinberg boardroom.

HIS MOTHER'S SON

Sam Steinberg's brief flirtation with formal education came to an abrupt end at the age of 14, when he was kicked out of school because of his annoying habit of always answering questions before the teacher had finished asking them. The expulsion never bothered Ida, who was pleased to have Sam helping out more around the store. Neither did it bother young Sam, who was delighted to have the chance to turn his full attention to the family business.

It did not take long for Sam to make his mark. That same year, on his own initiative, he undertook the first expansion of the family business. Seizing a sudden opportunity, he rented the store adjacent to his mother's grocery, knocked out the wall between the two, and in a single stroke doubled the size of both the store and the family's living quarters.

Soon after, Sam again moved to enlarge the business, buying another store in the more fashionable, fast-growing Outremont area of Montreal. He chose his younger brother Nathan to manage the new store, starting a pattern of using expansions of the business to provide jobs for family members. Sam called the new premises 'Store Number One'. Ida, who gave Sam the money for his new ventures, reminded him that the business was there to keep the family together. 'Sam, you must look after the boys,' she told him.

As Sam's star rose, Ida gradually faded from the company scene. Years of grinding work had taken their toll on her body, if not her spirit, and she suffered from angina and other complaints. In 1931, on the insistence of her family, she retired from daily operations and her first small grocery store was closed. Ida was never really happy on the sidelines, however; she missed the bustle of daily business. During Passover in 1942 she contracted pneumonia and died suddenly. She was 57 years old.

When the Great Depression hit North America, Steinberg's base of loyal customers allowed the company to continue to grow while the big grocery chains were retrenching. In 1931 Sam opened three new stores, filling market gaps left behind as the majors retreated. During these years, Sam also confirmed his reputation as an innovator in the Quebec food business by bringing the first self-service grocery stores to the province.

The expansion of the business was matched by the growth of Sam's own family. His wife Helen, who was the daughter of Ida's brother Lewis, bore Sam four daughters: Mitzi in 1929, Rita in 1932, Marilyn in 1933, and Evelyn in 1938. During these years, Sam worked tirelessly, traveling constantly and supervising every detail of his business; yet he somehow made time for family dinners and special events.

THE ENTREPRENEUR'S VISION

During the late 1940s, Steinberg's regained the momentum it had lost during the war, opening new stores and winning still more customers. During the war, the company had bought a lot of real estate at bargain-basement prices, looking ahead to later expansion. When the boom years of the 1950s arrived, Steinberg Inc. was ready.

By 1952, the company was booking over $70 million (Canadian) in sales and had profits of over $1 million. That year Sam launched by far the most ambitious expansion scheme in the company's history: a $15 million plan that would see 30 new giant supermarkets opened in just five years, one store every two months.

Key to the company's rapid growth in this period was another of Sam's innovations, the suburban shopping center. Steinberg's began developing integrated shopping complexes anchored around a company supermarket, the idea being that the presence of other retailers would increase the number of customers. Montreal's financial community was initially skeptical, but the resounding success of the first Steinberg shopping center in the new suburb of Dorval, west of the city, soon silenced the critics.

Until the 1950s, Steinberg's had financed its growth with internal funds. About to embark on another ambitious round of expansion in 1958, the company issued $8.5 million of participating equity. But still Sam would give up none of the control of his company; against the advice of his lawyers and bankers, he issued non-voting shares. By 1960 the company had 92 stores along with its burgeoning real estate and warehousing operations.

SAM AS A FAMILY BUSINESS LEADER

If Steinberg's began to look like a public company on the outside, on the inside it was quite another story. Sam still ran the company very much like a small family firm. Sam drove his employees as hard as he drove himself, and there were few executives who had not suffered one of Sam's characteristic tongue-lashings. His was a world of creative chaos, where formal management systems counted for little and his whim was the order of the day. As the company grew exponentially, Sam continued to keep track of every aspect, often taking decisions that circumvented those executives nominally responsible for a given part of the business. Sometimes it seemed that the whole company still reported directly to him.

Yet Sam also inspired enormous affection and loyalty among many of his employees. A man of great integrity, his personal code of behavior shaped the corporate culture of Steinberg Inc. Sam cared deeply for the welfare of his workers, helping them when they faced financial difficulties, calling on them in the hospital when they were sick, attending their weddings and funerals. He was a benevolent dictator, a man both loved and feared by those who worked for him.

Sam always said that business was built specifically for his family, and there would always be a place in it for family members. He firmly believed that if the business was destroyed as a result of that, so be it. Nowhere could Sam's contradictory nature be seen as clearly as in his treatment of his family. He was the unquestioned patriarch of his extended family, and he looked out for the interests of all its members to the point of interference. To his brothers and other family members who worked for the firm, Sam could present the image of the bullying father, shouting at them at the top of his lungs and disparaging their work in front of others.

However, although Sam was bossy and demanding with his family, he was also unquestioningly and aggressively loyal to them. Sam might berate his brothers, but he would defend them fiercely against attacks from others. Urgent family matters always took priority over business, and secretaries quickly learned that telephone calls from family members always went straight through to the boss, whatever else might be happening. He was always ready to help a family member in need. At home he was devoted to his wife, Helen, and he was an indulgent—maybe overly indulgent—father to his four girls.

Sam's paternalistic concern for his family's well-being carried over into hiring and promotion practices in his company. Sam was determined that there would always be a job for any family member who wanted or needed one, which turned out to be a lot of them. But there was a high price to be paid for using the company as a family job pool: the pervasive nepotism at Steinberg Inc. contributed in large part to a disturbingly high turnover among talented executives. Dozens of bright young managers cut their teeth at Steinberg's and then left for firms where they saw greater long-term potential for their careers. In Montreal, the company was known among its former employees as the 'University of Steinberg'.

Sam Steinberg may have been the absolute ruler of his family and his business, but not even he could withstand the march of time. He was getting older, and he knew as well as anyone that one day he would have to hand over control of his company to someone else. Finding someone to fill his central role in the company, Sam knew, would be an all but impossible order.

With no obvious solution in sight, and confident in his own abilities and stamina, Sam repeatedly swept the question of his successor under the carpet. It fell to his board and senior executives to raise the issue again and again at annual executive reviews, pushing Sam to prepare for a clear and orderly succession.

Sam would have dearly loved to have had a son to carry on in his footsteps and keep the Steinberg name at the head of the company. But to his regret, his marriage to Helen had produced only daughters, and, despite the shining example of feminine competence demonstrated by his own mother, Sam never seemed to consider his daughters as possible successors. He provided them with a luxurious lifestyle, and he never encouraged them to be anything other than housewives. When his oldest daughter, Mitzi, left home to gain a law degree and finally enter the family business, she did so entirely on her own initiative.

In 1969, Sam was 64 years old, and the unpleasant task of naming his successor could be put off no longer. He would have to decide whether to keep the job of running his company in the family, turn to one of his non-family executives, or to go outside the firm for a new chief executive. All the contenders would be present at Palomino Lodge that cold weekend in March at a meeting Sam had called to help him to choose his successor.

THE ENTREPRENEUR'S DILEMMA: PASSING THE BATON

'This is not the most qualified person we're selecting,' Sam Steinberg explained to one of his non-family executives shortly after naming his son-in-law Mel Dobrin to succeed him as president of Steinberg Inc. An accountant by training, Mel had joined the company on the grocery side and had climbed steadily upward through the corporate ranks. He knew the business inside and out and was a solid administrator.

Sam added, 'It may be in the best interests of this corporation to have a professional manager. But I've had so much fun building and running this business that I wouldn't deprive my family of doing it.'

With this blunt admission, Sam confirmed what many already suspected. As long as Sam was around—indeed, for the foreseeable future—family would always come first at Steinberg's, even though it was now a large public company responsible to thousands of shareholders. For Sam, appointing Dobrin was the least unattractive solution to an intractable problem. He was simply unprepared psychologically to either surrender control of his company or to see it pass out of family hands. Inside the firm, many said Sam was also incapable of standing up to his oldest daughter, Mitzi, Dobrin's wife. By appointing the solid, dependable, but uninspiring Dobrin to the presidency, he could keep family peace while maintaining personal control of the company through his compliant son-in-law. The appointment of Dobrin coincided with the beginning of a long, drifting decline at Steinberg's.

The most obvious effect of Sam's choice of a successor was a marked acceleration of the company's already serious problem of brain drain. For many talented executives, the appointment of Dobrin was the last straw. For his part, Dobrin never enjoyed any real power during his term as president and, indeed, was often undercut by Sam. At first, Sam routinely made executive decisions as if nothing had changed. Even when he finally started to withdraw somewhat from the daily operation of Steinberg's, he would still telephone his son-in-law several times a day just to keep tabs on everything.

Steinberg Inc. executives of the period remember Dobrin as a passive president who failed to provide the necessary impetus or direction. Little investment was made to counter the threat of rising competition, and combative unions ran roughshod over the company.

In May 1978, Sam died of a heart attack. When he was buried, his workers swelled the ranks of the 2000 mourners who filled the synagogue and lined the streets of Montreal to pay their last respects. In an emotional sense, as well as a literal one, the father of the company was gone.

THE NEXT GENERATION

In the weeks after Sam's death, Dobrin moved quickly to provide a sense of continuity and competence in the company and took over Sam's role as chairman and chief executive. However, Dobrin faced a number of serious problems. The competitive environment was getting ever tougher. The loss of Sam hung like a pall over Steinberg's, and his memory competed with Dobrin for authority and legitimacy in the company.

Following Sam's death, Mitzi had become the *de facto* head of the Steinberg family and the center of power within Steinberg Inc. The only Steinberg daughter with a university education, she was also the only one working in the family company: in 1973, Sam had parachuted her in to run Miracle Mart, the money-losing discount department store chain. At that time, Mitzi had no experience in retailing, and other non-family executives firmly opposed the appointment, telling Sam it was a bad idea.

Meanwhile, the core business went from bad to worse, and by the early 1980s the once unassailable Steinberg's had slipped into third position in the Quebec grocery business. In 1982, the situation at Steinberg's had become so grave that family members were prepared to contemplate 'the unthinkable': appointing a complete outsider to run Sam's firm.

IRVING LUDMER: PLAY IT AGAIN, SAM

The company seemed to be in free-fall. Without a vision or leadership, it was hemorrhaging money and talent. Analysts began to wonder if there was a future at all for the empire Sam had built. Into this desperate situation stepped the new president, Irving Ludmer.

A former Steinberg Inc. executive who had left the company in 1971, Ludmer had gone on to become one of Quebec's leading real estate developers and a rich man in his own right. In 1983, he had rejoined Steinberg's to take control of its drifting real-estate subsidiary, Ivanhoe Inc., after many months of concentrated lobbying by his old friend, Sam's nephew Arnold Steinberg. Intelligent, decisive and driven, Ludmer seemed to be the company's best hope in time of crisis. After much consideration, Ludmer had agreed to take the job as president, but only on condition that he be fully supported by Mitzi.

The situation at Steinberg Inc. was rapidly becoming critical: in the past five years, the company's share of the Quebec grocery market had slipped from 28% to 17%. The very depth and urgency of the crisis facing the company probably worked in Ludmer's favor, since executives and directors alike knew that serious changes were needed. And Ludmer, the former company *wunderkind* (and Sam's special favorite), was a man who could deliver change.

When he took over, many doubted that even Ludmer could halt the decline of Steinberg Inc. But he confounded all the skeptics: in his first full year as president, Ludmer quintupled profits, and Steinberg Inc. shares more than tripled in price. On his first day on the job, he flushed out the executive suites, pruning deadwood and cutting costs. He then began a huge program of renovating Steinberg's dilapidated stores. To many at Steinberg's, he was a messiah, anointed by his ancient association with Sam, to lead the company back to glory.

Ludmer was a determined man who would brook no interference in his running of the firm, be it from his executives or from the family. It was perhaps inevitable that he would eventually come into conflict with Mitzi. Her power base in the company was challenged by his ascendancy, and she began to reassert herself in company affairs. Push came to shove, and finally spilled over into direct confrontation in September 1985. Ludmer, the architect of the dramatic turnaround in the company's fortunes, bluntly (and not demonstrating much emotional intelligence toward the family) told Mitzi that if she did not resign, he would. The board of directors, which was chaired by Mitzi's husband, backed Ludmer. On September 6, Mitzi resigned as executive vice president, though she remained a director.

At last a Steinberg president had full power and a free hand to run Steinberg's his own way. Under Ludmer's leadership, the company began to pull together, free of the divisive presence of overt family power in the executive suite. The way looked clear for the company finally to become a truly professionally managed firm. However, as the Steinberg company began to recover some of its sense of purpose, ruptures in the Steinberg family became irreparable. Mitzi asserted herself in an ownership role and began looking for ways to sell the company. Her sisters did not agree with her. Family mediation failed, and the trust agreement set up by Sam was revoked. The feud became public when Mitzi filed a lawsuit to have her sisters and their husbands removed from the management of the family trusts.

For Irving Ludmer, the all-out war between the sisters made it difficult to ensure stability inside the company. Talk of take-overs always leads top executives to consider other employment options. This situation notwithstanding, as long as Marilyn and Evelyn were determined to block the sale of the company, Ludmer had a good chance of keeping it together. But he lost this advantage, touching off the final disintegration of Steinberg Inc., when he fired Marilyn's son Billy Pedvis during an executive shakeup in 1988 (demonstrating once more his lack of emotional intelligence). Billy was highly regarded in the family, and even the Dobrins objected when he was let go. Marilyn was furious at the treatment of her son, and gradually her attachment to the company began to weaken. This was a poor tactical move on Ludmer's part as he would need Marilyn's goodwill as a buffer against Mitzi's wrath. Ironically, the family began to find some unity again in its shared resentment of Ludmer.

As mentioned in the introduction, the final 18 months of Steinberg Inc. as an independent company were marked by an on-again, off-again battle for control of the firm. It began in earnest with a bid from a consortium of Toronto developers and financiers keen to get their hands on Steinberg's prized real estate assets. Then, Ludmer and Arnold Steinberg were deluged with proposals from leverage buy-out firms that wanted to finance a bid headed by the pair. Nothing came of this idea because of the family's refusal to enter such an agreement with Ludmer and Arnold Steinberg. The board then announced that it would seek other ways of 'maximizing shareholder value.'

This bought time, but not much. Ludmer turned to the powerful Quebec public employees pension fund, the *Caisse de depôts et placements*, in search of a long-term investor to buy out the Steinberg family and keep the company together. Jean Campeau, the head of the *Caisse*, wanted to keep control of Steinberg's in Quebec, but even more he wanted its prime real estate assets for the *Caisse*. Campeau found his solution in the person of Michel Gaucher, the high-profile Quebec entrepreneur. The *Caisse* agreed to back a bid by Gaucher, in return for the opportunity to buy the Steinberg real-estate portfolio. On July 8, the Steinberg family entered into a lock-up agreement with Gaucher. On August 22, 1989, some 71 years after Ida Steinberg opened her first grocery store on St Lawrence Boulevard, Gaucher bought Steinberg Inc. for $1.3 billion.

The epilogue to the whole story is rather sad. Michel Gaucher's regime was not to last for long. In retrospect, his takeover of Steinberg's was a disastrous move. He didn't know anything about supermarkets (his company having originally been a small shipping enterprise), and, furthermore, he terminated the employment of many of Steinberg Inc.'s key executives. Under his regime, the stores went downhill fast.

Gaucher went bankrupt only three years after the takeover, having financially overextended himself. The stores were sold off to various chains before the bankruptcy. While this was going on, thousands of employees lost their jobs. The politically charged decision of the *Caisse* (with its eyes on the company's real estate holdings) turned out to be a costly one. It is estimated that the

Caisse lost around half a billion dollars' worth of pension fund money, and the banks that were involved never recovered all their funds. In hindsight, it is clear that the price paid for the company to its shareholders was in considerable excess of its value. And the ultimate cost to the family? There is no longer a store with the name of Steinberg.

A FAMILY SYSTEMS PERSPECTIVE ON THE STEINBERGS

Important clues to the Steinberg family conflicts can be found in each of its member's unique life experiences, as well as the family's complex interpersonal relationships. Clearly much of the conflict was to do with Sam, the driving force for 50 years after his mother established the company.

Entrepreneurs are powerful people with special talents related to starting and growing business ventures. They have a high need for achievement, combined with a strong desire for personal control. They push themselves and their employees hard, always striving to exceed their own goals [1]. Ida Steinberg and her son Sam were both entrepreneurs in very different contexts and with very different outcomes. Ida's experience demonstrates how entrepreneurship can meet the basic survival needs of an immigrant family. Sam's entrepreneurial experience focused on innovation, growth, and wealth creation.

As we see in Figure 11.1, Sam Steinberg organized his business and ownership relationships to ensure that he was central to every aspect of his family enterprise.

Unfortunately Sam's business strengths as an entrepreneur brought with them some weaknesses in terms of creating supportive family relationships and developing meaningful roles for his children and other family or non-family members in the family business [2]. Entrepreneurs have a clear future vision: *themselves* as the eternal driving force and ultimate decision maker [3]. But what happens when these individuals are forced to transfer ownership and control to the next generation? How do they deal with their families and, especially, the emotional needs of their children?

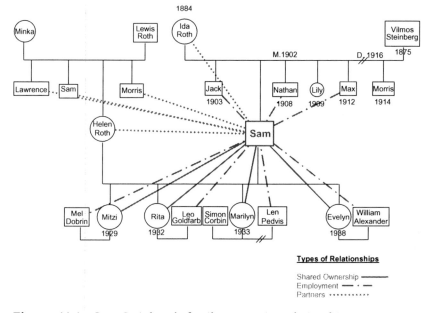

Figure 11.1   Sam Steinberg's family enterprise relationships

Using the Genogram with the Steinberg Family System

To help us to make sense of some of the decisions that Sam and his daughters made, we will use a genogram (Figure 11.2) to identify some recurring themes running through several generations of the Steinberg family. By compiling data to complete the genogram—such as birth and death dates, birth order, and family composition—we can gain deeper insights into patterns in the family's behaviour. As is usual in drawing genograms, we have used squares to indicate males, and circles to represent females.

From this simple family tree, we see that Ida—as the oldest girl—had adult responsibilities thrust upon her at a young age. We know from earlier in the chapter that the death of her parents in 1897 within a few weeks of each other forced Ida to assume her mother's role while still a teenager and become a 'parentified child', with responsibility for her five younger sisters. Despite her best efforts, she must have found this an impossible challenge. (Her siblings were soon split up and sent to live with relatives.)

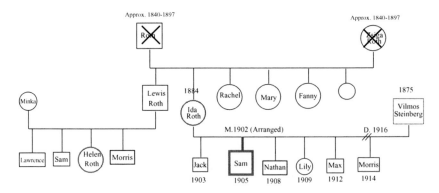

Figure 11.2   The Ida Steinberg family genogram in the early 1920s

Ida's loss of her parents and her inability to keep her sibling group together would clearly indicate why Ida valued family above all else for the rest of her life.

Sam later faced a similar experience because of his father's unwillingness to provide for the family and his mother's decision to divorce Sam's father. The genogram shows us that his parents had an arranged marriage, and divorced in 1916. At this point Sam assumed the role and responsibilities of father and provider while still really a child himself, nominated by his mother not only as the next leader of the business but also as the head of the family.

The genogram also shows that Sam was the second son (he had an older brother). Ida bypassed her oldest son, and designated Sam as the family leader. Ida's thinking was simple and direct, 'You whip the strongest horse and it will set a fast pace for the rest of the team.' The rest of Sam's life reflected his role as 'the strongest horse,' setting the pace for others.

In Figure 11.3, we have added yet another layer of information to the Steinberg genogram by depicting family relationships graphically. The triple line that we have drawn between Sam and his mother represents a very close emotional connection. The jagged lines between Ida's sisters and her husband represent a conflicted relationship. The two oblique slashes between Ida and her husband represent a cut-off relationship. Sam's relationship with Mitzi is shown as being close but conflicted by using

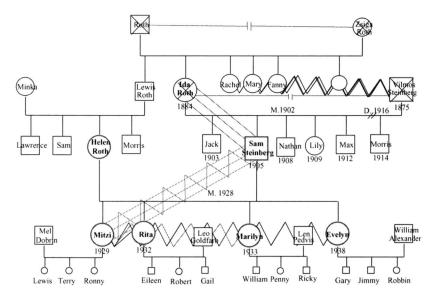

Figure 11.3   The Sam Steinberg family genogram with relationship symbols

three lines with a jagged line across them. Another factor to consider when assessing the Steinberg genogram is gender and birth order. Ida was the oldest daughter and replacement parent for her siblings, giving her an early exposure to family responsibility. Sam's role as the second son, anointed by his mother as the head of the family and as a replacement for his father, thrust Sam into a similar position as the one his mother had experienced.

Using the Circumplex Model

If we were advising or counseling Sam and his family, the genogram that we have drawn up would trigger many possible thoughts about family functioning around the three critical variables of the Circumplex Model: cohesion, flexibility, and communication (see Chapter 9 and Appendix 2). You will recall that this assessment tool allows therapists to rate a family's functioning based on a structured observation of their interactions. We would also use the anecdotes and examples from the case study to help us to develop a reasonable picture of how this family interacted and what values drove their behavior.

For example, we know from the case material that Sam was a strong and dominant patriarch who led the family based on a traditional model of high parental control. If we examine flexibility (leadership, discipline, negotiation, roles, and rules) on the rating scale of the Circumplex Model, we would place the Steinberg family in the extremely inflexible range, because leadership in the family was strongly centered on the father. An example of a family rule (as part of the family script) in the Steinberg family was that 'Sam has final say in most matters.' Other family rules also offered little opportunity for negotiation. Roles were clearly defined for men and women; women were 'delicate flowers' that were supposed to become homemakers, having no need for higher education. As stated in the case study, 'Most likely it never occurred to Sam that one of his daughters could take over the business one day.' However, men, even those who were in-laws and not blood relatives, were automatically ensured careers and leadership positions in the family business. We can ask ourselves, what type of message did this send to the daughters as they grew up following the family script?

The second variable on the Circumplex assessment is closeness, which includes emotional bonding, family involvement, marital relationships, parent–child relationship, internal boundaries, decision-making style, and external boundaries. The case study gives several examples to indicate that the Steinberg family is highly connected:

- Loyalty to the family is demanded above all else.
- Parents take an active role in the children's lives.
- The business provides many opportunities for Sam to exert control over his daughters' finances, and their husbands' careers and compensation.
- Sam also executed this level of control over his brothers and their families. The Steinberg family was at the center of their personal and social lives. Friday night dinner at Sam and Helen's home was not an option, it was an obligation. It was forced togetherness. Thus it becomes less surprising that after

Sam's death, his daughters would rebel, and (what was most disturbing) eventually would turn on each other.

Communication is another aspect important to the Circumplex Model. If we focus on the Steinberg family system in terms of their ability to communicate with each other, the communications patterns would probably score low in areas such as listening skills, self-disclosure, respect and regard, and high in areas such as speaking for others. This pattern of communication does not serve families well in a crisis.

As we saw in Chapter 9, the central hypothesis of the Circumplex Model is that balanced families are more capable of addressing stresses that challenge the family system than families that are overconnected, underconnected, inflexible, or too flexible. A family that has balanced flexibility and connections, and the ability to communicate, will have a more positive outcome.

At the time of Sam's death the Steinberg family still operated with a rigid and overconnected style. So when the family encountered this extreme situation, they lacked the emotional resources to talk about, or adapt to, the death in an appropriate way. Based on the events that followed Sam's death, including the sisters' lawsuits against each other and their mother, it is very likely that the family never developed a balanced family system or facilitating style of communication.

THE EFFECTS OF SAM STEINBERG'S INNER WORLD ON THE FAMILY BUSINESS

Though Sam's family-first philosophy was the main reason for his initial success, it was also the first nail in the coffin of Steinberg Inc. The first Steinberg store obviously grew out of the necessity for the family's survival. Sam's promise to his mother always to take care of the family guided his every move. It is hard to believe that Sam could really have failed to realize that his intention always to put the family first, even at the cost of the company, was in fact endangering the family's well-being. Did he really not understand that there would be no golden eggs to provide for his family if he let the hen that laid them die? What made a man of Sam's intelligence so unaware of the troubled dynamics in his own family?

The Lack of a Father Figure

There seems to be a direct connection between Sam's crucial childhood experiences and some of the mistakes he made later. The absence of a father figure, for example, is very likely to have affected his outlook and his behavior. Ida, her life made difficult by two weak men, seems to have compensated for this by purposefully raising her sons to be different from her father and husband: strong and capable of providing for the family. However, despite her intentions, what she actually created was an unholy alliance between herself and her son against the father—a form of triangulation likely to have strong consequences for Sam.

Furthermore, as favorable as the strong personality of his mother proved to be for young Sam's success as an entrepreneur, the lack of a father he could look up to, use as a role model, and provide boundaries during his childhood and early adult years seems to have affected Sam's attitude toward authority. In some ways, Sam became his own father, extremely independent-minded, not needing anyone. At the same time, he must at some (unconscious or subconscious) level have yearned for a strong, dependable male figure.

Ida Steinberg's Leadership Style

In Ida's case the parental role translated into a deep commitment to put her family first at any cost. The small family firm she led competed successfully on low-cost and trustworthy labor provided by the family. The jobs were unskilled, there was no need for professional management, and the family kept the profits. This early experience shaped Sam's management style and views of the family's role for his entire career. Unfortunately the scale and complexity of the business enterprise he created far exceeded the family's management pool and ownership capabilities.

However, despite the different contexts and scales of their respective firms, Ida and Sam's leadership styles were very similar. No matter how successful Sam became he still saw himself as an immigrant shopkeeper and believed he was the only person capable of making important decisions for the family and business. With his need to be in charge, and family relationships that reinforced this behavior, we can only imagine how it must have felt for Sam to try to imagine the (far-off) day when he would no longer control the company or the family. Endowed with an immense amount of energy and at the peak of his strength, he refused to face the fact that the day would finally arrive. His chosen solution was the conventional one: that of burying his head in the sand and depending on his own immortality. Sam was reluctant to let go of control because the company was so much a part of his core identity—no potential successor could ever replace him. Unconsciously, he may even have wanted the Steinberg business to go to the grave with him (as long as his family was provided for), so strongly did he identify with his stores.

Sam Steinberg and Women

Given the fact that his mother was an extremely hard-working and competent woman, Sam's attitude toward the roles of his wife and daughters in business was perhaps surprising. However, it is possible that witnessing his mother work day and night and destroy her health, triggered a strong protective desire in Sam not to let his wife or daughters experience similar hardships. Or perhaps his vision was clouded by stereotyping myths that meant he viewed his daughters as delicate individuals who needed to be looked after. Despite his mother's example, Sam's view was that women were the weaker sex and belonged in the home, not in the boardroom. Although he discussed important business issues with his wife (sometimes even following her advice) and often took his daughters with him when visiting the stores in an effort to instill in them pride in the family's stores, he seems never to have thought seriously about letting any of them take more than a token place in his empire.

Growing up in this climate, Sam's daughters were probably conditioned to believe that any aspirations to join the family business would be squashed and that they should content themselves with a more traditional female role. When Sam's oldest daughter, Mitzi, rebelled against her father's views about women and decided to study law, she encountered serious disapproval from Sam, who expressed his scorn about such 'unwomanly' practices.

The childhood environment of the Steinberg sisters also seems to have been characterized by tensions between them from early on. Four female children whose powerful father was absent most of the time must have felt an intense rivalry among them for his attention—a rivalry that surfaced later in the way they turned on each other.

THE INNER THEATER OF
SAM'S DAUGHTERS

Transmitting family values, especially about stewardship of family assets and concern for other stakeholders, is an important task of business families since it can help to prevent future family conflicts. So, it is remarkable to note how Sam and Helen Steinberg failed to instill in their daughters what they had grown up with themselves: a strong sense of keeping the family united. The Steinberg parents, after reaching a certain level of material comfort and security, fell into the same trap as so many other successful entrepreneurs before and after them have done: they spoiled their children rotten.

Having experienced the slums of The Main, Sam and Helen did not want their children to experience the fear of failure and poverty with which they themselves had grown up. Instead, their daughters were indiscriminately lavished with expensive gifts from very early childhood. Never learning to earn anything themselves, the girls developed a great sense of entitlement. The non-material values so important for their character development, as well as a solid education, and the appreciation of the value of work, seem to have been considered unnecessary. An upbringing like this does not make for healthy, stable, independent personalities.

Helen was the perfect complement to forceful Sam: her personality did not help to alleviate the situation. As a wife, she was everything a powerful and dominating entrepreneur like Sam could want. As a mother, however, she seems to have failed to provide what Winnicott described as the necessary 'holding environment' (see Chapter 1) for the girls while they grew up. She seemed to have been unable to contain the emotional outbursts in the family. Later on, she was batted from side to side in the war between her daughters and finally symbolically trodden on when her own brood took all her remaining power away. The viciousness of the daughters' fights, the strength of their vindictiveness, and the way they turned against their own mother raise disconcerting questions about the kind of emotional environment they experienced as children. It is characteristic that the only time they united was when faced with a common enemy in the form of Ludmer.

Like Father, Like Daughter

Mitzi's personality probably deserves the most attention. As the oldest daughter, and knowing Sam's attitude toward women, Mitzi may well have felt frustrated at never quite making it as Sam's 'son.' Extremely ambitious like her father, Mitzi is likely to have fantasized about life as Sam's rightful successor. Possessing a certain degree of ruthlessness and a strong fighting spirit, she did not easily accept the hopelessness of the situation, however. She invested all her energy into competing with her sisters for their father's favor and emerged the clear winner. Having achieved the position as the favorite of the most special and outstanding man she knew and admired would probably have reinforced any narcissistic fantasies she had of being special, different, and better than others.

It is unfortunate for Sam, Mitzi, and Steinberg Inc. as a whole that Sam was blinded by his own prejudices and did not recognize the potential he had in his oldest daughter. Instead of channeling Mitzi's ambitions in a constructive direction, Sam overlooked them, and Mitzi's bitterness over this became a destructive driving force. Her unspoken wish to follow in her father's footsteps drove Mitzi with a vengeance that neither Ludmer nor anyone else who tried to get into her way had reckoned on. She was out to win, even if winning meant the destruction of Steinberg Inc. A wrong had been done to her—the withholding of the coveted job of president—and nobody else was going to enjoy what she could not. In this situation, we see a clear example of how entrepreneurs can turn the constructive into the destructive, and potential into waste, when it comes to their children.

The Succession Decision

By appointing Mel Dobrin (Mitzi's husband and the most prominent male member of the family), it seemed as though from day one Sam had already made up his mind that the husband of his favorite daughter would run the company, whether he was competent to do so or not. In this way, his daughter would be the president by proxy, the next best thing to the old man himself. As a weak personality in awe of Sam, Mel was the easiest of the Steinberg Inc. executives to steer. Led by his need to remain in control, Sam could not help, consciously or unconsciously, but choose a weak successor. His personal interests blinded him to the effect his choice would have on the company, although the likely effect was quite clear to the other board members. This came to pass when many of the most capable and promising executives abandoned the company, causing a considerable loss of good executive talent.

In retrospect, it seems that nobody at all could have succeeded in taking over the leadership role after Sam, such were the innate dynamics of Steinberg Inc. and the will of Mitzi Steinberg. Steinberg Inc. was thus caught in a downward spiral after Sam's death.

However, the seeds of the company's destruction had been sown during its ascent and largely lay in Sam's own attitudes and actions. By failing to educate his daughters appropriately Sam ensured that the family business was deprived of capable, thoughtful successors, both as executives and owners.

WHAT IF?

Let's imagine for a moment that we could have sat down with Sam Steinberg on a day when he was in a good mood, and prepared to think about family transitions—perhaps motivated by a focal event such as a small incident of chest pain, which might have just reminded him of his mother's sudden, early death.

In such circumstances, we could have taken Sam through the Steinberg genogram and gently suggested that although both Sam and his mother had struggled valiantly with responsibility from an early age, it would be entirely appropriate for Sam to begin thinking about sharing the load so that the next generation would not resort to self-destructive activities.

We would also talk about adaptability, closeness, and communication. We would remind Sam that his mother was an unusual and exemplary role model for Sam's daughters. We would encourage him to consider one of his own daughters as a successor. If the meeting took place in the Steinberg boardroom, we could point to the painting of Ida that hung there, as a reminder of her values and strength, and suggest the appropriateness of one of her granddaughters following in her footsteps.

If we had been able to arrange further meetings in which the family was also involved, we would ask them to work together on renegotiating some of the family rules that gave Sam control over all aspects of his daughters' lives. A small step in changing family rules related to careers, for example, could have helped Sam and Helen see their daughters in different light and appreciate that they had aspiration beyond passive ownership of the business. We would also try to increase the cooperation between the four siblings in order to strengthen their power in the family.

Fundamental to this imaginary intervention would be an effort to improve the family's communication skills. The Steinberg family was unable to express their preferences about the types of family relationships they wanted, so consequently no planning or thinking about the future could take place. As facilitators, we would try to enable the expression of ideas (to bring the otherwise "undiscussables" out in the open) by those family members who felt intimidated by Sam.

One of our goals would be to help Sam to understand that it was possible to protect his family and, at the same time, preserve the company. We would talk about governance, and how to create a board of directors who would develop a strategic vision for the future. We would meet with the family and talk about their rights and responsibilities as owners. They might explore the idea of setting up a family council (see Chapter 12). They would feel free to raise their own ideas. We would discuss ways of bringing capable family members from the third generation into the company. In short, we would help them to identify new options and plans to meet the needs of individual family members within the family business.

Unfortunately, our meetings with the Steinbergs will remain in the realm of intellectual exercise. We have included the Steinberg case as a cautionary tale, but unlike the Steinbergs' story, our story does not end here. In the final chapter of this book, we will take you through an intervention we led with a family also facing a transition challenge. There, we will go into detail about the way a family and their business can move in parallel through a change process, with the help of advisers, to reshape the business and family for generations to come.

ENDNOTES

1. McClelland, D.C. (1961). *The Achieving Society*. Princeton: Van Nostrand.
2. Hubler, T. (1999). 'Ten most prevalent obstacles to family-business succession planning,' *Family Business Review*, **XII** (2): 117–121.
3. Collins, J.C. and Lazier, W.C. (1992). *Beyond Entrepreneurship*. Paramus: Prentice-Hall.

CHAPTER 12

PUTTING FAMILY BUSINESS INTERVENTION INTO PRACTICE

We hope that, having reached the last chapter of this book, you are now thinking about family business in a way that goes beyond the traditional management paradigm based on mere financial, strategic, and organizational considerations. In this chapter we will analyze a case study as a way of summarizing our conclusions as clinically informed advisers about the way well-functioning business families operate. We will share our insights about various techniques and processes that family businesses can use to improve their results. Finally, we summarize the role we believe advisers, consultants, and executive coaches can play in helping family businesses through the application of the insights of a psychodynamic-systems approach. This chapter is also designed to help business families to appreciate the role of outside advisers, consultants, and executive coaches and make better and more informed decisions when securing their services [1].

To facilitate the process of describing clinically informed interventions, we have chosen to share a consulting assignment with a family business to illustrate how psychological perspectives can help business families to address the social, economic, and psychological challenges confronting them. Our goal has always been to use the psychodynamic and family systemic paradigms to help family businesses to appreciate how the mindset of family members can influence their business actions. We will share a typical family business case, using a composite of several families with whom we have worked, and will then demonstrate how we would advise and coach the family to help them to identify options to strengthen their business effectiveness and improve their interpersonal relationships.

THE FAMILY ACTION RESEARCH PROCESS

As a tool to help you to understand the family business intervention we describe in this chapter, we will use a derivation of the *action research model* developed by Kurt Lewin. Figure 12.1 presents the action research process that begins with a family or business *triggering event*, followed by the *engagement* of an outside consultant or adviser. The subsequent phases are *data collection and family feedback*; *intervention and action planning*; and *implementation*. These phases reflect the change process suggested by Lewin of unfreezing, changing to new behaviors, and refreezing new attitudes. (In our intervention we will also be guided by the Kets de Vries change models on individuals and organizations, and those by Carlock on families, introduced in Chapter 10.) The process concludes with the *follow up and learning* phase, where the family tests its new behaviors, and the *disengagement* phase, where the family continues to learn and work on its own. We find this framework helpful in working with family business systems because the process is guided by information provided through

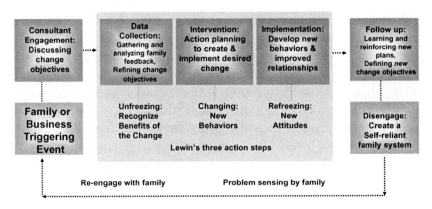

Figure 12.1   Family Action Research Intervention

an interactive process with various individual family members. The final outcomes are determined by the family's commitment to improve their performance and functioning.

THE SUCCESSION CONUNDRUM

Our contact with the XYZ Company was initiated by a call from a family member who had taken an MBA elective course in family business management that we taught at INSEAD. She was serving as the CFO of a family enterprise founded by her great-grandfather. She told us that her family was currently facing a succession dilemma because her father's cousins, the Chairman and CEO, two brothers aged 68 and 61 respectively, were planning to retire in less than 18 months. A major catalyst for their decision was the deteriorating health of the older brother. Family and board discussions about the transition were becoming increasingly acrimonious, with little progress in sight. To break the stalemate, our former student had suggested that her uncles should ask her professors for advice. The Chairman and the CEO reluctantly allowed their niece to initiate contact with us.

Our ex-student told us that the business had expanded dramatically under the two brothers' 25-year leadership, having become a global enterprise with sales approaching €1 billion. The company sold industrial equipment used in electric power generation and was organized into three divisions: manufacturing, European sales, and international sales. The Chairman, the CEO and their younger sister (a corporate lawyer, age 59), had inherited 50% of the shares from their father (the former Chairman) when he retired. Their cousin (son of the former CEO) age 52 and a medical doctor, had inherited his father's 50% ownership stake. The former Chairman and CEO had retired together 25 years ago. (See the family genogram, Figure 12.2.)

The previous year, the current Chairman and CEO had announced their joint intention to retire when the older brother reached 70. The two brothers (both trained as engineers) hoped their eldest sons (ages 43 and 41, and also engineers) who headed the European and international divisions would become the next

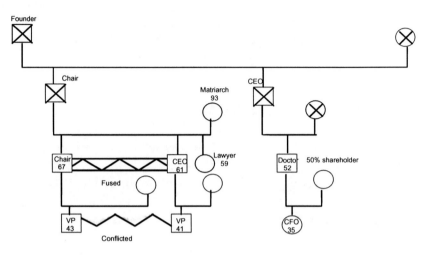

Figure 12.2   Genogram based on information shared during the telephone interviews

senior management team, working in tandem like their fathers. The family was concerned, however, because both their sons were highly competitive and often worked against one another's interests, in various subtle ways.

The niece explained that the business had a board of directors that included five family shareholders. The members were the Chairman, the CEO, their sister, their mother, age 93 (who was still a small shareholder but had not attended a board meeting in several years), their cousin (the medical doctor), and two retired executives. The two eldest sons from the third generation (who headed the two market divisions) had asked for board positions but the board (i.e. the Chairman and the CEO) had been reluctant to increase its size. The only shareholder willing to consider resigning as a director was the medical doctor, on the condition that his eldest daughter, the CFO (and our ex-student), was nominated to replace him.

The family met once a year at the home of the matriarch to discuss business and ownership issues; all family members over age 18 were invited. The family had written family agreements on employment, board membership, and selling stock. The firm paid a steady dividend. The Chairman's and the CEO's sister had suggested, however, that perhaps the time had come to organize more formal and more frequent family meetings. This idea was being considered.

As the conversation continued, our ex-student expressed her frustration with the fact that her family was not implementing many of the activities that we had discussed in her family business MBA course. She could not understand why her uncles planned to retire at the same time, although they were six years apart in age; and why the only succession discussions they were willing to have concerned their two sons, who had never worked well together. She added that although no one would say that openly.

The Engagement

After our discussion with our former student, we arranged for a conference call with the Chairman and the CEO later that month. After some small talk, the communication started in earnest with the two brothers talking over one another to explain their 'shared concerns' over management succession and the difficulty their sons had in working together. The Chairman added that they would *both* (his emphasis) be retiring in 18 months so it was critical that the younger men improve their relationship. During the telephone conversation we asked about the number of shareholders. The CEO replied, 'Four.' The Chairman quickly corrected him, saying that there were *five* shareholders, including their mother. The CEO countered that she was a shareholder in spirit only. The Chairman retorted that she was currently a shareholder of record and should be considered such in our discussions. The CEO replied, 'As you wish,' and moved to another topic: our fees. 'Will both of you be involved and will that increase the expense?' We told them, that to the best of our experience, it was more effective to work as a team. We also suggested that they should think about whether they would like to work with us. If so, we would discuss consulting fees. The Chairman immediately agreed that it was premature to discuss fees. 'But' he added, 'how do we know you can help us?' Our response was that a certain suspension of disbelief might be necessary but that we had worked successfully with many family firms.

We then asked: If we decided to work together, who would attend the first exploratory meeting? 'Just the two of us,' they replied in unison. At that point we explained that it would be best for us to work for, and report to, the *business* (the board of directors) or the *family owners group*, but *not* individual family members. Again the brothers replied almost at the same time, saying, 'We do the hiring and firing for this business.' We acknowledged their observation but noted that the issues we were asked to address could be bigger than only the business. We offered to send them some material on our work with business families, and think about the best way for them to move forward. The Chairman retorted, 'We're a *family business*, not a business family.'

Opening the Dance: First Impressions

Following these conversations, the two of us discussed our first impressions. The ability to compare notes is one of the main reasons why we find it very useful to work as a pair. An important question for us is how we feel when we are listening to the client. We are always cognizant of the fact that the client will be sending subliminal messages (based on transference reactions), and the consultant or coach is always reacting (having counter-transference experiences). Thus there will always be a struggle to make meaning and sense out of what takes place in an encounter, realizing that both parties are constantly tempted to *act out* perceived meanings rather than verbalize or mentalize them.

In the course of this struggle, every consultant or coach inevitably falls into the action trap at some point. This is especially likely to happen when strong fantasy material emerges during an encounter, prompting a mutual resistance to feeling and working with emotional data. We have learned from hard experience that when consultants and coaches do not recognize what is going on, and do not quickly enough make sense out of the subliminal messages that they are receiving, they may succumb to 'flight into action'—that is, they may react to information given by the client, without being aware of this acting out. After all, no matter how impeccably trained consultants, coaches, or therapists are, they are still human beings and still have emotions—and probably a number of unresolved issues of their own. If consultants, coaches, and therapists unconsciously accept a role ascribed to them by a client, they may respond by placing their own unacceptable feelings on the client without realizing that they are doing so. Working in pairs is one effective way of keeping a sense of perspective.

As consultants we have learned to listen to our clients at two levels. While not ignoring the content of what the client says, we continually ask ourselves a number of questions. How do we feel listening to the client? What is the client doing to us? Are we truly engaged? Do we feel comfortable? Are we bored? Do we feel uneasy? Do we feel in control? Do we feel confused? Are we getting irritated, angry? Do we feel seduced? And what do we find disturbing in our relationship with this client? In addition to these in-the-moment assessments, we try to assess how our feelings change over the course of our dealings with the client, evaluating our emotions and behavior in light of the client's behavior and the progress of the therapeutic relationship [2].

After sharing our initial reactions to the interview, we felt somewhat confused and anxious. We also realized that we could not readily remember who had said what. We asked ourselves what this signified. To what extent was this confusion and anxiety shared by the two brothers? To what extent had they transferred their confusion and anxiety to us?

To deal with our confusion, we began to sketch out a draft genogram (see Figure 12.2) using the preliminary information we had gathered. For example, after leading this firm for over two decades, the Chairman and the CEO (the brothers) obviously had a close working relationship, and yet their communication with one another during our conversation indicated a lack of clear boundaries between them. It was possible that they had a fused relationship, meaning that they were very close some ways, and yet conflicted in their interactions. It was as if they were bound in a 'dance of conflict'; their bickering was a way to maintain closeness but also distance. We also noted on the genogram that their two sons behaved in a similar manner, as we had learned from their cousin's (our student's) observations. This did not necessarily mean that there was serious conflict between them, but rather that this behavior pattern should be explored and discussed as a part of the data-gathering process during subsequent individual interviews with the fathers and the sons.

We explored the family's communication patterns using the Client Rating Scale from the Circumplex Model (see Appendix 2) to make our observations more objective. Assessing the two brothers' conversations with us based on such factors as *listening*, *self disclosure*, and *respect* and *regard* gave us some indication of how they communicated. For example, there was very little self-disclosure and several incidents when they spoke over each other or corrected each other in the short telephone conversation we had with them.

We had also learned about the involvement of the 93-year-old matriarch, who in the family setting would undoubtedly have some degree of emotional impact. In addition, she could provide first-hand knowledge of her husband as a former family and business leader. Consequently her insights on the family and the business could be important in helping the family to develop a better understanding of how it had functioned across generations. The discussion of her role also helped us to understand better how the brothers handled conflict. When the Chairman challenged the CEO about their mother's status as a shareholder, the CEO capitulated quickly ('As you wish') instead of pursuing the argument.

This short conversation also demonstrated the Chairman's and the CEO's strong need for control of the consulting process and, it seemed likely, of any decisions or plans for the family or business. The Chairman's comment, 'We do the hiring and firing for this business,' was not surprising, but it did indicate a concentration of power at the top of the organization and gave us further clues about the family hierarchy. The Chairman also offered a glimpse of his personal style when he corrected one of us by saying, 'We're a family business, not a business family.' This type of underlying current was exactly what we wanted to capture in the interview, and would later explore with each family member. His statement reflected a 'business first' philosophy that might not be appropriate for the next generation with an increased number of shareholders and fewer family members employed by the firm.

Two days later we received a call from our former student (the CFO), who reported that although her uncles were slightly put off by the discussion they had had with us, they were interested enough to instruct her to contact us to set up a meeting with the four shareholders (excluding the matriarch). We asked if anyone else should be included, and she recommended that the three next generation family members who were senior executives should also be involved, considering they would soon control the company as owners and executives. She added that her father was very supportive of the next generation and felt that the ownership issues needed to be discussed and resolved.

We suggested that since her uncles had involved her in organizing the meeting, she should consider discussing the planned meeting with her two cousins (the potential successors). If they agreed with her, then the three of them could approach the Chairman and the CEO with their request to participate. We explained to her that a multigenerational steering committee would be a step toward changing the family structure. We also mentioned that even if the uncles rejected next generation's participation, the cousins would have started communicating and working as a next generation team. The senior generation would soon realize that this was not business as usual; the topic of next generation participation could no longer be ignored.

Once again, this brief telephone conversation helped us to expand our view of the family and add some additional information to the genogram. We learned more about the family's communication patterns when the Chairman and the CEO asked a next generation family member to call us, rather than following up themselves. Perhaps their niece was dispatched to contact us because they did not want to admit or discuss the question of including other shareholders. We also noted that the Chairman and CEO were not controlling shareholders and that their cousin the doctor (our former student's father), who had never worked for the business, owned the largest block of shares. His daughter said that her father was supportive of the next generation, and felt that ownership issues needed to be discussed. We wondered whether this could reflect his anxiety over being the major shareholder without having comparable influence on the business itself. His comments also alerted us to the fact that some family members might feel that too much power was currently concentrated in the hands of the Chairman and the CEO.

The Family Audit: Gathering Information

The Chairman and the CEO decided that only the four major shareholders should attend this first meeting with the consultants. At that meeting, which took place at the company headquarters, the first item raised by their cousin, the doctor, was to inquire why the next generation had been excluded. The Chairman reported that he felt it was *not fair* to the rest of the family to only select three members of the next generation to participate. We proposed that there was no problem starting the process with the senior shareholder group, as long as the intention was to make the process more inclusive later.

We asked the shareholders to think about their objectives for an intervention and identified three specific outcomes for our work together:

1. To improve family communication and conflict management.
2. To develop a process for selecting the next senior management team.
3. To strengthen the participation in the business of next generation family members.

The discussion of these objectives stimulated the shareholder group's thinking about many of the issues and concerns facing the family. They all agreed that anonymous interviews with the family would be a good starting point. In fact, two of them strongly suggested that the first person to be interviewed should be the 93-year-old matriarch who was in remarkably good physical and mental health.

The Matriarch

This gracious woman still retained her position of quiet command. She met us in her mansion, ensconced in a comfortable wing chair. She began with an overview of the company's history. She told how the XYZ Company had been owned and operated by the family for over 85 years. Her father-in-law, the founder, was nostalgically remembered as 'the old tyrant.' His stone bust still guarded the entrance hall of the old manufacturing plant. He was an archetypal entrepreneur; he had gone bankrupt a few times but came back to launch the XYZ Company, and in a matter of a few years had become a millionaire. She recollected how he knew every employee on a first-name basis and was proud of the fact that he could do any job in the factory himself. She recalled that, during a strike, he had helped to teach the replacement workers each of the production steps himself. There was a general consensus that in spite of his toughness, he cared deeply about the employees and valued loyalty above everything.

She also talked about a bitter dispute that had occurred decades before between her husband, who was Chairman at the time, and his youngest brother, who served as director of manufacturing. The youngest brother (the middle brother was in the position of CEO) had firmly believed that the company should open an international division, but his two brothers had refused. Finally, behind his brothers' backs, he started making plans and finding new customers. When her husband found out, he accused his youngest brother of betraying the company, and with the support of his middle brother the CEO, they forced him out of the company and purchased his shares. These actions created a serious rift in the family: it was as if the youngest brother had been excommunicated. For his brothers, he no longer existed. The matriarch also noted that it had become taboo to talk about this part of the family history. It had been a traumatic experience that had affected the way that family members had dealt with each other ever since. It had created a strong sense of 'never again.' She mentioned in passing that from then on, whatever happened in the family, harmony had to be maintained. Real, overt conflict could not be tolerated.

The matriarch said that, ironically, the youngest brother was the most charismatic of the three. People used to say that he was an entrepreneur, just like his father, the company founder. She added that, many years later, his two brothers had implemented his plan for what was now the international division that accounted for over 70% of the company's sales. Sadly, the youngest brother had died unexpectedly several years after he was ousted. The dispute had never been resolved.

When we prompted her to tell us about her children, the matriarch said that their daughter had been her husband's favorite. She indicated that she tried to be fairer in expressing her affections to the children but her husband's favoritism had been a problem. She recalled that her two boys used to fight bitterly. Their fights became so destructive that, eventually, her husband gave them an ultimatum: either they shaped up or he would send them to a special military-style boarding school. His threat seemed to have worked. It was her impression that their common fright had the effect of bonding them together. Although they developed a kind of bickering way of interacting, their sister then became the object of their wrath. Their mother recounted sadly that they never developed a good relationship with her.

After the expulsion of their brother, the matriarch's husband and his brother made it known that family members would always hold the two top jobs in the business. In light of this family rule, it was her husband who forced their oldest son to give up a promising career in aeronautics and come back into the family business. Her brother-in-law's son had always had an interest in science, and when he chose to become a doctor, the burden fell on her two boys to lead the firm. She told us,

I always felt sorry for my sons, particularly the oldest, because my daughter and my nephew both had more choices in their careers. My daughter became a very successful corporate attorney and my nephew is a well-recognized surgeon. I think my two sons are happy but I sometimes feel I let them down by not taking a stronger position with my husband and allowing them greater freedom in their choice of careers.

The Chairman

Following our interview with the matriarch of the family, we interviewed the Chairman. The first thing he communicated to us during his interview was not in words. After we asked him to share his thoughts about his career, he paused for quite a long time before responding, 'That's not something I think about very often.' He noted that he had not intended to work in the family business, and that his passion had always been aeronautical engineering and flying. Trained as an Air Force pilot, he told us that the three most exciting years of his life were spent with a NATO air squadron in Europe. He then said that he had made a decision to continue a military career, but his father, knowing that his re-enlistment was coming up, sent him instructions to return to the family business within 90 days. He recalled how coming back into the family business had been a real shock. As a pilot, he had experienced the ultimate in personal autonomy. Suddenly, at the age of 28, he found himself reporting to his father and uncle for everything he did. Being in a position he was not really trained for had been difficult. He admitted that for the past 40 years, there had been many times when he felt like an impostor.

He spontaneously mentioned that his relationship with his father reminded him a bit of the way his father treated his brother. When we asked a clarifying question, 'In that case, how did the two men manage to work together?' he was startled, and replied, 'I wasn't thinking about his brother CEO, but his youngest brother, who he forced out of the business.' Our follow-up question received a belligerent reply of, 'That's old history; there's no use going into that now. I prefer not to talk about it.' It made us wonder, however, about his ambivalence about putting the younger generation in a leadership position. Was he afraid of what would happen if he let go of power? Also, why was he adamant that his brother would retire at the same time as himself? Was he afraid that history would repeat itself, albeit with a twist?

The CEO

Meeting the CEO without his brother, we found a very different person in terms of his communication style and ease with the situation. In our previous discussions, when his older brother had been present, the CEO always seemed slightly on edge, and cautious about how he responded or engaged in conversation. Alone, he was more open and friendly, displaying a warm personality.

He had always intended to join the family business, which he had done after five years' work experience as an engineer and executive with General Electric. He had hoped that his father would select him to take over the business, because his brother's passion was aviation.

Our first question was about how they had decided on their roles as CEO and Chairman respectively. His matter–of–fact answer was, 'We didn't. It was our father and uncle who slotted us into these two positions, then left us to figure out how to divide the work.' He added,

> We've been a good team in many ways, but I'm afraid it hasn't helped to mature our relationship as brothers because our styles are so different. As my brother has grown older, it is my perception that he has become more negative, especially in dealing with me. It is as if our conflict-ridden period during childhood is re-emerging.

When asked about the simultaneous retirement dates, he told us that his father and uncle had done exactly the same thing over 30 years earlier, and for some reason, his brother had declared that it was the right thing for them to do. He didn't really like the idea but, due to his brother's insistence, had given in. He wondered whether his brother was afraid that he would have too much power if he became the Chairman. Was he concerned himself about what he would do with this power? Off the record, he told us that he would personally like to work a few more years in a senior role to really help the next generation of the family to cement their positions and leadership roles.

The Doctor (the Largest Shareholder)

Our expectations were uncertain when meeting the cousin because in our previous discussions with the larger shareholder group as we were planning the intervention, he had very little to say other than expressing his concern that it was time to make room for the next generation. He shared his appreciation for the way in which the family business had allowed him to have a successful medical career and that he felt slightly unworthy owning a large asset that he had never worked for. He confided that he always felt that he could have made a contribution to the business beyond being a rubber stamp on the board, but that his two cousins had done such a spectacular job in developing the business that it made very little sense to push the point. His biggest concern was his eldest daughter's career. She had the professional training and skills for a very senior role, as demonstrated by her being appointed CFO at 33, but as her father, he did not want her to be drawn into the same unbalanced life as his cousins. He was also afraid that she felt some responsibility for continuing her grandfather's legacy as a senior leader in the business.

The Chairman's and the CEO's Younger Sister (and a Corporate Attorney)

The 59-year-old sister of the Chairman and the CEO, a successful corporate attorney, expressed comfort with her role in the family business. While she felt a commitment to the business, she had accepted early on that her father and uncle saw no place for a woman in the business, so she had pursued a legal career, and made it to the top of her profession, specializing in corporate law. Her reputation in the legal community was outstanding and her advice was sought by many large corporations and their boards. On a personal level, she was somewhat relieved that her two daughters had career interests completely unrelated to the family business, because she really saw her responsibility as helping to sustain the family legacy and connections, but the business was simply one aspect of that for her. She mentioned that she had always respected her older brothers, and recognized that compared to many of the other senior managers she had worked with, they were exceptional business leaders.

Next Generation and In-Laws

We met next generation members employed in the business individually, with group interviews for in-laws and the family members not employed in the business. The logic for the different methods of data gathering was that shareholders and employed family members have more information to share about the issues but may also be domineering in discussing the business and family challenges, giving us little opportunity to talk to the others. The group interviews provided social support for family members less connected to the business and also enabled participation from the entire family group, including those members who chose to say nothing during the interview process. It was agreed that each interviewee would share their perception of the family's values, critical issues facing the family, and questions the family needed to answer. The group interviews gave us a more rounded view of the family and business situation.

Below is a summary report of the interview results, organized by major topic themes, and including family members' specific questions. The information shared was not attributed to any individual.

The Family Information

Summary Report of Family Interviews

Business Values

- We are a family-owned and managed company.
- We should avoid conflict to protect the family and business.
- We must transmit our family values to future generations.

Family Values

- Stewardship of family legacy and wealth.
- Our strength is that we have 'a little bit more than common business sense'.
- Modesty and recognizing others.
- Harmony among members of the family is critical; real conflict is pushed underground.

Family Relationships

- Our family are not always honest with one another.
- The family needs to meet more often, once a year is not often enough.
- Who is head of the family?
- How can the business create opportunities for younger family members?

Ownership

- The ownership is not fairly divided among different branches of the family.
- The ownership group has no appetite for risk.

Third Generation (3G)/Fourth Generation (4G) Relationship

- 3G must give 4G more responsibility for ownership.

- 3G is dominated by (particularly) the Chairman and the CEO.

Governance

- The directors are not directing; they're a rubber stamp for management.
- The board includes no representation from the fourth generation.

Management

- How are we going to decide who will be the next senior leaders?
- What is the career path for 4G family members in senior operating roles?
- The current Chairman should retire; he's been in the job too long.

The Consultants' Reflections and Analysis: Developing an Action Plan

It was clear from the interviews that a strong theme within the family was conflict avoidance. The ousting of the younger brother many years ago had had an enormous intergenerational impact. The incident had never been properly metabolized, leaving a legacy of shame and guilt about what had happened. As a consequence, any Oedipal conflict or sibling rivalry was suppressed. This had contributed to a major rule within the family that real family fights were to be avoided at all cost. The suppression of conflict had not been completely successful, however; this was indicated by the bickering style prevailing among the brothers and cousins. Furthermore, the negation of conflict had also led to the postponement (or avoidance) of difficult family decisions.

Keeping this information in mind, we created a new genogram (Figure 12.3) showing all the family members' positions by generation, with specific indications of family dynamics, alli-

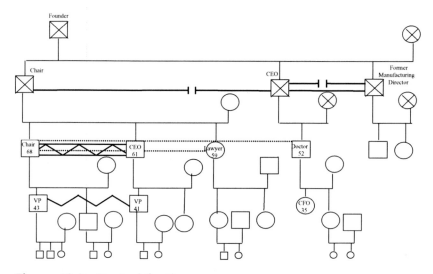

Figure 12.3 Revised family genogram

ances, or conflicts. Again, this genogram represented multiple snapshots of how different family members perceived relationships and interactions. It shows that it was possible for one cousin to consider a relationship with another as distant, while another cousin saw it as more satisfactory.

The interviews indicated several interrelated family and business challenges that needed to be addressed beyond the initial presenting problem of management succession. The bump under the carpet was the prevailing myth of harmony, the reluctance to address conflict within the family. Our challenge was to gauge the extent to which we could make the unconscious conscious. How far could we go in addressing the prevailing issues of sibling rivalry, Oedipal concerns, and fear of retaliation that we detected during our interviews? Recognizing some of these issues (and taking them into consideration) was one thing; bringing them out into the open, and dealing with the inevitable resistances, was another matter altogether. Our philosophy has always been, 'When in doubt, keep your mouth shut.' The strategy we chose was peeling the onion: we would start with surface material, and if the situation warranted it, go deeper. Whatever happened, we would keep our credo—strike when the iron is cold—in mind.

As always, the timing of bringing certain issues to the fore would be critical.

Starting to peel the family onion, there was strong agreement from the interview data that the family needed to explore its family and business governance processes for decision making; discuss future ownership challenges; and develop plans for improving family participation, especially next generation development. Given the emphasis that the two senior managers had placed on the succession process, we needed to make a slight redirection of the family's thinking to explore first how to mobilize the family's commitment and second how to agree on a process for identifying and confirming the next generation of leaders. The current focus on the two cousins, nominated by their fathers, reduced the size of the pool and limited the family's options. Historically, the family had a shared leadership model with a Chairman and a CEO. It had been an effective way to avoid making a choice about which individual should be in charge; it was a way to maintain the myth of harmony. In going forward, however, a better distinction needed to be made between the Chairman's role and responsibility for governance, and the CEO's role and responsibility for strategy and operations.

It made very little business or practical sense for the current Chairman and CEO to retire simultaneously, simply to conform to past tradition, to maintain the illusion of equality, and to calm the Chairman's fear about what would happen when he was no longer in power. The current CEO was several years younger, had extensive top management experience, and could play a significant role in supporting the transition to the next generation of family leaders. He also seemed to function better when not under the influence of his older brother. We also felt that he would not abuse his power (despite his brother's fears) if given the Chairman's position. It might also be helpful in terms of both family relationships and leadership continuity to think about possible roles for the current CEO, the largest shareholder (the doctor), and the sister (the corporate attorney).

Thinking about the family's participation, it was also important to consider who could take a leadership role in helping the family and the expanding ownership group to become more engaged with the business and other enterprise activities such as philanthropic actions, new investments, preparing the next generation, and perhaps a family office. The sister (the corporate attorney) was obviously well qualified to play a leadership role in this, and could perhaps be considered as a Vice Chairman supporting her brother (the current CEO) who could assume an Executive Chairman's role with his son, nephew, and niece creating a senior leadership team. This team would allow the next generation to strengthen their relationships and at the same time consider new options for growth under the guidance of the Executive Chairman/father and Vice Chairman/aunt.

One of the obvious weaknesses revealed by the family interviews was the lack of strong governance for the business and any form of governance for the family. The current board of directors was nothing more than a shareholders' assembly. With no outside members, it was unlikely to add much value to the strategic thinking of the management team.

Family governance represents a more difficult situation because previously the family had very little need for governance beyond some simple family agreements and the strong leadership of the Chairman and the CEO. Again, it was clear from the family interviews that many of the family needs were not being met. For example, the comment 'The family never works on anything as a family; our only concerns are business issues' represented the growing frustration of the group of family members not employed by the firm, who may or may not be owners in the future, but will remain part of the family group. A family of wealth and power needs to find ways to express its 'familiness' beyond the business and to articulate its family values. Behind this may lie the concern to stay 'with the facts,' rather than deal with potentially messy family issues. The family history showed that those who rocked the boat could come to a very bad end.

Meeting the Four Shareholders

Before the full family meeting we asked all five shareholders to meet us and review the interview report, the major educational themes, and most importantly the family genogram. A summary report that we had written was discussed by the shareholders and it was agreed that it would be distributed to the family group two weeks before the group met. In addition, we suggested that some material on effective family business management would also be included in the pre-reading. A mini-lecture was included in the package.

A large part of the meeting was spent discussing the draft genogram that we had developed based on our interviews with the family. During this discussion, several major areas of concern were identified. First, the unresolved conflict between the three brothers in the previous generation that resulted in the youngest brother being cut off from the family. In particular, we explored the effect it had had on the family, raising the issue of inter-generational repetition. Second, we brought up the relationship between the Chairman and the CEO. Third, we explored the relationship with their sons. And fourth, we asked about the distant relationship of the Chairman with their cousin, the largest shareholder. What was scheduled to be a two-hour meeting was extended into late in the evening as the five senior generation family members wrestled with not only the genogram interpreta-tions, but also the larger implications of these various relationships on the family. The Chairman and the CEO were particularly concerned. As the discussion became more emotional, they became more aware of their subtle bickering as a relational style, given their wish, perhaps unconscious, to suppress conflict in the family. Fortunately, we were able to bring to the surface some of the positive elements of their relationship. They explored what they had in common and what they liked about each other.

What became clear to them during the encounter was the extent to which their example could have (or had had) an impact on their sons and created the foundation for future damaging conflicts. After full consideration, and with some reservations, the group agreed that the genogram should be presented at the full family meeting to demonstrate the senior generation's commit-ment to openness, and to help the family to focus on specific relationship issues that needed to be addressed.

The Intervention: The Family Meeting and Action Planning

The intervention with the entire family was designed around a two-day meeting that included preparatory reading, mini-lectures and discussions, feedback and discussion of the information collected from the interviews, and time for family action planning [3]. This intervention acknowledged that the family as a group was in transition from its current patterns of behavior to new behaviors based on the concerns and issues identified in the interviews and the new practices suggested by the readings and mini-lectures. The action planning phase represented the family's synthesis of this new information with the family's values and vision for the future.

It is important to begin a family business meeting with a mini-lecture and discussion of possible business tactics and family processes that support the resolution of the family's issues. In any family group, especially when ownership and management are separated, there can be a wide discrepancy in people's knowledge and experience of the family business, so it is helpful to 'teach' the family about key concepts that support the family's action plans. This educational step also gives the family a shared vocabulary with which to discuss their issues and stimulate their thinking about solutions. The following mini-lecture opened the two-day family meeting with XYZ Company.

Mini-Lecture for the Family Meeting

It is clear to us from our interviews with you that your family has a competitive advantage in the areas where your values, goals, and actions are well aligned. The dramatic growth of your business and your leadership in innovation and people development clearly display your effectiveness in doing so. Often, business families are in a better position in terms of professionalizing the business, while leaving the family somehow to take care of itself. The interviews show that your family has done a strong job of strategic planning for the business but has not needed (or wanted) to take much action related to the family.

As families grow and the number of owners increases, the family needs to create a *parallel planning process* that creates a sense of belonging and ensure that family members are willing to make sacrifices if doing so will benefit the group as a whole [4]. In these families, the members are concerned about one another's needs, they care about each other, they communicate properly, and they go out of their way to help each other. These families can enjoy certain traditions, without becoming inflexible or overly controlling.

At times, even in the best-functioning families, there are, of course, conflicts of various kinds—family recognition and financial matters are major areas of conflict. Family relationships will never be perfect; there will always be the possibility that someone will feel he or she has been treated unjustly (major contributing factors are sometimes simple things like difference in birth order, and, in some cases, gender). Well-functioning families demonstrate a concern for fairness in the family's plans and decisions. We would like to suggest the concept of *fair process* as a useful philosophy for your business, and describe how *coaching* works in families like yours.

Fair Process as an Organizational Philosophy

Fairness is a fundamental issue in everything families do, whether they are deciding what to eat for dinner, where to go on holiday, or who should be the next CEO. Probably the most common response parents hear from their children, particularly young children and adolescents, is 'That's not fair!'

Actions that are perceived as fair are more likely to be accepted and supported if they follow the five fair process behaviors:

• *communications and voice*—giving each of the concerned stakeholders an opportunity to speak and be heard; creating the perception that each person can make a difference;

- *clarity*—offering timely and accurate information about family and business issues;
- *consistency*—applying rules in the same manner to all people;
- *changeability*—the willingness of the family to make adjustments in its family agreements based on new information or changing situations;
- *commitment*—practicing fair process in all activities [5].

The Use of Coaching

Effective business families use coaching or mentoring as a tool for improving business and family leadership and strengthening relationships. For example, senior family members can coach or mentor the next generation as a part of their gradual disengagement from business and ownership roles and help the next generation to learn more about the business and the family. Older family members can take vicarious pleasure in seeing the next generation develop their talents and capabilities, and next generation family members can focus on learning from the experiences of their elders.

The use of outside coaches helps to insure developmental experiences for the next generation. These will help them to explore their own interests and careers, even if these take them outside the family business. The family needs to think about multiple types of next generation personal development—activities covering management, ownership, philanthropy, and governance. Philanthropy is an excellent opportunity for younger family members to apply family values and use the assets and talents of their business for the good of others. Many families subscribe to the 'learning, earning, returning' credo. As next generation family members learn about the different dimensions of the family enterprise beyond the business, they find new opportunities for participation.

Processes for Helping Family Businesses Develop Effectively

It's clear from our interviews and discussions that until recently the family only needed an annual family meeting and informal family decision making to ensure effective business functioning. The increasing size of the family in the next generation, and the growing involvement of in-laws, means that the family needs to re-examine its participation and engagement as a family group. This could include more regular family meetings, the development of a family council, expanded family constitutions, and exploring new family activities such as philanthropy.

Family Meetings

The family meeting is the first organized forum for making decisions that affect the business and the relationship of the family to it. Typically, a family will begin holding such meetings when the children are in high school or college and start to show an interest in the family business. Topics presented at a family meeting can include the family's vision and values, how business ownership should be handled, and what agreements the family needs to make to ensure fairness and prevent conflict.

Family Councils

As the family grows in size, or further generations join it, family meetings are replaced by a representative body of elected or appointed family members who guide the family's planning and decision-making actions concerning the family's relationship with the business and each other.

The family council is a critical part of the governance process and while it can serve as a training ground for the next generation, it is important that it acts in a formal manner when addressing family planning, family training and development activities, and issues related to family agreements or conflicts.

Family Charters (Constitution)

One specific task of a family council is to help the family to develop and approve family agreements, also known as a family charter or constitution. These rules of the game encapsulate the family's values and vision and help to clarify decision making and problem solving. It is important for rules to be developed before they are applied to a specific family member or situation, so that they represent the family's intentions and are not an attempt to resolve a specific problem.

The family charter can lay down mechanisms for resolving future conflicts by answering questions such as:

- Who is a family member?
- How do family members pursue careers in the family business? Is everyone welcome to work in the company or is there a requirement for educational and outside experience?
- What is the authority of the family council?
- How are family members nominated for the positions on the board of directors?
- What is the family's code of conduct regarding family members' rights and responsibilities?

Boards of Directors

A strong board of directors will be particularly helpful in facilitating the management succession process because it adds objectivity and ensures legitimacy. In highly professional family firms a board and chairman will take the responsibility for nominating the new CEO as a part of a long-term planning and development process, thus avoiding conflicts between the outgoing president, family members, and influential shareholders.

Effective boards for family businesses are different to the boards of public companies, in that they must also play a bridging role with the family council, balancing the needs of the family and the corporate system [6]. Board members need to have an understanding of the relationship between the family values and goals and the company's culture, and they must strive to have empathy for the position of each of the various family members.

> The board's contribution is also important because powerful psychological processes can affect an outgoing president's judgment: it is important that he or she should not be the sole decision maker. (CEOs may well be familiar with the story of Shakespeare's King Lear and their actions may be motivated by fear of a similar fate, leading them to become overcontrolling in their decision making.)

Next, we presented the report, describing the three major themes: governance, family participation, and management succession, and the genogram identifying critical family relationships. The conflict in the previous generation and the cut off of the youngest brother had never been discussed. It gave us the opportunity to touch (in a more general way) on the issues of Oedipal and sibling rivalry and their implications. As the discussion progressed, we learned about other questionable forms of behavior by the previous generations. We pointed out that all these activities had contributed to the family myth of harmony.

The Chairman, who was visibly moved as these topics were discussed, explained how his father and uncles had mishandled some disputes about the business that affected several family members. When these issues came to light, we saw a very different side of this tough old family leader. There were still many questions about the conflict that remained unanswered, but one suggestion that came from one of the other participants was writing a family history so that we can 'set the record straight about a lot of things, and share our family's legacy and learning with generations to come.'

We recommended that the family create three task forces, and the family agreed. The cousins working in the firm, with their aunt, would head the governance task force. The doctor would lead the family participation task force. The CEO would head the management succession task force. The task force members would interview and discuss with all family members and key non-family employees and advisers. It was agreed they would report back to the family in 90 days.

Follow-up Learning and Reinforcing the Action Plans

Over the next year the three family task forces and owners' steering committee continued to gather information and draft and explore scenarios for addressing the three major issues. Table 12.1 provides a summary of the decisions they made, and the actions that were recommended and/or implemented.

Table 12.1 Summary of decisions

Focus	Intervention	Rationale
Governance	Strengthen board with outside members	Provide objective input to improve decision making
	Replace matriarch, Chairman, and cousin (largest shareholder) with the three next generation family executives	The next generation needs to learn and influence governance with the support of the senior ownership
Family Participation	Develop a family council	Inclusive body for family members
	Continue the work of the three task forces: • Management succession • Governance • Family participation	Formalize a way for family members to contribute
Doctor, age 52 Largest shareholder	Head of family council: attends family business conferences and executive education program	Develop strong understanding of family business functioning to lead family
Daughter, lawyer, age 59	Vice chairman of the board: attends family business conferences and executive education program	Develop a stronger interface between family and business governance

Table 12.1 (*Continued*)

Focus	Intervention	Rationale
Management Succession		
Chairman	• Become Chairman emeritus • Take on a mentoring role	Chairman work on coaching next generation and leads a family history project
CEO	• Become Executive Chairman • Take on a coaching role	Develop a new executive role. Mentor the next generation family and non-family executives
Next generation son, age 43 and executive	• Mentoring by CEO and/or external coach • Team-building sessions	Work closely with his uncle on developing executive and teamwork competencies
Next generation son, age 41 and executive	• Mentoring by CEO and/or external coach • Team-building sessions	Develop leadership and teamwork capabilities
Next generation daughter, age 33 and CFO	• Mentoring by CEO and Vice Chairman and/or external coach • Team-building sessions	Develop leadership and teamwork capabilities and explore career/life options
Next generation executive team	• External coach • Team-building sessions • Explore their plans for a senior leadership team	Develop teamwork and communication skills

THE ROLE OF THE OUTSIDE ADVISER

As we have demonstrated in the family intervention outlined above, tensions and unresolved conflicts within the family system can seriously affect future prospects for the family business. Family members who fight each other often have little emotional energy left to address the business issues like succession. In our experience it is clear that most business families can benefit from professional support in addressing the ways in which their family relationships affect their business. Professionals can help to lead an objective research and facilitation process whereby the family is more able to explore its values, goals, strengths, and weaknesses. Furthermore, advisers can help to disentangle knotty emotional issues and look for win–win situations.

Four different types of professional adviser typically serve family businesses: teachers, consultants, coaches, and therapists. Each of these brings a different, yet often related, approach to change based on various tools and disciplines of origin (see Figure 12.4 below). The approaches can be from:

- teachers transmitting knowledge;
- consultants offering expert advice;
- coaches supporting new interpersonal and work skills; and
- therapists working on new behavior and deep insights.

Teachers and consultants tend to be more directive and focused on what they perceive as rational thinking processes, and coaches and therapists are usually more reflective, addressing the non-rational/emotional, sometimes even unconscious, dimension.

ADVICE TO FAMILIES SEEKING HELP

Unfortunately, it is not possible to design a template or scorecard that can help a family to make a decision on the type of adviser they need, since the most important criterion for any type of consulting, advising, or therapy relationship is a degree of trust (the ability to establish a working alliance) between the client and the adviser. Nonetheless, there are several factors that families can take into consideration when hiring an outside adviser:

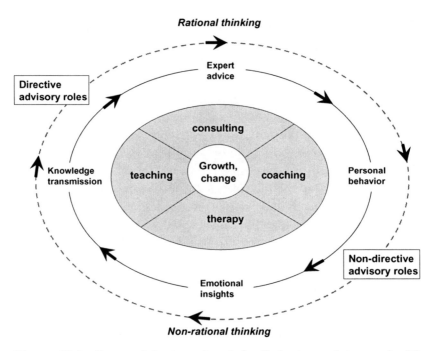

Figure 12.4   Four social-science based, family-business advisory roles [7]

- What are the adviser's values when working with business families? It is important that he or she is capable of recognizing and respecting that each family has its own unique set of values. The adviser should seek to understand the ways in which the family is successful; what is important to family members, and how they see their relationship to the business.

- Can the adviser support the family across a range of family and business issues? Does he or she understand the context in which this particular business family is operating? Most business organizations are designed to create wealth, which provides a unitary measure of performance, and strongly aligns the values and perspectives of the business. In the family business context, however, there can be multiple influences beyond financial performance. Any family business adviser must understand that family relationships and dynamics, family emotions and feelings, or family business history and legacy may be just as important as wealth creation, or even more important, to the players involved.

- What theoretical model of change will the adviser use to guide his or her work and engage with the family? Typically, a therapist will work with the family on assessing family interactions and developing a plan for helping the family to create new behaviors. Strategic business consultants, on the other hand, will make a professional assessment of the problem areas and make specific recommendations for action. Coaches will look at critical incidents and teach new skills.
- How will the outside adviser gather data? How will he or she share this information with the family? Who will be privy to this information? And how will the adviser and family develop action plans?
- How does the outside adviser see his or her role in relation to the family? Is the adviser a facilitator? Does the adviser see his or her role as a process consultant, helping the family to improve the way they do things, or a content consultant, providing the family with expert advice?
- Does the adviser appreciate the impact of cultural and societal influences upon the family in business? Some advisers work on a global basis and therefore have a working knowledge of many different business cultures. Others specialize in a given type of industry or market. It is important for the family to ascertain whether the adviser's cultural and work experience match their own.
- What does the adviser understand by confidentiality? Perhaps surprisingly, many people in the advising world lack professional guidelines in the form of a code of ethics that ensures confidentiality. Confidentiality is particularly important in the family business setting, and especially in some cultural settings, so outside advisers must understand what confidentiality actually means to each family. Some families have confidentiality rules that apply both inside the family and outside, in the wider external environment. In these cases it is vital that the family make their expectations plain before developing a confidential relationship with an adviser.

THE BENEFITS OF A PSYCHODYNAMIC SYSTEMS PERSPECTIVE

We have tried to demonstrate throughout this book how the psychodynamic systems perspective enables business families to create better business outcomes by gaining insight into how their family's emotional needs are affecting their business decisions. We have tried to show how owners, individuals working in a family business, and others interacting in one form or another with family businesses can benefit from psychodynamic systemic insights. For example, an attorney hired to develop a trust for a multigeneration family business would be able to provide a stronger legal document if he or she could help the family to ensure that it reflected not only the best legal and economic thinking but also the emotional concerns of grantor and beneficiaries. Taking into consideration the family's relationships and other issues could well change the attorney's recommendations— for example, ensuring that a trust allows the beneficiaries more, and eventually full, control of the family's assets. The term 'trust fund baby' conveys the clear image of an adult under the control of the parents for much, if not all, of his or her life. An attorney with some grasp of the psychodynamic systems perspective could help the family to consider whether this type of legal arrangement will in fact meet the needs for the differentiation and autonomy of the beneficiaries. Does it strengthen the family's flexibility or simply represent another example of the parents' need to control things, perhaps even from beyond the grave?

A family group or management team that recognizes the importance of considering psychodynamic systems perspectives in a family business will be able to build an additional base of support for their proposed actions, and foresee where they are likely to hit obstacles. For example, an investment banker might be hired by a founder/CEO to explore the sale of the family business because the founder perceives the next generation as uninterested or incompetent. The banker can consider more options with the CEO and other family members by assessing the next generation's capabilities, either alone or with the help of others.

A psychodynamic systems perspective can also be used to complement other planning, problem-solving, and consulting approaches undertaken by businesses. For example, a process consultant working in the area of quality who expands their definition of the client to include the whole family system (rather than just the management of the business) could identify how family demands affect the firm's quality processes. By offering to communicate with the whole family through a short write-up, or even conducting an overview of quality practices as a part of the family meeting, the consultant could motivate the entire family to support a quality program. Family members who do not work in the business do not always appreciate the challenges involved in, for example, maintaining quality in the manufacturing plants. A consultant who ensures that the wider family is helped to understand these issues can ensure that the larger family institutionalizes a commitment to quality as a specific family value.

Finally, a psychodynamic-systems perspective can provide a tool for explaining to the family any uncomfortable but necessary actions or outcomes that are needed within the family business. Good communications, facilitated if necessary by a family systems therapist, can be invaluable in helping family members to address the emotional issues associated with difficult decisions or actions.

FINAL WORDS

In the words of George Santayana, 'the family is one of nature's masterpieces.' In the journey we have made through this book, we have tried to show that a well-functioning family business can also be a masterpiece. Our discussion also has made clear that owner-managers of family businesses cannot run a family like a company. They need to take a much more balanced approach. Owner-managers of family businesses sometimes forget that they are human beings first and business people second. Success implies having a balance of success stories across the various areas of our lives. Many family business owners have discovered that it is very difficult to be a success in their business life if their home life is a mess, and vice versa.

George Bernard Shaw once said, 'If you cannot get rid of the family skeleton, you may as well make it dance.' In this book we have suggested that to deal effectively with knotty family business issues, we need to address the 'undiscussables'—we need to make family skeletons come out and dance. To put it another way, if there are bumps in the family carpet, it is better to lift it up and check for hidden snakes, who will not go away of their own accord. In life as in business, there are two cardinal sins: the first is to act without thinking and the second is not to act at all.

We hope the reader realizes that studying families is like looking at magic mirrors. In these mirrors, we can see the past, the present, and the future and we need to remember that no image should be left out. To be more effective in the present and future, we need to acknowledge the past. Becoming successful in a family business is not a matter of how much money you make, who your parents are, or what you do. It is essential, rather, to study the family mirrors, and use the reflections to help all members of the family business to create indelible strokes that contribute to the beauty of the family masterpiece.

ENDNOTES

1. Kets de Vries, M.F.R. and Miller, D. (1984). *The Neurotic Organization*. San Francisco: Jossey-Bass; Carlock, R.S. (2007) 'Leadership coaching in family business,' in Kets de Vries, M.F.R., Korotov, K. and Florent-Treacy, E. (eds) *Coach and Couch: The Psychology of Making Better Leaders*. London: Palgrave.
2. Kets de Vries, M.F.R. (2007). 'Are you feeling mad, sad, bad or glad?' INSEAD Working Paper, Fontainebleau, France.
3. For example, we ask families to read: Blondel, C. and Carlock, R.S. (2004). 'Fair process: Striving for justice and fairness in the family firm,' *Families in Business* (April–May): condensed version of academic article on the five principles of Fair Process; Carlock, R.S. and Ward, J.L. (2003). 'What every family needs to know about strategy,' *Families in Business* (April–May).
4. Carlock, R.S. and Ward, J. (2001). *Strategic Planning for the Family Business: Parallel Planning to Unify the Family and Business*. London: Palgrave.
5. Van der Heyden, L., Blondel, C. and Carlock, R.S. (2005). 'Fair Process: Striving for justice in family firms,' *Family Business Review*, **XVIII** (1): March.
6. Carlock, R.S. and Ward, J.L. (2001).
7. Carlock, R.S. (2007). See note (1).

DEVELOPING A BUSINESS FAMILY GENOGRAM

The basic concept that lies behind the genogram is that many of the problems families face have been created within the family system and are repeated over and over again across different generations [1]. Many business families, despite exceptional talents in management or other areas, are unable to recognize objectively that their particular family's patterns of loss, conflict, communications, and use of power have led to ineffectual family behavior and, eventually, to problems for their business.

The genogram is a tool that enables a family and their advisers to facilitate discussion about the family's biological and emotional past. Completing and discussing their genogram helps a family to clarify, interpret, and create meaning about their behaviors and attitudes across generations. A well-crafted genogram exercise serves the business family, helping them to address three questions:

1. How does our prior experience shape our collective behavior and interactions?
2. What can we do to make our current relationships (both positive and conflicted) more meaningful?
3. What values and behaviors will help the next generation to construct more positive future interpersonal relationships?

CREATING THE GENOGRAM

In business terms a genogram is the equivalent to an organizational chart showing people's rank or hierarchy within a business organization. If asked to produce a schematic of their members, families will typically produce a family tree. This could be considered a form of genogram, but family trees tend to be super-ficial, in the sense that they simply show family position and do not really provide any demographic facts or relationships to explain how the family functions.

The genogram is best constructed to show three or more generations, with each family member placed by generation. Typ-ically the genogram is positioned as an upside-down tree with the roots (the senior generations) on top, cascading down in the multiple branches as the family expands across generations. The basic method of organization is around couples in the family of origin (parents and children), with the father shown on the left, symbolized by a square, and the mother by a circle. The couple are connected by a line and their offspring are shown below.

Individual demographic and historical information about the biological events that shaped the family's experiences is then added to this family structure, including dates of marriages, births, and deaths. Although one would usually consider births, marriages, and deaths to be factual information, historical facts are often disputed and in some families there is often significant misunder-standing or even conflict about whose grandfather was the oldest son or whether an in-law worked in the family business before he or she married a family member. In this case, notes can be made on the genogram to indicate the divergence in opinion.

Additionally, information about careers, ethnic or religious background, education, and health issues can be entered on the genogram, although it is important not to overload the genogram with too much information. The goal is to be able to spot pat-terns of relationships and behavior, not to create a comprehensive family history.

THERAPEUTIC APPLICATIONS OF THE GENOGRAM

The drawing up of the genogram provides a unique opportunity for the family to discuss, interpret, and hypothesize interpersonal relationships involving both living and dead family members. A therapist or adviser can suggest different perspectives on interper-sonal relationships among family members and discussion about these can act as a powerful intervention in the family process. Often the most difficult relationships in the family involve dead family members whose behavior and influence are misunderstood because the family has created different versions of their history (or narratives) to protect family beliefs, identities or values. For example, a grandfather who was in fact an overbearing bully and destroyed a whole generation's interest in working for the family business, might be 'remembered' as a driven and visionary entrepreneur.

The genogram can also help a family to explore how gender, birth order, or branch membership influences positions of power within the family. A four-generation genogram of a large family with many branches could make it clear that in the past three generations the CEO has always been the oldest son from the same branch. This gives useful information about the way gender and power are treated in this family.

Clearly most family members are aware at some level of the existence of these family patterns or arrangements, but being cognitively aware of something and appreciating its full significance can be very different things. The same is true with seeing a conflicted relationship depicted on the genogram at a family meeting. The jagged line used to symbolize a conflicted relationship between an individual and his or her father creates a different emotional response than simply discussing that relationship on an intellectual basis.

USING THE GENOGRAM TO IDENTIFY FAMILY SCRIPTS AND THEMES

The human side of family business issues is often described as a soft topic, meaning it is hard to identify, quantify, and address. Indeed, this is the argument that some family members use for avoiding an attempt to address the family's emotional issues or conflicts. They fear that people issues are a swamp that will drag the family down and prevent them from addressing the 'real,' hard business issues, not realizing that the soft issues *are* the hardest issues—and that there is nothing soft about soft issues. They know that family conflicts or rivalries are likely to be played out in the business setting. The business meeting provides a perfect venue for a frustrated son, daughter, sibling, or cousin to express a family hurt or rivalry by communicating with another more powerful family member about business weaknesses and their poor leadership performance. Frustrations that cannot be expressed within the family system can be made into agenda items for the board meeting and then used as an opportunity to confront or challenge a more powerful family member.

Business families can develop other scripts or myths (i.e. rigid patterns of behavior) that are reinforced because of the overlap of family and business systems. For example, some families strive to avoid conflict by never discussing certain business topics, like salaries, on the basis that not addressing this issue will prevent bad feelings and smooth family relationships. Other rigid patterns that develop in the business family can be:

- sibling or branch rivalry;
- gender stereotypes (with males preferred for both ownership and leadership roles);
- high parental expectations (with oldest sons being assumed as the next leader);
- cut-off relationships where family can no longer bear ongoing conflicts; and
- enmeshed relationships where family members are unable to develop a sense of autonomy.

The genogram can help to address these challenges by focusing the family's energy in a constructive way and finally address the 'undiscussables.' Instead of allowing a general conversation about a lack of communication to continue, an adviser can change this into a focused exploration about the origins of aspects of the family scripts or myths. This way the family can come to appreciate those aspects of their current experiences and beliefs that support old behaviors. They can then review whether their attitudes (a) are still relevant and make a useful contribution to the family's functioning, or (b) need to be changed.

The genogram can be also be used to identify whether any family members have significant power in the family. Power is often allocated on the basis of rank in the business or experience and seniority as a business leader. Looking at a grandparent's attitude to power can shed light on current power systems in a family. Take, for example, a business family that is struggling with ongoing conflict between the father, his daughter, and his two sons who together form the senior management team of a growing global family business. The father, now aged 64, joined the business at 17 and took over as Chairman and CEO on his father's death. The three children were hired as the division heads for the firm's three business units with full responsibility for strategy and financial performance. Two of the children hold MBA degrees and the third is a lawyer, all from prestigious American universities. Before joining the family firm they worked in other large organizations for at least five years.

The conflict started soon after they joined the family firm at their father's request to support the reorganization of the company into three geographic divisions and to begin the succession process. At first the children accepted their father's interference as a phase of the transition; however, when it did not improve after two years, the oldest son told his father that he intended to resign unless he stopped interfering with the siblings' business operations.

Things improved for a period of time but their father then reverted to his old behavior and created a major bust up when he countermanded his daughter's instructions on a major decision without consulting her. Things are now at the point where personal relationships are being harmed and three children are reluctant to socialize with their father.

In this case the family script on power, roles, boundaries, and communication is no longer working for several reasons. However, the family is beyond attempting to communicate about their differences and needs a serious outside intervention that engages them constructively in addressing the conflicting family scripts and myths about roles and boundaries.

If an adviser can get the family to work together to understand where dad learned his rules about family business interactions, they will have an opportunity to change their family scripts or myths. Appreciating that their grandfather's script was boss-subordinate, top down, and on a need-to-know basis may help the siblings to appreciate their father's behavior. The three children only remember their grandfather as a doting man who bought them gifts and took them on trips; they were too young to see him running the family business, which he did until the day he died. It is also possible that their father does not appreciate quite how competent his children are as executives and feels the need to second-guess them because he wants to protect them from failure.

An adviser working with the family on their genogram could help all four executives to gain a shared understanding of their family's history. Often the younger generation is ignorant of their parents' and grandparents' lives, making it difficult for them to appreciate the senior generations' values and views. This exercise would help them to appreciate their father's behavior, improve family understanding, and provide an opportunity for exploring new patterns of behavior.

HOW GENOGRAMS IMPROVE COMMUNICATION

Another very important aspect of genograms is that they can provide a means by which all family members can gain a voice in discussing the family. Often younger family members, or those members who do not actually work in the business, feel unable to communicate their feelings. A genogram levels the playing field by changing the context from the business to the family, where everyone is an equal member. Genograms use words that all members can understand rather than business terminology.

The demographic information contained in a family genogram might appear benign, simply presenting facts, but there is very little in family history and relationships that is not emotionally powerful. Discussing their genogram may be the first time that a family has addressed losses arising from death, divorce or interpersonal conflict. Sharing thoughts and feelings about an important family event or conflict can have a cathartic benefit for the family. However, intense emotional responses are often aroused and advisers, coaches, and therapists facilitating such discussions must ensure that the family feel safe as they learn to work together.

ENDNOTE

1. McGoldrick, M., Gerson, R. and Shellenberger, S. (1999). *Genograms: Asessment and Intervention* (2nd edition). New York: W.W. Norton.

THE CLINICAL RATING SCALES AND THE CIRCUMPLEX MODEL

The clinical rating scales (CRS) are useful ways of exploring family functioning in terms of flexibility (change) and cohesion (closeness) based on the Circumplex Model discussed in Chapter 9 [1]. The CRS are ideal for working with business families because they use interviews and behavioral observation rather than an assessment instrument and computer scoring. The trained clinician with a working knowledge of family systems theory and the Circumplex Model can use the CRS to help families to understand how they function, and what actions could help them to improve their family interactions.*

We have included this introduction to the CRS in this appendix because the scales can provide very helpful guidelines on diagnosing the likelihood of improving interpersonal and group communications in the family. For example, if family members do not listen to each other, send inconsistent messages, or speak for others, the likelihood of change, in the family or in the business, will be limited no matter how good the intentions or the urgency of the issues being discussed. A blocked communications process prevents the family from sharing clear messages and staying on the topic. The family's inability to be flexible may also

---

* We included only a sample of CRS materials for review here, since a full clinical intervention methodology is beyond the scope of this book. Materials on the Clinical Rating Scales are available from Life Innovations, Inc. at www.facesiv.com.

be a contributing factor to their failure to make required changes. If the family's discussions always end with 'We can't do that because . . .' there will be limited opportunity for new options to be explored, and the family is likely to remain stuck.

Using the information from the CRS, activities like family meetings, or structures like boards of directors, may be designed to improve the family's process skills, such as sharing feelings and information, with the goal of putting new information into the family system. The result of positive communication behavior is an improvement in the family's effectiveness and the strengthening of family trust and the underlying family relationships.

HOW THE CRS WORK

The CRS use a semi-structured interview with questions designed to facilitate a discussion of critical family behaviors. The CRS are completed under the supervision of a therapist or adviser. The following are sample questions for the two dimensions.

I.   *Questions for assessing family closeness*
   - *Separateness–togetherness*: How does your family balance separateness and togetherness?
   - *Marital closeness*: How emotionally close are the parents?
   - *Family closeness*: How close do family members feel to one another?
   - *Loyalty*: How loyal are family members?
   - *Activities*: Do people usually engage in activities alone or together?
   - *Independent–dependent*: How independent (or dependent) are family members?
   - *Other questions*: How does your family celebrate birthdays and holidays? What are typical evenings and weekends like in your family?

II. *Questions for assessing family flexibility*
   - *Leadership*: Is the leadership shared between parents/ adults?
   - *Discipline*: Is (was) the discipline strict in your family?

- *Negotiation*: How are differences or conflicts negotiated in your family?
- *Roles*: Are family members restricted to certain roles?
- *Rules*: Do rules seem age-appropriate for family members? Have the rules evolved over time?
- *Change*: In general, how open is your family to change?
- *Other questions*: How organized is your family? Who is in charge of your family?

In discussions and informal conversation generated by these and other questions, the therapist captures information about the family members' interpretation of their functioning and also the behaviors that confirm or challenge the family's reported dynamics. The therapist then assesses the family or couple using the Couple and Family Map (see Figure A2.1) and the Family Profile Summaries (Figures A2.2–A2.4) to measure three profiles:

- cohesion (e.g. family closeness, family activities);
- flexibility (negotiation, change); and
- communications.

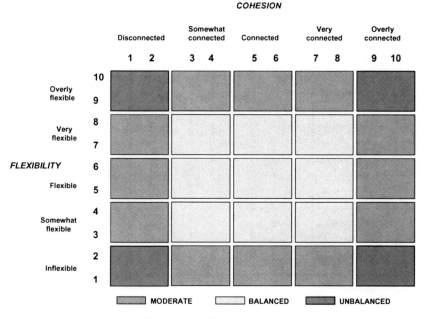

Figure A2.1 The couple and family map

CRS	Disconnected (disengaged)	Somewhat connected	Connected	Very connected	Overly connected (enmeshed)
Closeness (cohesion)	1 2	3 4	5 6	7 8	9 10
Separateness / togetherness	• •	• •	• •	• •	• •
Marital closeness	• •	• •	• •	• •	• •
Family closeness	• •	• •	• •	• •	• •
Loyalty	• •	• •	• •	• •	• •
Activities	• •	• •	• •	• •	• •
Dependence / independence	• •	• •	• •	• •	• •
Global rating					

Figure A2.2 The Family Profile Summary—Closeness

CRS	Inflexible (rigid)	Somewhat flexible	Flexible	Very flexible	Overly flexible (chaotic)
Flexibility	1 2	3 4	5 6	7 8	9 10
Leadership	• •	• •	• •	• •	• •
Discipline	• •	• •	• •	• •	• •
Negotiation	• •	• •	• •	• •	• •
Roles	• •	• •	• •	• •	• •
Rules	• •	• •	• •	• •	• •
Change	• •	• •	• •	• •	• •
Global rating					

Figure A2.3 The Family Profile Summary—Flexibility

CRS	Poor		Good		Very good	
Communication Score:	1	2	3	4	5	6
Listening skills	☐	☐	☐	☐	☐	☐
	Poor listening skills		Appears to listen, but feedback is limited		Gives feedback, indicating good listening skills	
Speaking skills	☐	☐	☐	☐	☐	☐
	Often speaks for others		Speaks for oneself more than for others		Speaks mainly for oneself, rather than for others	
Self-disclosure	☐	☐	☐	☐	☐	☐
	Low sharing of feelings		High sharing of feelings		Moderate sharing of feelings	
Clarity	☐	☐	☐	☐	☐	☐
	Inconsistent messages		Clear messages		Very clear messages	
Staying on topic	☐	☐	☐	☐	☐	☐
	Seldom stays on topic		Often stays on topic		Mainly stays on topic	
Respect and regard	☐	☐	☐	☐	☐	☐
	Low to moderate		Moderate to high		High to very high	

Figure A2.4   The Family Profile Summary—Communication

The individual communications rating scale (Figure A2.4) can be used to explore specific positive behaviors such as listening, self-disclosure and respect. The global rating that the therapist assigns to the family should reflect not only the four profiles, but also the therapist's overall impression of the *gestalt* of the family situation.

ENDNOTE

1. Olson, D.H. (2003). *Clinical Rating Scale for the Couple and Family Map*. Minneapolis, Minnesota: Life Innovations, Inc. Tables reproduced by permission of David Olson.

INDEX

Index compiled by Indexing Specialists (UK) Ltd

Lightning Source UK Ltd.
Milton Keynes UK
01 March 2011

168481UK00001B/1/P